SO-BIY-866

VOICES OF RESISTANCE
Editorial Board

Benjamin Pimentel

REBOLUSYON!
A Generation of Struggle in the Philippines

Foreword by
RAMSEY CLARK

Afterword by
EDICIO DE LA TORRE

MONTHLY REVIEW PRESS
New York

In memory of Freddie Salanga

To my parents

To Carlos, Karen, Red, Grace, Alex, and Mara
That they may understand . . .

Library of Congress Cataloging-in-Publication Data

Pimentel, Benjamin, 1964-
  [Edjop]
  Rebolusyon! : a generation of struggle in the Philippines /
Benjamin Pimentel.
    p. cm. — (Voices of resistance)
  Reprint with new introd. Originally published: Edjop.
  Quezon City: Ken, 1989.
  ISBN 0-85345-822-7. — ISBN 0-85345-823-5 (pbk.)
  1. Jopson, Edgar, d. 1982. 2. Philippines—Politics and
government—1973–1986. 3. Philippines—Politics and
government—1986– 4. Students—Philippines—Political activity.
5. Communists—Philippines—Biography. I. Title. II. Series.
DS686.6.J67P54 1991
959.904'6'092—dc20   90-46928
[B]   CIP

Monthly Review Press
122 West 27th Street
New York, N.Y. 10001

Manufactured in the United States of America

10 9 8 7 6 5 4 3 2 1

CONTENTS

FOREWORD

Ramsey Clark

Not many Americans have ever heard of Edgar Jopson. This valuable book offers an opportunity to learn of his short, remarkable life and perhaps better understand how our foreign policy affects others. The U.S. presence in the Philippines has been the dominant fact in the lives of the four generations of Jopsons who have lived their lives in this century.

Edjop's grandfather was a child living in an impoverished peasant family on the fertile island of Negros when the United States seized the Philippines in 1898. Then, as now, most of the population of Negros suffered malnutrition though its rich soils could feed one hundredfold its population and have provided sugar for tens of millions of people in North America and Europe.

Our benevolent purpose was discovered by President William McKinley through prayer and recorded by him for posterity. Having defeated Spain, he said, there was "nothing left for us to do but take them all, and to educate the Filipinos, and uplift and civilize and Christianize them, and by God's grace do the very best we could by them, as our fellow-men for whom Christ also died."

Just how conscientiously we pursued this commitment was revealed in the ensuing years of the Philippine American war. Secretary of War Elihu Root assured the American people: "The war in the Philippines has been conducted by the American army with scrupulous regard for the rules of civilized warfare," he stated, "with self-restraint and with humanity never surpassed. . . ."

The truth was otherwise. General Franklin Bell estimated one-sixth of the population of Luzon, 600,000 human beings, died as a result of U.S. military campaigns. In Batangas Province 100,000 died out of a total population of 300,000. On Samar, General Jacob Smith ordered, "kill and burn," and said the more he killed and burned the better pleased he would be. Major Waller asked General Smith to define the age limit for killing, and Smith replied, "Everything over ten." For General Smith, it was just like "killing niggers." Villages were systematically burned. Torture, including the notorious "water cure," was official policy. Prisons overflowed with Filipinos. In Bilibid Prison in Manila, administered by the United States, the death rate among inmates rose to 438 per 1000 in 1905.

For a decade the peasant struggled in Negros for independence, land reform, and economic justice, not unlike the struggle Edjop joined two generations later. The decades before World War II were full of turbulence, poverty, and unemployment. But every decade since the U.S. intervention in 1898 has seen flare-ups of violent struggle for independence and land reform.

Hernan Jopson, Edjop's father, left Negros, joined the army, and was a sergeant when the Japanese invaded. He survived the battle of Bataan, escaped from the ensuing Death March in 1942, joined the resistance and fought the Japanese throughout their occupation. By contrast, the father of Salvador Laurel, now Philippine vice-president, served as president during the Japanese occupation. Corazon Aquino's father-in-law served as speaker of the House of Representatives under the Japanese while her family preserved and expanded its land-based wealth.

On July 4, 1946, the Philippines formally attained its political independence. In fact, its political, economic, and psychological dependence on the United States was greater than it had ever been. Physically devastated by the war, reeling from a harsh three-year military occupation and wartime condition, all major Philippine political figures openly vied for U.S. support as the one means to convince the people they could bring about recovery. The first president had the backing of powerful American interests, including his wartime boss, General Douglas MacArthur.

Edjop's parents were just starting a small grocery store and desperately poor when he was born in 1948, fifty years after Admiral Dewey destroyed the Spanish fleet in Manila Bay. After years of hardship, sacrifice, and a bankruptcy they established themselves as successful, wealthy entrepreneurs.

By the time Edjop was five years old, the CIA had hand-picked and largely created Ramon Magsaysay as a political figure. He was predictably elected president in 1953. The Pygmalion of this particular work was the CIA's Edward Lansdale, who went on to similar efforts in Vietnam and Cuba. President Eisenhower, who served as General MacArthur's Chief of Staff in the Philippines before the war, approved the CIA election operation and sent a note of congratulations to the CIA station in Manila after its success.

Still the Philippines was a nation of great potential. Imbued with generations of American rhetoric about freedom, democracy, and education, the people had a high capacity for self-government under democratic institutions. They created diverse political parties and conducted rigorous campaigns, developing able and articulate politicians. Their large population was energetic and productive. Awareness of the need for land reform and the effect of widespread U.S. military bases on their soil and sovereignty was high and growing. There was every reason to believe the Philippines would become a major country and economy among the rapidly growing Pacific nations.

The two decades of rule by President Ferdinand Marcos, from the mid-1960s through the mid-1980s, were the most demoralizing and finally the most destructive of the century for the Philippine people. Democracy and the rule of law were not only mocked but destroyed, ending in a decade of martial law. The monopolization of political power and investment opportunity stifled economic growth. Half the national income was received by one-fifth of the population. The majority lived in terrible poverty. Malnutrition was a national plague. By the end of the 1980s per capita annual income was $590 in the Philippines, the major U.S. Pacific ally in World War II, while in Japan, which lost the war, it was $15,000. Other Tigers of the Pacific had per capita incomes 3 to 15 times that of the Philippines: Hong Kong, $9,600; Singapore, $8,000; Taiwan, $6,000; South Korea, $2,700; Malaysia, $1,800. The Philippines' long and intimate relationship with the rich and powerful United States had left it crippled economically and politically at war with its own people.

President Jimmy Carter, our Human Rights President, supported Marcos, proclaiming U.S. human rights policies inapplicable in the

Philippines. Vice-President George Bush, visiting Marcos, a long-time personal friend of the Reagans, praised his democracy in the midst of martial law.

It was in this environment that Edjop grew to manhood. An only son and first-born in a home of many sisters, he was deeply loved and supported by a close and strong family. While the Jopsons were finally wealthy, he remembered want, economic adversity, sacrifice, and long hours of work as a child.

Edjop was keenly intelligent, an excellent student in a highly competitive elite Jesuit school among children of the aristocracy and a natural political organizer and leader. He was also deeply religious. Under less turbulent circumstances, he might have been the priest or businessman he thought of being. His position and abilities suited him for success in either pursuit.

Edjop was profoundly affected by Pope John XXIII and Vatican II, which stimulated an abiding and deep concern for the poor he knew from childhood in the streets of Manila. Soon he was swept up in the tormented conflicts of the times. As the top student from the best high school in the country and later of his university, and then elected head of the major national student association, Edjop was forced to make hard decisions about what he should do. Because he was honest, informed, intelligent, moral, and strong he made the difficult choices that are the heart of this book. For him 1972 was a year of anguish, when martial law was declared and he visited Beijing, nearly breaking with his best friend and wife-to-be in Tiananmen Square from the terrible tension of choice. Life is choice.

Edjop chose total sacrifice for the people, the *masa*, for whom he bore profound respect and love. He left social approval, wealth, comfort, assured success by the values of the society in which he was raised, access to parents, sisters, relatives, friends, his own children. He suffered long periods of separation from his wife. He chose physical danger, privation, ostracism because he wanted a better life for the poor. He worked to exhaustion thankless, under hopeless conditions. He struggled pragmatically without ideology, applying his experience and intelligence to change a government.

He joined the New Peoples Army (NPA), a Philippine communist armed military, in its struggle against Marcos.

In spite of all and in what could rationally be seen as the near sure pursuit of death, he performed well. He made real differences. He advanced an effort he thought essential to the welfare of his people, the poor.

Called a traitor, a terrorist, and worse, Edgar Jopson was the true Philippine patroit. Seeing his government was wrong, he said so. Seeing it persist in its deadly course, he defied it. Against all selfish interests, he sided unafraid with the true nation, the people, against a tyranny that impoverished them. In the face of maximum adversity, Edgar Jopson maintained his idealism, stood by his convictions, practiced his beliefs, raised however precariously his children, told his parents and his sisters in fleeting ways, he loved them. He remained gentle, modest, always constructive, even a scholar, with one honest, simple desire, to serve his people as he understood he ought to. When governments that terrorize their own people speak of terrorists, we should remember Edjop.

In the heart of Makati, a prosperous business district outside Manila, there is a powerful, heroic statue of Benigno Aquino, murdered on behalf of Marcos less than a year after Edjop was gunned down. It is an ambiguous statue. Ninoy is falling forward down stairs to portray the circumstances of his assassination.

There ought to be a statue of Edjop. It might be facing the Malacañang Palace to remind its occupant there will always be champions of the people. It might be at the Ateneo, the elite Jesuit school where Edjop excelled, to bring out the best in future generations of students. It might be in Tondo, the sprawling Manila slum of more than a million poor, to remind them there are those who care. The people of the Philippines should choose. But there ought to be a heroic, public statue of Edgar Jopson.

Only then will we know that the Philippine government understands what NPA leader Joma Sison meant when he wrote from prison, "A system that hunts down and kills a man like Edgar M. Jopson is thoroughly wrong and unjust." Or what a great human rights lawyer and Philippine patriot José W. Diokno, Jr. wanted us to know when he spoke at the wake in the University of the Philippines chapel: "we should mourn for ourselves and a society which has made it necessary for a young man like Edjop to give up his own life." He might have added "and mourn for the United States which led us to these extremes so it could prosper, for U.S. policies made Edjop's acts necessary and his death inevitable." José Diokno believed that.

Corazon Aquino, miraculously president of the Philippines, speaking of her martyred husband, "Ninoy used to say that Marcos would leave so many problems behind that whoever followed him wouldn't last six months."

In the Philippines after four years as president, we see a good and loving woman clutching to her own family's vast, privately guarded plantations. Corruption consumes a large part of the government's whole income while babies starve. American consumerism dominates the culture. Paramilitary organizations mostly backed by the government, Alsa Masa, Nakasaka, Tad-Tad, the cry of Filipinos resisting U.S. forces nearly a century ago, roam the country killing people and striking fear. The military, uncontrolled by civil government, is a constant threat to its leaders and continuity.

From Negros, where the Jopsons began the century, a saintly Bishop, Antonio Fortich, speaking in the wake of the military's Operation Thunderbolt, observed: "There is no peace in the Philippines. . . . Since 1987, the total war policy of the government against the insurgents makes all of the country a battlefield."

To look at Liberia, India, Pakistan, virtually any country of Africa, most of Asia, and Central or South America, shows us that the legacy of colonialism and latter day foreign political and economic domination is devastating for a people. That even if let alone to solve their problems for themselves, a condition that rarely occurs, adverse effects can endure for generations. Colonialism in all its forms disturbs the cultural self identity or soul of a people and it is difficult for them to know who they are and what they want to be.

For the Philippines, U.S. military bases mean they have no sovereignty. Without divestment of the huge colonial land holdings, the people are imprisoned in their own country from access to the foundation of economic prosperity. Hungry, homeless, ignorant and poor, the people cannot be free. The rush for markets, cornering of resources, competition to produce unnecessary necessities and desire to dominate other peoples for profit will lead to disaster.

The lessening of East-West tensions and proclaimed victory of capitalism will not solve the problems of the earth's poor. Still in this century a billion more persons will be added to the planet's population. Eighty percent will have beautiful darker skin. The majority of these will live short, miserable lives of violence, hunger, want, sickness, ignorance and pain—unless we act.

In this lesson from the Philippines and the life of Edgar Jopson, we may learn something of what we must do and act to offer Edjop's children a chance for peace he never had. If so we may yet save ourselves from William James' curse: "God damn the United States for its vile conduct in the Philippine Isles."

Acknowledgments

In writing this book, I relied mainly on interviews with Edjop's family, friends, and comrades. I wish to thank all the people who shared their recollections of Edjop and their insights into his life and times.

I also made use of other interviews conducted by Boni Ilagan and Jose Cuaresma, director of the prize-winning documentary film on Edjop's life.

I am particularly grateful to the Jopson family, especially Edjop's parents, Hernan and Josefa Jopson, and Edjop's sisters, Inday and Marie, for their cooperation and the enthusiasm they showed for the project.

I also owe a lot to my editor Pete Lacaba who took time out of his hectic schedule to go over a draft of the biography, and to Greg Brillantes for his comments and suggestions.

It was the late Freddie Salanga who encouraged me to pursue this project. That I never got to share with him the things I learned about his dear friend is something I shall always regret.

I am also grateful to Edith Galve, who proofread the final text, and Audie de la Cruz, who helped in the selection and reproduction of photographs.

I wish to thank John Cavanagh and Robin Broad, dear friends who urged me to make Edjop's story known to more people in North America.

Joy Jopson tops the list of the people I must thank. She helped arrange most of the key interviews with underground personalities and served as an inspiration and guide in writing this book. Her gentle strength and courage I will always admire.

To her I say, "*Natupad din ang dalawang taon nating pinaghirapan! Mabuhay ka!*"

Prologue

There had been signs . . .

Once, a *kasama* (comrade) on his way home noticed he was being followed by two men. He decided to walk on, past the neighborhood. After a few blocks, he suddenly turned around and walked the other way. The two strangers, he noticed, looked startled.

Another time, the kasamas noticed a red car parked in a nearby vacant lot overgrown with tall cogon grass. There was nobody inside.

On the night of June 13, 1979, the kasamas met to discuss security measures. It was time, they decided, to move to another address. But no date was set. They would stay in the house a few more days.

"But in case of a raid, what do we do?" one of them asked. "Do we fight?"

"It depends on the situation," answered another. "No use shooting it out if we are already surrounded."

"Besides, we only have two handguns. Not much we can do with that."

In one corner of the living room were two steel cabinets filled with documents: reports on the underground organization, in Manila; files of *talambuhay* (short biographies of cadres); and copies of *Liberation* and *Ang Bayan* (The People).

"What will be our story, our *prente?*" a kasama asked. "A research group," somebody said.

The others nodded.

"If worse comes to worst, I'll admit that I'm with the National Democratic Front," said Rodel, a short, stocky cadre with a round chubby face. He was the leader of the collective. He looked at his comrades, and affirmed, "Yes, that's what I'll do."

They adjourned at around midnight. Rodel went to the room where his four-year-old son lay asleep. He gently lifted the boy to one side of the bed, kissed him on the forehead, and got into bed beside him. Also in the room were the boy's *yaya* (nurse-maid), and two other comrades, Tessie and Lito. The rest slept in another room. Rodel's wife, who had given birth only days before, was staying in another house.

Carlo was still up, writing a manifesto on some labor issue. His *talambuhay*, too, had to be written before morning. Rodel was strict with deadlines.

The night was humid and quiet in the exclusive subdivision in Las Piñas.

It was almost four o'clock when Carlo heard dogs barking outside. Carefully, he stood up and peeped through a crack in the window.

He saw shadows moving about. Then he discerned figures with white bands tied around their foreheads. They were in civilian clothes and rubber shoes, they carried rifles. Swiftly, they surrounded the house. Three men were hugging what looked like a large iron beam. There was a loud bang as the men charged, using the beam as a battering ram, at the front door.

Tessie, in the room with Rodel and the others, was keen to sudden, unusual sounds at night—a discipline she had developed in guerrilla zones. She woke up with a start. From the rear window she saw relays of armed men climbing over the concrete fence and dropping into the backyard.

Lito was disoriented. When the armed men struck at the front door, he thought the noise came from garbage collectors on their early morning rounds.

Just then, Carlo came running into the room. "Raid! Raid!" he yelled.

Tessie, Rodel and the other comrades tore up notebooks, address books, other sensitive documents. Some letters they chewed up and swallowed.

The armed men—members of the Constabulary Security Group—came crashing through the front door. Another team, broke through the back. One trooper grabbed Carlo by the neck.

"Dapa!" the trooper yelled, throwing Carlo to the floor.

As he lay face down on the kitchen floor, Carlo remembered the handguns. They were hidden under the beds in the room occupied by Rodel and the others.

The soldiers found the pistols. They started beating Rodel and Lito, shouting, "*Putang-ina n'yo, lalaban kayo ha!* So you want to fight, you sons-of-bitches!"

Rodel's son didn't understand what was going on. When he saw a trooper push and slap his father, he screamed and started hitting the soldier with his little fists. Another soldier grabbed the boy.

"Let him go!" Rodel shouted. "Don't you dare touch him."
The troops ransacked the two bedrooms. They opened drawers and closets, scattering clothes and other items on the floor. Rodel saw some of them furtively pocketing the money they found in handbags. They broke open the filing cabinets and pulled out all the envelopes and folders.

Rodel and the other men were brought to the kitchen and made to join Carlo on the floor.

An officer looked Rodel in the face.

"Well, well," the officer said, smiling triumphantly. "Look who we have here. Edgar Jopson! We hit the jackpot!"

1
A Store in Sampaloc

He would someday be known to many as the rich kid who joined a poor man's cause. But Edgar Jopson, or Edjop, was not born with a silver spoon in his mouth.

He was born to a family which he would one day classify as lower petty bourgeois—that is, too rich to be considered poor, but not really rich enough to be in the social register. His father, Hernan Jopson, was the son of a poor peasant; his mother, Josefa Mirasol, was the daughter of a businessman who owned a small hat factory in Manila.

Born on the island of Negros, Hernan Jopson joined the Philippine Army at the age of 21, and was a sergeant when the Japanese invaded the country. He survived the fall of Bataan. During the infamous Death March to Tarlac, he escaped and joined the guerrilla resistance.

After the war Hernan Jopson came to Manila, practically penniless. But he had a strong body, a keen business sense, and the capacity for long hours of hard work. In the immediate postwar period, a time of rebuilding for a country ravaged by four years of war, these were enough to start with.

Hernan, a short amiable fellow who never lost his distinctly Visayan accent, went into business with an old army friend. They bought and sold U.S. Army surplus materials, and opened a sarisari store. His friend introduced him to his sister-in-law Josefa Mirasol, an optometry student at Centro Escolar University, who shared Hernan's enterprising nature. Hernan also went to college at the Far Eastern University, where he took up commerce.

They were still students when they got married, on January 5, 1947. Hernan subsequently asked his friend to buy him out, and with an initial capital of P870, he and Josefa put up their own sarisari store at 300 San Anton Street in Sampaloc, just a block away from where the Jopson Supermarket now stands.

Hernan and Josefa both remember the exact date their sarisari store opened: February 11, 1947. Their capital was obviously limited. "We could only buy one bag of sugar at a time," Josefa recalls. "This usually lasted for only a few hours, and I would have to rush back to the public market to buy another bag with whatever cash we had at hand." But the store was the beginning of a classic rags-to-riches story.

Josefa, then 23 years old, would graduate from college in March. Hernan, 27, quit school to devote all of his time to their store, where he worked as manager, accountant, carpenter, janitor, and all-around handyman. They lived in a small room in one corner of the store. The room served as kitchen, dining room and bedroom. The newlyweds slept on two *tejeras* (foldable army cots) which they bought at ten pesos each.

In front of their store was another store owned by a Chinese businessman, who gave the Jopsons their first taste of business competition. The Chinese storeowner laughed off the challenge posed by the young couple. "Don't you know," he sneered, "that all establishments put up in this area, other than mine, went bankrupt?"

But Hernan Jopson was convinced a Filipino could beat a foreigner at his own game. His strategy was to outdo the competition in every important aspect. The Chinese storeowner sold evaporated milk at 60 centavos a can; at the Jopsons' you could get three cans for a peso. "The Chinese opened at around five in the morning," Hernan Jopson recalls. "We opened at four. So long as the Chinese's store was open, we remained open. This usually meant closing at around one o'clock the following morning. My wife and I were so tired that we often fell asleep just sitting down."

A little entrepreneurial gimmickry—"things you don't learn in college"—didn't hurt. At five in the morning, Hernan could be seen in front of the store, heating *pandesal* laid out on a wire mesh held over a big metal tray of burning charcoal. Hot pandesal was thus one of the store's main come-ons. Customers could not resist the aroma of what seemed like freshly-baked bread. "Actually, the pandesal was delivered to us the afternoon before," Mr. Jopson chuckles. "But customers always thought that they had just come out of the oven."

Not surprisingly, more customers began buying from the Jopsons. As early as five in the morning, people were lining up outside their store. Hernan and Josefa had to give out tickets to accommodate everyone.

Ten months after they opened, their initial capital had grown to P11,000. "We're making more than congressmen do," Hernan informed his wife after making an accounting. Back then a congressman received—officially—P700 a month; the Jopsons were earning P1,100 a month. The store itself now looked more like a grocery, complete with display stalls, a soft drink cooler and a freezer. The Jopsons could now procure supplies, from canned goods to dairy products, by the cartons and cases. One of their suppliers, another Chinese entrepreneur, impressed with their performance, gave them extended credit, and even loaned them a few pieces of store equipment.

Among the Jopsons' patrons was Senator Emmanuel Pelaez, who told the couple, "Your store is like a fast-growing plant in a small pot. You need a bigger place."

As their Chinese competitor had predicted, the Jopsons closed down their sarisari store on San Anton Street—but only because it was time to move up. In 1953 they leased the top floor of a two-story building along Earnshaw Boulevard, right beside the Sampaloc church. It was actually an old dilapidated wooden apartment, home to cockroaches and termites; it was even older than the Sampaloc church. The Jopsons had the floor repaired and converted into a self-service supermarket. Because they could not afford stainless steel carts, they made do with push-carts made of rattan. Because they could not afford an artist, Hernan himself made the display signs, such as 'For a Healthy Strong Body' on top of a stack of canned milk.

It was the first self-service supermarket in the country—a fact, says Hernan Jopson, that is even mentioned in some grade school textbooks. The supermarket prospered, and in 1955, in recognition of his pioneering work in the supermarket business, Hernan Jopson, then in his early thirties, was named 'Grocer of the Year' by the Business Writers Association of the Philippines.

One indication of the supermarket's success was the number of important people who patronized the store. In addition to then Senator Pelaez, regular customers included Supreme Court Justices Roberto Concepcion, J.B.L Reyes, and Almeda Lopez, as well as future Manila Mayor Ramon Bagatsing. There were also Spanish-speaking matrons from the old rich families of Manila, who, at first, sneered at the "self-service" policy and would simply point to items that store employees picked up from the shelves and placed in their carts.

As a boy Edgar Jopson would perform similar services for these rich ladies. He was also given to more theatrical performances. At age six or seven, he would often be seen clambering atop a supermarket counter and declaiming, "O Captain, My Captain, the fearful trip is done . . . ," or "Dirty hands, I love my dirty hands . . . ," to the delight and applause of supermarket customers.

2
Boyhood

Edgardo Gil Mirasol Jopson was born on September 1, 1948. His mother named him after Edgar Rice Burroughs, the author of the Tarzan novels, which she had grown fond of, and Saint Gil, whose feast day falls on September 1.

He was the couple's second child. The first, Zenaida, nicknamed Inday, was born in October 1947.

When he was two years old, Edgar suffered a bout of asthma. Josefa Jopson feared that, as a result of the illness, her son would grow up weak and sickly. But the boy recovered after a year. Much to the relief of his parents, he no longer had serious health problems after that.

He grew up robust, running around half-naked in short pants, playing in the streets of Sampaloc. Independent, full of energy, he was uninhibited by people, places, or things unfamiliar to him.

The whole city was his playground. At the age of five, alone and unassisted, he boarded jeepneys without knowing where they were headed. Standing on the running boards, hanging on to the railings at the back entrance, he would get as far as Divisoria or Quiapo. The jeepney drivers, amused at the carefree little boy with a toothy smile, let him ride with them for free. Sometimes the drivers didn't even notice his presence, because he was so small; the passengers took him for a street urchin or a vendor.

Ed never got lost and always got home in time for lunch or dinner, with a ready excuse to tell his parents. He found an ally in his elder sister, Inday, who, though aware of her little brother's adventures, never told on him. In return, Ed always came home with a *pasalubong* for Inday—sweet bread or candy, or figurines of saints or the Blessed Virgin, bought at Quiapo Church.

Coming home with a little gift was, says Inday, a habit she and Ed picked up from their parents. Years later, when Ed was in

23

the underground, he would still bring his sisters and friends gifts from the far-off places he had been to—*pastillas* from Pampanga, native jewelry from the Cordilleras, *malongs* from Mindanao.

Ed and Inday also pooled their money to buy birthday gifts for their parents or for any of their younger sisters—a fountain pen or cheap perfume—which they bought with savings from their daily allowance of 25 centavos each. "We never asked from our parents," says Inday. "To save, we sometimes skipped *meryenda* or forwent the toys we wanted to buy."

As a boy, Ed loved the movies, often sneaking out of the house to see one in downtown Manila. He routinely took a bath once he got home, to remove the smell of the moviehouse from his body. His sister Marie remembers being taken along on one of these movie trips when she was only four years old. It was her first time in a moviehouse, and she was afraid of the dark. But each time she asked Ed to take her home, he would take her to the door to show her it was till daytime.

The second to the eldest of twelve children, Ed was, for twenty years, the only boy in the family. And he was the leader of the Jopson brood in the games of childhood—teks, sipa, marbles. "Ed could mobilize us for whatever activity he had in mind," says Inday. "I sometimes felt like a tomboy, playing those rough games." Ed even took his sisters swimming in the flooded streets of Sampaloc. "We had lots of fun," Marie recalls, "even with all the garbage and human waste floating around us."

Inday describes her brother as *"sutil na bata,"* an incorrigibly naughty child. Indeed, the extremely active Ed had a penchant for mischief that worried his parents.

When the Jopsons went to the movies, Ed would bring along a flashlight, and would use this not only to find a seat but to flash at people seated behind them. The Jopsons often sat in the balcony section, where lovers traditionally make out.

With a soft-drink straw for a blowpipe and mongo seeds for ammunition, Ed and Inday would sometimes snipe at store customers they disliked—the mestiza matrons who wouldn't carry their own grocery bags, grouchy priests, altar boys who bullied Ed in church. He also led his sisters in mock battles, using rubber bands and paper "bullets," against the other kids in their neighborhood.

Inday was implicated in many a prank which Ed master-minded, and the two of them often got a spanking. But Ed had a way of putting one over his parents: he padded his buttocks with his baby sisters' diapers. While being whacked, he would cry and moan, pretending to be hurt. When his mother or father wasn't looking, he would wink triumphantly at Inday, who ended up with a sore behind.

Besides being Ed's partner in mischief, Inday was also her brother's closest childhood friend. Ed tended to dominate the relationship, but there was no sibling rivalry between the two of them. Inday was always willing to follow Ed's adventurous lead, to play second fiddle to her kid brother.

"Whenever we played cowboy and Indian," Inday recalls, "Ed was always the cowboy. I was always the one who got shot and tied up. Whenever we played house, he was always the 'mother,' because he always had to be the bida, the good guy."

Ed and Inday were alike in many ways and shared many inter-ests. They both had a passion for books, and often pooled their savings to buy the latest edition of the *Nancy Drew*, *Hardy Boys* or *Bobbsey Twins* series. They collected Tagalog comic books, which they asked their father to read aloud. Hernan Jopson, an Ilon-ggo, got his tongue all twisted up trying to pronounce the words, to the amusement of his children.

The two elder children's tastes developed as they grew older. Inday tells of a card game called "Authors," which listed novels by writers like Nathaniel Hawthorne, Mark Twain, and Charles Dickens. "We became curious about the book titles," says Inday, "and we began reading some of them."

Ed developed faster. While in elementary school, he had al-ready read *The Scarlet Letter*. In high school, he and Inday pored over books on literature, history, and the sciences. Ed was always conscious of the quality of the books he read. Once he saw her reading an Emily Loring romance novel. "How trite," he mocked. "Why do you read such trash?"

Another time he came home with books he had bought at a

bargain sale in school. Many of them were far too advanced for him. When asked by Inday what he planned to do with all of them, he said, "They'll be of some use someday." Years later, in the underground, Ed would be instrumental in making some of his comrades appreciate the value of reading in waging revolution.

Ed and Inday showed their affection and concern for each other in many ways. Late one afternoon, the elder sister came home to discover that her younger brother was nowhere in the house, though it was getting dark. Due to some miscommunication and a hectic schedule at the store, her parents had forgotten to pick him up in school. Inday and her parents rushed to the Ateneo grade school campus on Loyola Heights, where they found Ed seated patiently on a bench. The worried Inday ran to the little boy and gave him an emotional hug. "It was only about six-thirty in the evening," Inday recalls. "But I really thought that I had lost my little brother."

The bond between Inday and Ed, formed and strengthened during their childhood, would help them both see their way through the major crises they faced together and separately. Years later, Inday would continue to watch over Edgar, providing him with whatever support she could—money, clothes, a place to stay for the night, a secret dangerous ride to a remote barrio controlled by the clandestine movement her kid brother had joined.

3
Family Crisis

In 1955 the owners of the newly opened Philamlife Homes in Quezon City asked Hernan Jopson, who had just been named Grocer of the Year by the Business Writers Association of the Philippines, to put up a supermarket in the exclusive subdivision, home to movie stars, government officials and other public personalities. It was an offer Hernan and Josefa found difficult to resist. Their warehouse was filled to the ceiling, and their capital investment was by then worth over half a million pesos—an enormous amount in the 1950s. "We didn't owe a single centavo to any bank," Hernan Jopson recounts with pride. "We really had it made."

That same year, a branch of the Jopson Supermarket opened in Philamlife Homes. The Jopsons bought a house in the subdivision, as well as a Mercedes Benz. They sent their children to exclusive private schools—Ed to the Ateneo and Inday and the other girls to Holy Ghost College (now College of the Holy Spirit). Hernan Jopson started playing golf at a first-class country club.

The years spent in a modest one-room apartment in a not-so-fashionable neighborhood in Sampaloc seemed to be over. For the Jopsons, who by this time had seven children, there seemed to be nowhere to go but up.

But they found out the hard way that moving up did not necessarily mean moving forward. In 1958, three years after they moved to Quezon City, the Jopsons went bankrupt. Husband and wife have different explanations for the tragedy.

"I was to blame for what happened," says Hernan Jopson. "I thought we could manage two supermarkets at the same time. But we couldn't do it. We were overstretched. Many of our employees at both stores lacked discipline. They usually lounged around doing nothing when I was not around—shoplifters had a field day robbing us."

27

Josefa Jopson herself thinks the problem was that they put too much trust in their new neighbors: "The residents at Philam were always trying to outdo one another. The Santoses always wanted to do better than the Cruzes. So they were always giving these luxurious parties, and always buying groceries from our store on credit. We were new in the subdivision and we wanted to fit in, so we gave most of them credit—*pakikisama.* But most of them never paid us back."

Inday remembers the agony her parents went through at this time. "Mommy went around the subdivision every day, trying to collect from the people who owed us money. But all her efforts were in vain. She got sick and eventually had a nervous breakdown. Daddy tried to raise money with which to salvage the business, but he had nowhere to go."

It was, says Hernan, a period of "enormous mental and emotional stress." They had to sell almost everything—the house, the Mercedes Benz, most of their appliances. Hernan had to pawn his golf clubs and give up playing golf. They were heavily in debt, owing P160,000 to suppliers; their inventory had shrunk from half a million to P19,000.

They kept the piano, Josefa Jopson's only family inheritance. The Jopson children were able to continue with their education at their respective schools. The Jopsons also managed to hang on to the store in Sampaloc, which became their sole means of livelihood.

They had more than what they had when they were just starting. But the load seemed heavier this time. From a comfortable, luxurious home in an exclusive subdivision, the Jopsons suddenly found themselves in what seemed like a hell hole. They had moved back to Sampaloc, all nine of them, and were staying in a dingy, rundown one-room apartment on the lot where the new supermarket now stands. The apartment used to be a meat shop; Inday recalls it always had a foul smell. The Jopson children developed skin rashes. On hot nights, Josefa Jopson had to stay up late, fanning her children and driving insects away.

The family could no longer afford to hire employees to run the supermarket. To keep the family business afloat, Hernan and Josefa had to rely on their two eldest children: Inday, 11 and Ed, 10. "One day, our parents called Ed and me to a meeting," Inday relates. "They explained what had happened, why we went broke. They needed our help."

The two kids found themselves playing key roles in their family's struggle out of the pit. Ed was then a fourth grader at the Ateneo, and every morning, before going to school, he and Inday helped open the store, sweeping floors, replenishing and arranging displays, running errands. At lunchtime, Inday, whose school was only a few blocks away from the supermarket, came to mind the store so that her mother could go home to feed the younger children.

After school, Ed and Inday took over the entire supermarket, while their parents went home to rest and have dinner. Hernan and Josefa would return at around seven, so the two kids could go home to do their schoolwork and help their younger sisters do theirs.

But on hectic days the two kids stayed until closing time, which was around ten p.m.; they brought their books and notebooks to the store and did their schoolwork behind counters or by the shelves whenever there was time. On weekends they spent the whole day at the supermarket. On Sundays the store usually opened at around five in the morning, in time to catch the crowd coming from the first mass at Sampaloc church.

As in the past, the Jopsons worked with very limited capital, and the supermarket stock had to be replenished several times a week. There were days when Ed had to wake up at three in the morning, to accompany his father to Divisoria, where they procured supplies.

Ed and Inday worked the cash registers, to the amusement of their customers, who grew especially fond of the little boy standing on a box of apples, making computations and giving out change. Customers sometimes teased the little grocer. "You shortchanged me," one would pretend to complain. Ed would count again and, convinced of the accuracy of his original computations, would lose his temper and tell his "unsatisfied" customer, "Now, let's go through this together. You gave me fifty pesos. You bought this and this and this. So that means you owe me this much, and so I gave you the right change."

As sackers, Ed and Inday loaded grocery items into bags and cartons and carried them for their customers. "We were like their maids," Inday recalls. "We were small children then, but we carried bags which our customers could have carried themselves."

Ed also worked as the store butcher, preparing cold cuts in the supermarket freezer section. One morning, while preparing ham pieces with an electric knife, he accidentally sliced off part of the index finger of his right hand. "I was then at the cash register," Mr. Jopson relates. "Ed just came up to me and said 'Daddy, look.' I saw his finger almost cut off, and I felt my knees weaken. He wasn't crying or panicking. He was quite calm about it. But there was blood all over his clothes. I immediately closed down the store and took Ed to the hospital."

The accident affected Ed's parents more than it did the boy. "We began to worry," Mr. Jopson recalls. "Was it worth it to put our children in danger just to succeed?"

The store remained closed for a time, until Ed—and his parents—recovered from the incident.

There were times when Inday and Ed were depressed over their situation. While working on weekends or during vacation time, they would see their friends and classmates outside the store, playing and having fun. They could only sigh, " *Ay naku, bakit naman ganito?* Why does it have to be this way?"

But they found ways of making the toil less tedious. The store became their playground. They played hide and seek and pretended that the stacks of boxes and sacks of rice in their warehouse were castles or mountains for them to climb and conquer. They secretly made fun of their customers, giving them names based on the way they looked, their mannerisms, and even the time they usually came to the store; a man who regularly came at seven o'clock, for instance, was dubbed Mr. Alas Siyete.

"The games helped take our minds off our burden, so Daddy and Mommy put up with them," says Inday. "We never complained. We knew our parents were working hard for us and the whole family. They served as good examples for us. If there is anything that our experience in those years taught us, it is the value of hard work and hard-earned money."

The experience also taught them independence. When Inday was in fifth grade and Ed in fourth, they took care of enrolling themselves and their younger sisters, and shopping for the needed textbooks and school supplies.

On his tenth birthday Ed got a wristwatch from his father. One day, while Ed was being punished in class for some misdemeanor, his teacher accidentally hit his watch with a pointing stick. Furious, Ed grabbed the stick and hit back at the teacher. "Ed had not been a particularly violent or aggressive child," Inday recalls. "But when the teacher hit his watch, the first thought that probably came to his mind was, My father worked hard for this watch and you dare break it!' He got a D for conduct that semester, but I don't think he regretted what he did."

After three years, the Jopsons were back on their feet. They had paid back all their debts, and their supermarket was once again a thriving concern. Since they could once again afford to get hired help, Ed and Inday began to spend less time at the store. As a reward for their commitment and hard work, Mr. Jopson sent his wife and two children on a tour of Japan.

"Many people were surprised to see us recover so quickly," says Mrs. Jopson. "Some of our relatives even asked if we had won in some sweepstakes raffle, or if I had received some sort of inheritance. But the truth is we owed a lot to the efforts and sacrifice of Ed and Inday."

In 1965 the Jopsons bought the whole building on Earnshaw Boulevard, which they had renovated. They also decided to buy a house on Paraiso Street in Quezon City. Formerly owned by an American engineer, the elegant two-story house had well-furnished rooms, a garden with a variety of plants and flowers, a big lawn and a swimming pool.

The Jopsons hired maids to maintain the house and to take

care of the children. But to instill in their younger children the values of responsibility and hard work—values which their two eldest kids had learned and practiced splendidly—Hernan and Josefa required them to spend some time working in the supermarket.

One leisurely afternoon, as Ed and Inday watched their younger siblings play noisily in their swimming pool, Ed, then in his teens, said to his elder sister, "Look how happy they are. They'll never know the pain and hardships we had to go through. But I wonder if that is good or bad for them. On one hand, they are lucky never to have to work as hard as we did. But on the other hand, they will never know how it is to struggle and succeed like we did. In many ways, that is also their misfortune."

4
Atenista

Edgar Jopson's first school was the Telly Zulueta Albert Kindergarten in Malate, Manila. As the most outstanding pupil of his class, he was given the honor of delivering a speech at his kindergarten graduation in 1954. After the ceremony, a Jesuit priest who had attended the affair, impressed by the six-year-old boy's eloquence, approached Hernan Jopson and encouraged him to enroll his son at the Ateneo Grade School.

At first Mr. Jopson hesitated—the Jesuit-run Ateneo was known as a school for the rich. But the family business was going well, and he thought it right to let his son have the kind of education he himself never had.

The school was also known for its high standards, and on the day Ed took the grade school entrance examinations, his father was "a bit nervous." Afterwards, Hernan asked his son how it went. The boy seemed uncertain. "I answered all the questions," he said. "But I'm not sure if I got two of them right. I was asked for the names of my father and mother. So I wrote *Daddy* and *Mommy*."

Ed passed the exams and entered the Ateneo in 1954. He would stay there until college. The sprawling picturesque campus on Loyola Heights, Quezon City, overlooking the Marikina Valley, became his second home, far from the hustle and bustle of downtown Manila.

It was at the Ateneo, in high school, that Ed got the name "Edjop." As the story goes, his geometry teacher, an American Jesuit named William Kreutz, would often mispronounce his family name, giving the J the English rather than the Spanish pronunciation. His classmates began aping Father Kreutz's mispronunciation, and Ed Jopson got a new nickname.

Under Jesuit tutelage, Edjop went through a rigid academic training. In high school he took up a strict study routine, starting on his homework after dinner and staying up until midnight.

When his parents wondered why he was so relaxed during exam periods, he assured them, "I've been studying every day for the whole semester." To help him concentrate, his parents had a private den built for him, complete with air-conditioning, wall-to-wall carpeting and its own separate entrance and bathroom.

Ed kept index cards and took notes on everything he read. According to Inday, he also kept some sort of dossier on his friends, classmates, teachers, and acquaintances, noting down how and where he met them, their characteristics, his impressions. It was a practice he would carry with him as an underground cadre, and when he was detained in 1979, he compiled information on the notorious military officers he met in prison, documenting their personal backgrounds, work habits, and favorite torture methods.

The Ateneo was the perfect setting for the young boy's intellectual growth. Traditionally a school for the elite, the school boasts a proud tradition of excellence, having produced national heroes such as Jose Rizal and Gregorio del Pilar, and contemporary leaders in business and politics. Ateneans were the best elocution speakers and debaters. They won inter-school quiz contests, science competitions, and art festivals. They spoke English fluently, with the patented "Arrneow accent." Even in sports, at the annual games of the National Collegiate Athletic Association, Ateneo was always the team to beat.

But the tradition of excellence also bred arrogance. Many Ateneans looked down on students from other campuses, most especially from their arch-rival, La Salle. To the question, "Why is the sky blue and the grass green?", an Atenean would answer, "Because Ateneo is better than La Salle." Ateneans saw themselves as the best and the brightest, and their school as the greatest. As Raul Manglapus, foreign secretary under Corazon Aquino, put it in a rousing song which he wrote as a student and which was to become a popular school anthem: "You are the King! Blue Eagle, the King!"

As a young Atenista, Ed developed airs. Hernan Jopson recalls that, in high school, his son "began to carry on like he was better than other people." During meals, Ed would sometimes complain about the food. Marie remembers an instance when there was only corned beef on the table; Ed opened a kitchen cabinet, took out something he liked and ordered the maid to cook it.

Sianing, a helper who came to work in the Jopson household when Ed was in sixth grade, describes the boy, during this period, as *suplado* (snotty). He did nothing but study in his room, and he would sometimes ask her to wake him up at a certain hour, only to snap at her for disturbing his sleep. Yet he showed concern for Sianing's situation. One afternoon he asked her why she had to work as a helper.

"Because I come from a poor family and, in our place, we have no means of earning a living," she explained.

"Don't you have land in your province, where you can grow crops?"

"Yes, but we live in a mountainous place. We have to wait a long time for the rains to come, so that we can plant."

"Don't worry, Sianing," the boy said. "Someday I will discover ways for you to get more out of your land."

At the Ateneo in those days, students were required to speak in English and were fined for using Tagalog. Ed tried to impose this policy on his sisters at home. The girls found their brother's policy an enjoyable game, until the fines began to eat into their allowances. The "English campaign," as Ed called it, was eventually scrapped.

When he was in his third year in high school, Ed asked his father to buy him a car. Pressed to give "one good reason," Ed replied, "Well, most of my classmates have cars." Hernan pointedly reminded his son that his classmates belonged to rich families—the Aranetas, the Yulos, the Padillas. "We are not like them," said Hernan, "and I don't like your attitude." Ed was ordered to take the bus from then on. Not until he was in college would he get his own car.

Despite his snottiness as a young Atenean, Ed was humbled by his own background. His family—and what it had gone through—kept his feet on the ground, reminding him always of the value of humility and hard work.

"Ed wasn't, in a sense, rich like the others were rich," writer Alfredo "Freddie" Salanga would reminisce years later. Salanga, who died in 1988, was a year ahead of Edjop in college, and would later become his best friend. "The other Ateneans had fathers who were hacenderos, lawyers, doctors, professionals. Ed's father was a grocer—*iba talaga*. It was really different.

"The others belonged to 'old' Ateneo families, and had fathers, brothers, uncles who had gone to the Ateneo. They had an Ateneo tradition in their respective families. Their family names appeared several times on the alumni roster. There were those whose family names began with the letter J, like Jardeleza, Jereza, and Jalandoni. These were the Bacolod-Iloilo families. Then there were those with Spanish family names, like Araneta and Buencamino. Ed and I were Jopson and Salanga. *Mga bago na*. Ours were new names."

Ed was one of the few students on the high school campus who had to work. "To most of us, having to work was embarrassing," Freddie Salanga would later recall. "But Edjop made a show of his responsibilities in their family grocery."

Ed's circle of friends in high school was not of the party-every-weekend "burgis" type. He was in class 4-A, the honors section. Many of his classmates were skinny, or short, or incredibly fat, and wore thick eyeglasses. They got straight A's in their report cards, were the best declaimers and debaters in school, and submitted the most intelligent term papers and science projects in their batch. They were, in other words, nerds and squares.

"Edjop," Freddie Salanga would later recall, "was the typical square guy. The guy who went to mass. The guy who went to confession. The guy who, in the junior-senior prom, brought his sister as his date . . . He was a good boy, which to the other students, meant a *sipsip* [someone who likes to suck up to figures of authority]. The Jesuits would find nothing wrong with him. He was their model student. He was perfect in almost everything. The only thing he couldn't go in for was basketball, because he was short."

Edjop did go to parties, but he was the type who would sit quietly in a corner. He had to be forced to mingle or dance with the girls. Once he dared to ask an attractive girl to dance—only to find out, when she got up from her seat, that she was about five inches taller than he. The girl, according to Inday, was Mitch Valdez, who would one day become a famous entertainer.

At 16, Ed stood at five feet one, and finding a girl who was not too tall for him was a difficult task. This was also one reason why he didn't go out on too many dates or parties, or why he never had a high school sweetheart.

Ed remained close to his sisters. While brushing his teeth at night, he would walk from his den to his sisters' rooms, where he would rinse his mouth and join in the chit-chat. But as the only boy in the family, he was wary of feminine influences. He would later admit to Marie that one of his reasons for joining so many organizations in high school was so he could get out of the house more often, and not spend so much time with his sisters.

In high school, Ed joined groups like the Math Club, the Debating Society and the Dramatics Club. He was a staffmember of the Blue Book, the high school annual. But he was most involved in religious and service-oriented organizations, like the Ateneo Catechetical Instructors League (ACIL), which taught catechism in public schools in Marikina; the Sodality of Our Lady, a spiritual brotherhood; and the Student Catholic Action, which held fund-raising and welfare programs.

Edjop was a very devout young man. Piety ran in his family: one uncle was a priest, several cousins were priests or nuns; Ed's immediate family always went to Sunday mass and observed all religious holidays. Ed himself was an altar boy at the Sampaloc church, and at home he regularly gathered and led his family in prayer. Aside from religious images, he was fond of giving his sisters estampitas, Bibles, and rosaries of different kinds, from the plain wooden types to the luminous ones.

The Jesuit education reinforced his faith. Every morning, before classes started, he attended and served mass at the high school chapel. He always carried a rosary in his pocket, and on all his books, notebooks, test papers and diaries, he would write the initials AMDG, for *Ad Majorem Dei Gloriam*—"For the Greater Glory of God." He served as a model for the "Hail Mary Boys"—as Ateneans were called. The priests at the Ateneo liked and admired Ed, and would fetch him from the Jopson residence for some religious activity in school.

At the Ateneo, Ed's religious convictions acquired a new dimension: service. An Atenean, according to the Jesuit ideal, is supposed to be a "man for others." He comes from the elite, but, as a Christian, he is expected to share with the poor and the deprived the blessings and good fortune he has received from God. Of all the lessons learned at the Ateneo, this one had the greatest influence on Edjop's personality.

In fact, at one time he had his mind set on becoming a priest. Hernan Jopson—with ten daughters and only one son—began to worry. "*Brainwashing* is perhaps too harsh a term," he says. "I didn't really have anything against the priests. But they were really grooming my son for the priesthood."

Hernan tried to divert his son's attention, by taking him out to golf games and other leisure activities. But "nothing seemed to work," Hernan recalls. According to Inday, their father at one point thought of sending Ed to a military academy in the United States. Josefa went to the parish priest of Sampaloc to seek his advice on their "dilemma." But all the pastor would say was: "Give Ed his freedom, and God will reward you."

As it turned out, Ed realized for himself that "many are called, but few are chosen." Josefa recalls that Ed, coming home from a retreat in Baguio, said to her, "I have been praying hard, Mommy, and I realize that I can help people even without entering a seminary."

Hernan has a different explanation for his son's change of mind. In the summer of 1965, he took Ed to the island-province of Mindoro. They rented a room in the sleepy town of Mamburao, moved around in the only jeepney in the town or in karetelas, and sometimes rented a pumpboat to go to other towns and barrios.

One day, their host took the Jopsons to see a piece of land up for sale in another part of town. Father and son were awed by what they saw. The 300-hectare land was bounded to the east by a river, and beyond it was a forest. A stream flowed into a lagoon, where the water was clean and pure. The land abounded with animal life—deer, wild boar, monkeys, birds. "The place seemed untouched by civilization," says Hernan. "We had never seen anything like it before."

When they came back home to Manila, Ed urged his father to buy the land. "What would I do with it?" said Hernan. "I'm a businessman, and my work is here in Manila. Who will take care of the land?"

"I will," Ed said.

Hernan Jopson was unimpressed—it seemed like another one of his son's flights of fancy. "How can you take care of it, when you yourself said that you plan to become a priest?"

"I've changed my mind," said Edjop. "I don't want to become a priest anymore. I want to become a farmer instead."

Ed's words, to Hernan Jopson, "sounded like they came from heaven." He immediately closed the deal on the land in Mindoro. (The Jopsons now own a handsome vacation house in Mamburao, and Mr. Jopson recently went into prawn-farming there.)

Ed graduated the next summer. He was chosen class valedictorian, which came as a surprise to him, but not to Inday and some of his schoolmates. Freddie Salanga called Edjop the "logical choice." According to Inday, her brother did not have the best grades in his batch, but he excelled in both academic and extracurricular work, making him a model, well-rounded Atenista.

In his valedictory address at his high school graduation on April 30, 1966, Edjop declared, "We will not just dream our goal in life without doing anything about it. We shall develop all our talents and gifts to the fullest, in order to serve you, our neighbor, and our country, to the best of our abilities."

And at the end of the ceremony, the graduates, their clenched fists raised proudly in the air, sang the school hymn:

We stand on a hill, between the earth and sky;
Now all is still, where Loyola's colors fly . . .
Down from the hill, down to the world go I,
Remem'bring still, where the bright blue eagles fly . . .

As a reward for his son's achievement, Hernan Jopson took Ed on a vacation trip to Hong Kong in the summer of 1966. There, father and son had another heart-to-heart talk. Hernan told his son about his plan to retire at the age of 55, "to rest and enjoy the fruits of my labor." He said he would be happy if one of his children would take over the supermarket.

Ed replied, "Daddy, if that's what you want, then I'll take up a college course which will be of use in running the store."

That, says Hernan, was why his son took up management engineering at the Ateneo. "But as things turned out," Hernan adds, Ed "put his education to use in something else."

Right after being named class valedictorian, Edjop also told his father how he wished he had been named salutatorian instead. Surprised, Mr. Jopson asked why, and Edjop answered, "Because as valedictorian, many people will expect a lot from me, and will turn to me for leadership. I can no longer relax, and my life will no longer be normal. Now I must show them that I deserve this honor."

5
Loyola Heights

Before Edjop got involved in movements and causes, the Jopsons were not really a politically-inclined family. Hernan Jopson did not translate his prosperity and reputation into some form of political clout; nor did he ever think of running for public office. For the family, politics was confined to dinner-table talk about the scandals splashed in the newspapers or on television about cabinet officials accused of taking bribes, senators exposed for having connections with criminal syndicates, congressmen flayed for going on too many lavish junkets abroad.

Marie says that one of the first political phrases they learned as kids was *graft and corruption.* "The image of the politico that was inevitably formed in our minds was that of a dirty, scheming person, who made use of his position in government to advance his own interests. He stole from public funds, lied about wanting to help the people, and bribed the police to bully and protect himself from ordinary citizens."

One afternoon, in the summer before he entered college Edjop brought a few of his friends to their house on Paraiso street. They spent the whole afternoon in the basement living room, analyzing the state of Philippine politics. Inday had just entered the room when Edjop asked her, "What about you, Inday—what do you think would be the best type of government for the Philippines?"

"For me, it was simply another playful conversation," says Inday. "But Ed was really caught up in the discussion, serious about his ideas and proposals."

"As we all know, the Filipinos are not a disciplined people," Edjop declared that afternoon. "That's why simple democracy cannot be effective in this country, for this leads to confusion. But then, we also cannot have tyranny or dictatorship, for our people love freedom, and they rebel when it is taken away from them. So we must have a government that takes into consideration the needs and aspirations of the people, but is, at the same time, firm in implementing policies based on these needs and aspirations. That's why I say that we must have guided democracy."

At the height of the First Quarter Storm in 1970, as she read news of student protests and Edjop's sudden rise to national prominence, Inday, then studying in the United States, would recall the summer her kid brother had talked so seriously about the changes he envisioned for Philippine society. "This is it, this is the start," she said to herself.

But before that turbulent year—when Edjop became a much-admired, and much-maligned, public figure—there was a period of tranquility when he viewed society, not from a platform in street demonstrations, but from the serene and secluded campus on Loyola Heights. In the calm before the storm, Edjop's blue feathers were unruffled by the turmoil of the times.

As a college freshman, his main concern was to define the balance between, on one hand, the business career he had set for himself and, on the other, his commitment to God and country. In his Ateneo college application, he wrote, "I want to enter business. . . . By succeeding in the business field, I hope to help the Philippines progress, and also to assist my fellowmen in my own little way."

In his freshman year, Edjop finally got a car, a reward from his parents for being high school valedictorian. His friends recall watching out for the short fellow driving a cream Le Mans, though it was only his head that they could see from afar. Not too many college freshmen owned cars, and the Le Mans made Edjop quite popular. He was, of course, well-known for other reasons. As high school valedictorian, he became the logical choice for class president, and he easily won a seat in the university student council.

He was taking up management engineering, the toughest course in the college, combining two strict disciplines: business management and mathematics. But Edjop maintained a notable level of excellence. A look at his transcript of records shows

Edjop more inclined to the social sciences, history, and religion (grades of "A" in subjects like "History of Western Civilization," "The Filipino and Philippine Society" and "The Sacraments, Grace and Eschatology") than to mathematics and the natural sciences (grades of "C" in "Fundamental Concepts of Algebra," "General Chemistry" and "Introduction to Statistical Theory"). Edjop's lowest grade was a "D" in physical education in his last semester.

Edjop was a sophomore when he met Maria Gloria Asuncion. Joy, as she is called, was the seventh of nine children of a customs broker. Her family lived a short distance from the Jopson house on Paraiso Street. But though they were practically neighbors, it was only in 1968 that she and Edjop met. He was then a member of the Ateneo Student Catholic Action, and had been assigned to do extension work at the Sergio Osmeña High School, where Joy was then enrolled. "Ed had a crush on Joy, and he often described her to me," Inday recalls. "I helped set them up for a date. My boyfriend and I went along, as chaperons."

Joy was two years younger than Edjop. She was petite and attractive, *kayumanggi* (of brown complexion), with a sweet, dimpled smile and a warm, tender voice. Gentle and childlike in her manners, she nevertheless projected strength and a sense of self-assurance. Like Edjop, she was an outstanding student in high school, graduating valedictorian of her class. Like him, she came from a staunchly religious family, and was reared as a devout Catholic.

As valedictorian in a public school, she would have logically gone to the University of the Philippines. But her father decided against sending her to a campus which, by then, was known as the center of student activism. Instead, Joy got a scholarship at Saint Theresa's College, which her parents considered "safer."

This was in the late 1960s, when, amid the rising tide of radicalism led by students from the UP and the Lyceum University, middle-class parents looked to Catholic schools as sanctuaries to protect their children from the "Red menace." Meanwhile, at the Ateneo, the prevailing mood was one of ambivalence.

"The atmosphere was very consciously elitist," Freddie Sa-langa would later recall. "*Masuwerte ka nasa Ateneo ka, hindi bale na ang iba.* You were lucky to be in the Ateneo, other people didn't matter. You felt safe and secure, and privileged to be there. You didn't have to worry about your future—and you knew this. No Atenean would ever go hungry. No Atenean would ever be unemployed. No Atenean would ever be poor. You knew this and felt safe. The sense of guilt—*Why are we privileged, while the rest of the world are not?*—came only later. But in that kind of atmosphere, you can imagine that everything really worked against concern and involvement."

Romy Chan, another of Edjop's closest friends in college, says the Ateneo campus in the sixties had a "country-club atmo-sphere." The Ateneans bought their shoes from Walkover De-partment Store; their ties and shirts from Soriente Santos or Aguinaldo's. They hung out at Botica Boie or on Escolta, the financial and business center, where most students hoped to land a job after graduation. They danced to hit songs by the Beatles and the Rolling Stones, wore bellbottom pants, and had favorite expressions like "Groovy!"

Edjop, however, was *baduy*, out of key and old-fashioned. He wore shirtjacks and straight-cut black pants. But now he went to more parties, some of them held at the Jopson residence on Paraiso, where he and his sisters had friends over for punch and finger food. (They got most of their refreshments from the supermarket.) They danced to music played on portable turnta-bles, although Edjop, Inday says, was a rather awkward dancer. He began to show more interest in girls, often conspiring with Inday to have a slow song played right after he had asked a girl to dance; Edjop would return the favor, when his sister was asked to dance by a boy she liked. In the evening, as the youngsters got tired of dancing, the party would move to the swimming pool, where it would continue late into the night.

6
Activism

Edjop was still in high school when the seeds of the movement he would one day oppose, and later lead, were being sown.

In 1964, the Kabataang Makabayan (KM) was founded by a University of the Philippines academic named Jose Maria Sison. Born in 1939, Joma, as he is more popularly known, came from a rich landed family in Ilocos Sur. He also went to the Ateneo de Manila High School, but was dismissed for supposedly being a delinquent student. In fact, he was an intelligent young man, with an unquenchable thirst for knowledge—the type who spent the whole day reading books in the library.

But he also had a penchant for defying conventions. At the University of the Philippines in Diliman, he made friends with young people who, like him, were fascinated with new and unorthodox ideas about the arts, culture and philosophy. The group, says a "KM original" who prefers to be known only as Anna, was the *"barkada ng mga baliw na baliw sa ideas"*—gang of people crazy about ideas. They congregated in the basement of the Liberal Arts building, where they analyzed and debated the ideas of Jean-Paul Sartre and Albert Camus—and where Sison wrote erotic poems with titles like "By Cokkis Lily Woundis."

Later, the group ventured into political theory and history, following closely the latest schools of thought in Europe and the United States, and studying the revolutions ablaze in Central America, Asia and Africa. In the 1950s, "nationalism" was a dangerous cause to espouse. But Sison and his friends read, and were moved by, the writings of Senators Claro M. Recto and Lorenzo Tañada; Sison would later become secretary-general of the Movement for the Advancement of Nationalism (MAN), chaired by Tañada. Sison got hold of even more radical literature and, with a number of his friends, eventually accepted Marxism-Leninism as the "most comprehensive and scientific framework of analysis" in viewing Philippine society.

He was, by then, the undisputed leader of this pack of budding revolutionaries, intellectual rebels who had finally found a cause. Sison was no James Dean—he wore thick-rimmed glasses, had a thick upper lip and was awkward in his movements—but he had a sharp analytical mind, and he evinced a tremendous self-confidence which earned him the respect of his colleagues.

U.S.-based writer Ninotchka Rosca, in an interview in New York in 1983, said: "The one person who really affected my generation and, I suppose, the generations that came after ours, there can be no question—Jose Maria Sison. When you come down to the bottom line about who has been the major influence in my intellectual and literary development—Jose Maria Sison. He taught us how to think, how to view the world as an interconnection of phenomena. . . . When the question is asked: Who has affected the post-war period most? Jose Maria Sison. No question about it."

As an association of ideologues and polemicists, Sison's group was harmless. But Sison was no armchair revolutionary engaged in endless fancy talk. In forming KM, he aimed to translate abstract concepts like "nationalism" and "democracy" into a material force.

In his founding speech, delivered at the YMCA Youth Forum Hall on November 30, 1964, Sison said:

"Kabataang Makabayan, as the vanguard organization of the Filipino youth, should assist in the achievement of an invincible unity of all national classes and forces and to push further the struggle for national and social liberation in all fields—economic, political, cultural and military—against the leading enemy, U.S. imperialism, and against the persistent and pervasive main enemy, landlordism, both of which have frustrated the national democratic aspirations of the Philippine revolution of 1896 and have made the suffering and exploitation of our people more complex and more severe. . . .

"This generation of Filipino youth is lucky to be at this point in history when U.S. imperialism is fast weakening at all significant levels of conflict: that between capitalism and socialism;

that between the capitalist class and the working class; and that between imperialism and national independence movements in Asia, Africa and Latin America."

Had he made such a public statement in the 1950s, Sison would have been instantly put in jail. By the 1960s, however, the *Partido Komunista ng Pilipinas* (to which Sison then also belonged) had been effectively neutralized, its key leaders captured or dead. The *Hukbong Mapagpalaya ng Bayan* (People's Liberation Army or HMB), the PKP's armed wing, had been almost totally decimated in their base areas in Central Luzon. The left, in short, was perceived as a boisterous but, on the whole, impotent force. KM itself was seen as nothing more than a curious bunch of fiery, bright-eyed student intellectuals and activists who held regular noisy demonstrations.

But the 1960s also saw a resurgence of student activism in the world, particularly in the United States, South Korea, China, and Mexico. In Paris in 1968, a rebellion spearheaded by students, and supported by workers, nearly brought down the government of French President Charles de Gaulle.

This worldwide trend in student militancy had its effect on the Filipino youth. But Joma Sison took pains to draw a more comprehensive blueprint for the student nationalist movement in the Philippines. In an article entitled "Student Power?" published in his collection of speeches and articles entitled *Struggle for National Democracy* (1972), Sison wrote:

"It appears that the common notion of student power is that students all by themselves can develop their own power, independent of other social forces outside of school walls, and also that, all by themselves, they can hit the streets to make and unmake governments. . . .

"If the meaning of the term *student power* be limited to mere autonomism, then we need to raise serious disagreement in the light of an analysis of the social status of students. Students who truly stand for revolutionary change should always strive for integration with larger and even more dynamic social forces, that is to say, the exploited masses of the people."

In 1966, a summit meeting between leaders of Southeast Asian states and U.S. President Lyndon Johnson was held in Manila. On October 24, at least 500 UP students, mostly KM members, demonstrated in front of the Manila Hotel, the site of the summit, to protest U.S. involvement in the Vietnam war. They burned effigies of Ferdinand Marcos and the American president, and chanted slogans made popular by the anti-war movement in the U.S. and in Europe—"Yankee Go Home!" and "Hey, hey, LBJ, how many kids did you kill today?"

The riot police tried to break up the demonstration, and a skirmish broke out. One student was shot in the neck; seven others were arrested and charged with breach of the peace. Congress subsequently held special public hearings to investigate the melee. Though the students were also blamed for the violence, they nevertheless won the sympathy of some legislators, who filed a bill seeking to protect the students' right to peaceful assembly and free expression.

Then Congressman Emmanuel Pelaez, in explaining the proposed bill, said, "We should make a distinction between ideas as ideas and subversion per se. Our students are looking for new ideas. As long as they employ democratic methods to convince people to adopt their ideas, and as long as no laws are violated to propagate those ideas, they should not be punished."

The Manila Hotel incident gave birth to the October 24 Movement, which was in the headlines for a week. Edjop was then a college freshman. On December 6, 1966, in a symposium sponsored by the Ateneo Political Society and the Ateneo student council (of which Edjop was a member), Edjop met and heard the controversial Joma Sison speak for the first time. The KM chairman opened his talk with a tribute to the Filipino youth heroes of the 1896 Revolution, who committed themselves to "push out the decrepit colonial system and give form to a new nation."

"If the brilliant students—Dr. Jose Rizal, Emilio Jacinto and Gregorio del Pilar—had merely concentrated on stale academic studies, pursued successful professional careers and married well—in the accomplished style of Señor Pasta in *El Filibuster-ismo*—they would be worthless now to this nation, as worthless and unremembered as the captain-general and the archbishops who dominated the pages of the colonial press and the salons of the social elite. Our elders, who take pride in their sheer age and their sense of caution, should learn from the youth, from the revolutionary and nationalist youth movement of 1896 and of today. The elders in the reactionary government should not now assume the function of the censors and the black judges who condemned Rizal, del Pilar, Bonifacio and all other patriots of the old democratic revolution as subversives and heretics."

Sison affirmed the three main objectives of the October 24 Movement: to "wage a national democratic education campaign; defend civil liberties; and expose the nature of state violence." He described the congressional hearings to investigate the October 24 incident as "more dangerous than the accomplished fact of police brutality, because they not only divert attention from and white-wash the acts of police brutality, but also encourage the further commission of such acts. In effect, these congressmen are trying to uphold the fascist character of the state."

"The principle of violence lies with the state first of all," Sison asserted, mentioning, "the police, the armed forces, the courts and the prisons and the reactionary congress" as the "instruments of coercion necessary to maintain order and to guarantee the freedom enjoyed by the ruling class in this society." The KM, he said, had "earned the most bigoted and intolerant ire of the powerful" because it was committed to "the continuation and realization of the unfinished Philippine revolution."

"It is the best reassurance for a genuine anti-imperialist and anti-feudal patriot that he is doing well if he is placed under attack," Sison argued. Defiantly, the KM chairman declared, "We belong to the tradition of the national democratic and revolutionary youth, who merge themselves with the masses under the red banner of the Philippine revolution."

Sison's words found fertile ground in the consciousness of some young Atenistas; in a few years Ateneans such as Emmanuel "Eman" Lacaba, Ferdie Arceo and Nick Solana would be active on the radical side. But declarations about "the fascist character of the state" and "the red banner of the revolution" hardly aroused the majority of students. Edjop himself was unimpressed by Sison's rhetoric. He took a sullen view of the UP brand of activism; when Inday, who went to college at the state university, told him about the demonstrations that students like Sison and UP Student Council Chairman Enrique Voltaire Garcia led, Edjop commented, "Instead of shouting about it in the streets, why don't they do something concrete?"

The first sign of awakening on the Ateneo campus came in 1968, when Edjop was in his sophomore year. A group of students led by Freddie Salanga, Gerry Esguerra, and Eman Lacaba came out with a manifesto entitled "Down From the Hill." The statement, published in the college paper, *The Guidon,* was essentially a call to social awareness and involvement. The drafters criticized the Western orientation of Ateneo education, pushing for a greater emphasis on the study of Philippine society and history, and the use of Pilipino on campus. They also questioned the predominance of American Jesuits in key academic and administrative positions in the university.

With "Down From the Hill," according to teachers and students of those days, the nationalist movement came to the Ateneo. The statement became the subject of a campus controversy. Some of the Ateneo Jesuits reacted negatively to the manifesto, and a tit-for-tat debate ensued among students, teachers, and administrators.

It is not clear how the incident affected Edjop. Nevertheless, he was a very active campus figure. Besides being a member of the Ateneo student council, he was one of the founders, and the first president, of the Ateneo History Club; one of the initiators of AISSEC-Ateneo, the prestigious international organization of business students; the co-chairman of the first Ateneo-Sophia (a Japanese university) Student Exchange Program; and the overall coordinator of the Boys Town Adopt-a-Boy-for Christmas Program. He would later lead student campaigns for fairer Spanish exams, and against school regulations requiring students to wear neckties, to always speak English, and to attend mass every morning. (Though religious, Edjop apparently believed that going to mass should be an individual decision, not a compulsory activity.) He also helped in the Filipinization campaign on the Ateneo campus, and even decided to drop, or at least tone down, his "Arrneow accent."

His election as student council president in June 1969 came as no surprise to anyone at the Ateneo. One of his classmates compared him to a Volkswagen, "small but dependable." Salanga, who served as Edjop's campaign manager, would later recall: "By the time he was in third year, Ed was already a popular and respected figure at the Ateneo. His opponent's campaign was actually more of a token opposition. Edjop won by a landslide."

According to Inday, Edjop had been reluctant to run, since he "hated" the idea of having to flaunt his credentials in order to convince people to vote. But, as Salanga would later point out, "Edjop was the most qualified student for the position. Everybody knew this, and, I guess, Edjop did, too."

By then, a mood of restlessness was sweeping the campus. "There was a feeling that we had to be involved," Salanga explained. "But we didn't know in what. The NCAA games, which by then were wracked with controversies that resulted in schools bolting the league, were no longer that exciting to us. Though there were still parties, we wanted something more than the Beatles or being hip and groovy."

In God, sensitive students found the first step to greater fulfillment. In Edjop's first two years at the Ateneo, a kind of spiritual revival swept through the campus. He joined "Days with the Lord," a junior *cursillo* movement, where, said Salanga, who also joined the group, students went through "examinations of consciences and a lot of psychological browbeating." Salanga added. "It was a very emotionally-draining experience. But the movement became very popular on campus. It was then what the born-again movement is today. Everybody was in it. Everybody went to mass in the mornings and received holy communion. The college chapel was always full of people."

During this period, Edjop stayed clear of political issues; the causes he got involved in were not colored by any political or activist orientation. But this changed with a major development in the sixties. The Vatican's Ecumenical Council (Vatican II), from 1962 to 1965, and a series of encyclicals issued by Pope John XXIII, set the tone for sweeping reforms in the Catholic church in the sixties.

Vatican II, according to Penny Lernoux in her book *Cry of the People,* "sought to modify institutional rigidity and anachronistic liturgy." Pope John emphasized "the human right to a decent standard of living, education and political participation" and challenged the "absolute right to private property and the Church's allegiance to capitalist individualism in the cold war against socialist collectivism." Said Lernoux: "Vatican II widened the floodgates by establishing two radically new principles: that the Church is of and with this world, not composed of some other-worldly body of celestial advocates, and that it is a community of equals, whether they be laity, priest, or bishop, each with some gift to contribute and responsibility to have."

In the wake of Vatican II, bishops from third world countries lobbied for a "church of the poor." In Latin America, the theology of liberation began to take root in Basic Christian Communities set up in the barrios and poor communities of workers and peasants.

Though it did not have as big an impact on the Philippines as it had on Latin America, Vatican II helped focus attention on the Philippine church and its role in society. Filipino radicals, suspicious of religious involvement in the clamor for social change, belittled church people and students who took up the banner of Vatican II, branding them as "clerico-fascists." But for students from private Catholic schools, the Vatican II reforms provided the groundwork for a kind of activism they could relate to and accept.

In 1968 the Laymen's Association for Post Vatican II Reforms

(LAPVIIR) was formed by students from the Ateneo, La Salle, Holy Spirit, and other Catholic schools, and by members of religious organizations such as the Young Christian Socialist Movement. Edjop joined LAPVIIR. This, said Freddie Salanga, "was a portent of things to come."

"His involvement, however, didn't make Edjop less of a traditional Ateneo student leader or, for that matter, a Catholic-bred activist," Salanga explained. "Of course, we didn't call ourselves activists at the Ateneo. We were simply Christians trying to get involved in society. The activists were those from the University of the Philippines and other secular settings."

Like KM, LAPVIIR launched education campaigns to spread the "good news" of a new church based on Vatican II reforms. Its members held pickets calling for reforms in the church and its hierarchy. They demanded an accounting of the properties of Rufino Cardinal Santos, then Manila archbishop. A picture of a LAPVIIR picket in Intramuros shows Edjop holding a placard that says, *Kaisahan at Kalayaan sa Simbahan* [Unity and Freedom in the Church]. Another placard at the same picket reads, "Live up to true Christian witness."

At first, the LAPVIIR seemed like just another religious organization of the youth. Its members protested graft and corruption in government, though their denunciations were not as strongly-worded, or as political, as those of the radicals. Because of this, they had less of a problem with the authorities. Jose F. Lacaba, then a reporter for the *Philippines Free Press*, wrote of a demonstration by radical students protesting Philippine involvement in the Vietnam war. They were blocked by riot policemen from staging their rally in front of Congress. When students from Catholic schools and members of religious organizations held their own demonstration the next day: "The cops were less tense and nervous. The demonstrators were attacking a safe, obvious, uncontroversial target: graft and corruption."

But one activity which created a stir among the rich was a picket put up by students from the Ateneo, La Salle, and other Catholic schools during the wedding anniversary party of millionaire Eugenio Lopez Sr. at his house on Quirino Avenue in Parañaque. The celebration was a magnificent extravaganza, with hundreds of guests and an exotic fountain from which champagne gushed. For Edjop and the other student protesters, it was a vulgar display of opulence amid abject poverty. The picket was played up in the newspapers, generating a lot of public contempt for the affluent classes. It also sent shivers down the spine of the members of high society; though they had turned a deaf ear to the cries of protests of peasants, workers, and radical students, they could not ignore these clean-cut boys and girls from prominent families who were now calling into question the morality of their lifestyles.

Amid these protest actions against the elite. Mr. Jopson told his son that he could have a new car. Edjop declined the offer. "What would people say about me if I get a new car while we are protesting the extravagance of the rich?" Edjop said.

"I began to have more respect for him after that," says the elder Jopson.

In LAPVIIR and in the causes it led, the moderate student movement began to take root. By then, the lines between those advocating revolution and those calling for reforms were being drawn more clearly, with members of each camp eyeing the other's motives with suspicion and arrogant disdain. Influenced by the anti-communist hysteria of the fifties, the moderates saw the radicals as scheming godless Communists out to build a totalitarian state. Revelations about sponsored trips to China of some radical students, mostly from UP, reinforced the belief of the moderates that KM was actually a creation, and was under the direction, of the Chinese Communist Party.

On the other hand, the radicals suspected the Jesuits, in connivance with the Central Intelligence Agency, of being involved in counterrevolutionary activities in different parts of the world. A Jesuit priest by the name of Jose Blanco was widely believed to have been involved in the 1965 CIA-sponsored coup in Indonesia which ousted Sukarno and led to the massacre of hundreds of thousands of Indonesians. That the Jesuits were at the forefront of the Vatican II reform movement made many radical activists conclude that the rise of the moderate student organizations was actually a counterrevolutionary scheme.

By the end of the sixties, these two camps were on a collision course that would set off an explosion in the turbulent, historic year that was 1970.

7
Student Leader

In 1969, the same year that Edjop was elected Ateneo student council president, Ferdinand Marcos won a second term as president of the Republic, in one of the dirtiest election campaigns in Philippine postwar history. Just four years earlier, Marcos had been a charismatic and popular leader. But now his credibility was fading fast. The United States still considered him an important ally, one whom U.S. President Lyndon Johnson called his "right arm in Southeast Asia"; but to a growing number of Filipinos, Marcos was the cause of a worsening political and economic crisis and a brewing social upheaval.

Earlier, on December 26, 1968, the birthday of Chinese leader Mao Zedong, Jose Maria Sison and 10 other young radicals had formed the Communist Party of the Philippines (CPP), which they proclaimed as the vanguard of the "national democratic revolution." Sison had by then broken off from the Partido Komunista ng Pilipinas (PKP), which he branded as "revisionist" and "counterrevolutionary." PKP leaders reportedly sent hit squads to assassinate him; with the military also hot on his heels, Sison went underground.

On March 29, 1969, Bernabe Buscayno, alias Kumander Dante, another PKP "renegade," linked up with Sison and the newly-founded CPP to establish the New People's Army (NPA). It was not much of an army, with only 60 youth and peasant guerrillas, armed with 35 functional firearms. Pitted against it was the 50,000-strong Armed Forces of the Philippines. But in the countryside the rebel band steadily increased in number, and in the cities Dante and the NPA captured the imagination of radical activists, who began calling for "people's war" as the answer to the problems of Philippine society.

By 1969, the streets had become an important political arena, and street actions were powerful political statements. The activist fever spread to Catholic schools, including the Ateneo. "By then, we were getting cues from UP," Salanga would later explain. "We also wanted to know what was going on at the national level. We had become open to politics and political issues." With a chuckle, Salanga added, *"Pero open lang*—but just open. We were still apprehensive about getting too involved, especially with the Reds. We were not ready for that. *Takot pa kami noon sa Pula.* We were still afraid of the 'Reds.' "

In mid-1969 Edjop decided to run for president of the National Union of Students of the Philippines (NUSP). The election was to be held at the organization's national congress in December. Edjop told Salanga of his decision. "It's a different kind of campaign," Salanga remarked. "Are you willing to work for it?" Edjop said he was ready. "So we started working," said Salanga.

Back then, anybody seeking the presidency of the biggest student organization in the country had to campaign like any politico running for mayor or congressman. Edjop's bid began months before the NUSP congress. He went on sorties to different provinces and cities in the country, trying to win the support of other student council officers of different schools.

In the provinces in the sixties, student activism was an extension of traditional politics. On some of his sorties, Edjop had to deal with student council officers old enough to be his father. They were, in Salanga's words, "professional student leaders" who were on the payroll of politicos in their provinces or cities: "They just kept enrolling every year, taking any course available, while the politicos took care of them. Some of them were even older than the deans of colleges. We met one student council president who was also the provincial sheriff of Bacolod."

NUSP politics then was also the game of students from the elite. They used national student politics, according to businessman Alex Aquino, a former Ateneo student, "as a springboard from which to launch their political careers." Budding politicians from three prestigious schools—Ateneo, La Salle, and UP—dominated organizations like the NUSP and the College Editors Guild of the Philippines (CEGP).

The Ateneo, according to Salanga, won the presidency every other year. In 1969 it was the Blue Eagles' turn once again. Edjop found no difficulty getting the support of his Ateneo classmates. Romy Chan, who helped in Edjop's campaign, admits, "The NUSP elections, for us, were a matter of grabbing power for the glory of Ateneo."

That year, from December 26 to 30, more than 250 student council representatives from 69 schools nationwide attended the 13th annual congress in Iloilo. The gathering was "like a fiesta," Salanga would later recall. "NUSP congresses were always happy occasions. Everybody had fun. Everybody got to know one another."

Two people Edjop met at that time would later play short but important roles in his life: a young dentistry student from the Southwestern University in Cebu who prefers to be known only as Angelo Buenavista; and a political science student from the Notre Dame University in North Cotabato named Nelson Estares.

The NUSP congress was Estares's; first exposure to students from Manila. Now a colonel in the Philippine Constabulary, Estares relates with amusement his first encounter with Manila colegialas: "*Dyaheng-dyahe ako.* I was so embarrassed. They spoke slang, which I could not pick up. On the other hand, I spoke like a lawyer or a politician from the province. I spoke what they sometimes called 'Liberation English.' *Inabogado at de-kahon* — legalistic and stereotyped. I could not integrate with those girls."

Edjop did not speak with an "Arrneow" accent, and this made Estares and other students from the provinces feel more comfortable with him. "Of course, Edjop spoke very good English, but he pronounced his words clearly, with no twang, unlike other students from Ateneo and La Salle. He was soft-spoken, a real gentleman."

The 1969 NUSP congress is sometimes referred to as the start of the open conflict between the radical and moderate camps in the student movement. Estares, speaking as a military man nearly 20 years later, tells how his school supported Edjop's bid

and shared his concern about radical influence in the convention. "Edjop was afraid that the KM would eventually take over
the NUSP. *Magaling kasi talagang magmaniobra ang mga Komunista.*
The Communists were good at maneuverings."

But others remember the conflict as just another manifesta-
tion of the traditional Ateneo-UP-La Salle rivalry. "It seemed to
have been all a question of who was the better speaker, who had
the better organization and things like that," says Cynthia "Cha"
Nolasco, then a delegate from Saint Joseph's College, who also
helped Edjop in the campaign. "The personalities were there,"
said Freddie Salanga. "But they were not political persons. They
were more school partisans. It was not yet an ideological
conflict."

Like the Ateneo, La Salle was an elite Catholic boys' school.
But on political issues, the Lasalistas of the time tended to side
with the radical bloc led by UP students. This could have been
simply a case of siding with the enemy of one's enemy. But,
according to banker Jun Miranda, then of La Salle, the reasons
went deeper than that. Something had happened at La Salle, he
explains, which made radicalism acceptable to its students. In
1966, freshmen students, led by people like Chito Sta. Romana
and Miranda, boycotted their classes to protest the dismissal of
a La Salle brother who was advocating academic reforms in the
college. The campaign caught fire on campus. Though the dismissed brother was not reinstated, the students won on their
other demands, including an autonomous student council and
an independent student paper.

By the time they were in their senior year, the students who
led the 1966 strike, Chito Sta. Romana in particular, had become
the recognized leaders on the La Salle campus. Sta. Romana,
like Edjop, was an exemplary student and public speaker. (Jun
Miranda compares him to John F. Kennedy.) He was also of a
devout Catholic background and had been involved in the LAP-
VIIR movement. But Sta. Romana and Edjop were different in
their political outlooks. During discussions at the 1969 NUSP
congress, both agreed on the need for greater student involve-

ment in national political affairs. But on prescribed solutions, on the question of which road to take—the "what is to be done" part—Edjop and Chito, the moderate and the radical, were seriously disunited.

This was evident in the major debates at the NUSP congress, which had for its theme "Youth and the Philippine Constitution," in preparation for the Constitutional Convention (Con-Con) to be held in 1971. Edjop and the moderates saw the Con-Con as the "last chance for democracy," the only hope left in achieving meaningful social changes. They believed that the nation's basic law and the the rules of politics in the country could be altered to serve the interests of the masses, and they would lobby to have politicos and traditional power-wielders barred from participating in the convention. "In a sense it was an antipolitical time," says Salanga. "*Galit ang mga tao sa pulitiko.* People were angry at politicians. This made the call for a nonpartisan convention popular, especially among the middle classes."

But for Sta. Romana and the radicals, reforms through the Constitutional Convention were illusory. The ruling classes, they asserted, would surely use the Convention to firm up their dominant and privileged position in society. The rules may change, but they would still be in favor of the powers that be. The elite would never permit the basic law of the land to serve the interests of the majority, for this would mean losing many of the privileges they enjoyed. Therefore, to pin one's hopes on the Convention was, in a way, to take part in this grand deception of the people.

"I think that Edjop never wanted this conflict with the radicals," says Cha Nolasco. "As far as I can remember, he was preoccupied with a singular crusade, and that concerned constitutional reforms."

The student delegation from La Salle and UP supported the candidacy of Francis Jardeleza of UP-Iloilo. Edjop had the support of other Catholic schools such as Saint Joseph's, Saint Scholastica's, and Maryknoll. Students from these schools, Salanga explained, always took a staunchly anti-communist stance.

"When the nuns in convent schools would not send a delegation from their schools, we would tell them, '*Gusto ba ninyong manalo ang mga Komunista?* Do you want the Communists to win?' and they would immediately send their students."

The election was close and riddled with controversies. But Edjop, according to Cha Nolasco, conducted his campaign "with utmost tranquility."

A news story published in *The Guidon* (January 12, 1970), the official Ateneo student newspaper, wrote of the campaign: "During the last five minutes of the time allotted to Jopson, his opponents presented a letter from an Atenean to a cousin in one of the Manila delegations offering free accommodations at the conference. They then asked Jopson if he had offered free board and lodging to some congress delegates. Jopson answered with a terse, 'I deny it!' The letter caused a momentary furor, but after several minutes, the situation eased up when a challenge from the Ateneo side to prove that any of Jopson's supporters were actually receiving free board and lodging was not taken up."

Economist Manuel Montes, then the finance officer in Edjop's campaign, commented in the same news item: "The charge was obviously last-ditch mudslinging by the opposite camp an hour before the voting. Everyone we billeted paid ten pesos a day and we have the receipts to show you." According to Colonel Estares, "The KM delegates spread all sorts of black propaganda against Edjop. They accused him of having been bought by Marcos, of having been given a Mercedes Benz, of having traveled from Manila to Iloilo using a Philippine Air Force plane."

Cha Nolasco says the night of the counting was like a scene from a suspenseful movie. "It was a neck-and-neck race," she relates. "There were two ballots left, and Edjop was ahead by just one vote. Then there were protests about some of the ballots, so the counting was temporarily delayed. It was still not a comfortable margin for Edjop. But when the counting resumed, the first vote went to Edjop, so that already sealed his victory."

Edjop won by a hairline: 27–24.

During the congress, the student delegates had agreed to spearhead the formation of a new alliance called Students United for Constitutional Convention Reforms (SUCCOR). They also decided to call a nationwide mass action on January 26, 1970, the opening day of Congress, to push for a "non-partisan Constitutional Convention."

Among the other NUSP projects mentioned in "Page for the Young at Heart," Ethel Soliven Timbol's column in the *Manila Bulletin* (January 13, 1970), were "picket rallies with informative and not rabble-rousing speeches."

Maximo Soliven, in his column in the *Manila Times* (January 21, 1970), wrote:

"The forthcoming rallies and other demonstrations to be held by different youth (moderate) groups are an indication that the young are unhappy over the way their elders have been behaving . . .

"They showed me a copy of their manifesto and I was impressed to find it a very sober one. In fact, they avoided the use of the word 'DEMAND' and instead stated that their intention was 'to appeal' and to 'pledge faith in our last great hope—the rebuilding of our society according to the Constitution.' I trust that our leaders will not allow the meekness of language employed by these youths to lull them into false complacency. For if we do not listen to these kids when they speak softly, we may eventually find them massed at the barricades. Should that day ever come, we shall realize with a sense of shock that they no longer wish to parley or to talk—but to fight."

When he took hold of the reins of leadership in the moderate camp, Edjop had proudly proclaimed: "Here is the alternative to the Communists!" To students from convent and Catholic schools, he would, from then on, be the symbol of the kind of involvement that they wanted and could get into—committed but moderate.

Barely a month after he was given a victory ride by his friends and supporters in Iloilo, Edjop would go through the most trying time of his youth.

8
January 26

The January 26, 1970 rally was to be the first nationwide student demonstration in the Philippines in recent history. In the first few weeks of the year, Edjop and the other NUSP officers busied themselves with preparations for the event, drawing up plans, organizing committees, and coordinating with the different student councils and organizations in the provinces.

It was at about this time that Dicky Castro, then of the University of San Jose Recoletos in Cebu, first met Edjop. He had imagined the student leader at the forefront of such a big event to be a "tall guy with a big build." But the person he met was short and a bit chubby. He also met Freddie Salanga, whose bulk was already unmistakable. Dicky remembers thinking: "*Bakit ganito, puro maliliit at matataba?* Why is everybody here so short and fat?"

Ed del Rosario, or Edros, was a staff member of the San Sebastian College student paper and a member of the College Editors Guild of the Philippines (CEGP). "At that time, Edjop was just like any other student council president," he recalls. "He had more drive than the other student leaders and was consistently active. But, otherwise, I wouldn't say that he struck me as someone absolutely extraordinary."

Aside from the NUSP and SUCCOR, the other participating groups, in what was dubbed as the January 26 Movement (J26M), were the National Students League headed by Portia Ilagan; the College Editors Guild of the Philippines; the Young Christian Socialist Movement; Citizens for a Filipino Convention; and the Christian Social Movement. The KM, SDK, and other radical formations had also signified their intention of joining. Radical student leaders, like Chito Sta. Romana of La Salle and Gerry Barican of UP, were members of some of the committees formed to prepare for the rally.

According to Nelson Estares, then of the Notre Dame University in North Cotabato, Edjop had warned the other groups about "the danger of infiltration by the KM," saying that "the radicals wanted the rally to become violent."

Edros recalls, "In the series of teach-ins held in different schools before the January 26 rally, we noticed other groups making different calls, like *Rebolusyon!* They had their own agenda. But we didn't call them radicals or leftists or anything like that."

"I guess the radicals already called us moderates at that time," adds Jun Pau, then of the Mapua College Student Council. "But we were not aware of this. Right before the January 26 rally, there were no clear distinctions between radicals or moderates, rightists or leftists. We were simply *aktibistas*."

On January 21, 1970, the NUSP called a press conference at Saint Joseph's College. Leaders of both radical and moderate blocs came to the presscon. Edjop laid down the plans for the rally. There is a picture of him before a blackboard, explaining how the students would march six abreast from 14 assembly points and converge in front of Congress. The plan for the demonstration, said Freddie Salanga, was simple enough. "We were just to present ourselves in front of Congress, listen to speeches, and go home. *Martsa, salita, 'tapos uwian na,*" he explained.

"It was five minutes past five in the afternoon, by the clock on the Maharnilad tower, when I arrived at Congress," begins Jose F. "Pete" Lacaba's report on the January 26, 1970, demonstration; the report is published in his book *Days of Disquiet, Nights of Rage,* a collection of his *Philippines Free Press* articles on the First Quarter Storm. "The President was already delivering his State of the Nation message: loudspeakers on both sides of the legislative building relayed the familiar voice and the equally familiar rhetoric to anyone in the streets who cared to listen. In front of the building, massed from end to end of Burgos Drive, spilling over to the parking lot and the grassy sidewalks that form an embankment above the Muni golf course, were the demonstrators. Few of them cared to listen to the President. They had brought with them microphones and loudspeakers of their own and they lent their ears to people they could see, standing before them, on the raised ground that leads to the steps of the legislative building, around the flagpole, beneath a flag that was at half-mast. There were, according to conservative estimates, at least 20,000 of them, perhaps even 50,000. Beyond the fringes of this huge convocation stood the uniformed policemen, their long rattan sticks swinging like clocks' pendulums at their sides; with them were the members of the riot squad, wearing crash helmets and carrying wicker shields."

The rally had actually started at around one p.m., when members of the NUSP and other moderate groups started massing up at the different assembly points. At three, they marched to Congress, where 50,000 students, including some high school students from Catholic schools, began to hold a program.

Among the rallyists were four of Edjop's younger sisters: Beng, then a college student at the UP, and Adel, Marie, and Sucel, high schoolers from Holy Spirit, who had come to the gathering in their beige uniforms. "We were very proud to see his name in the papers, and we just wanted to be part of the rally," Marie recalls.

The radical student groups, like KM and SDK, arrived at around four p.m., when the program was about to end. "The KM made a sort of grand entrance," relates Dicky Castro. "There were about 500 of them in wedge formation. In front of them was a jeepney with loudspeakers on top. They marched right through the center of the assembly, splitting the group in two and taking the most prominent position in front of the rally."

Suddenly, Edjop found himself in an emotionally-charged confrontation with the radicals.

"There were two mikes, taped together; and this may sound frivolous, but I think the mikes were the immediate cause of the trouble that ensued," Pete Lacaba would write afterwards. Edjop, who was in a polo barong with a red armband that bore the inscription "J26M," was the program emcee. He had announced that the next speaker was Gary Olivar of the *Samahang Demokratiko ng Kabataan* (Democratic Association of the Youth or SDK) and the UP Student Council. But Olivar was nowhere to be seen.

Instead, Edjop said that Roger Arienda, then a radio commentator, would address the crowd. Arienda began delivering a speech in Tagalog, but before he could finish, the students, led by the KM activists, started chanting, "We want Gary! We want Gary!"

"Arienda retreated," wrote Lacaba, "the chant grew louder, and someone with glasses who looked like a priest took the mikes and in a fruity, flute-thin voice pleaded for sobriety and silence. 'We are all in this together,' he fluted. 'We are with you. There is no need for shouting. Let us respect each other.' Or words to that effect. By this time, Olivar was visible, standing next to Jopson. It was about a quarter to six.

"When Jopson got the mikes back, however, he did not pass them on to Olivar. Once more he announced, '*Ang susunod na magsasalita ay si Gary Olivar.*' Olivar stretched out his hand, waiting for the mikes, and the crowd resumed its chant; but Jopson after some hesitation now said: '*Aawitin natin ang Bayang Magiliw.*' Those seated, squatting, or sprawled on the road rose as one man. Jopson sang the first verse of the national anthem, then paused, as if to let the crowd go on from there; instead he went right on singing into the mikes, drowning out the voices of everybody else, pausing every now and then for breath or to change his pitch."

"Olivar stood there with a funny expression on his face, his mouth assuming a shape that was not quite a smile, not quite a scowl. Other demonstration leaders started remonstrating with Jopson, gesturing toward the mikes, but he pointedly ignored them. He repeated his instructions to NUSP members, then started acting busy and looking preoccupied, and all the while clutching the mikes to his breast. Manifestoes that had earlier been passed from hand to hand now started flying, in crumpled balls or as paper planes, toward the demonstration leaders' perch. It was at this point that one of the militants grabbed the mikes from Jopson."

According to Gerry Esguerra, who was with Edjop on the platform, some KM leaders (he thinks KM Chairman Nilo Tayag may have been one of them) actually pulled on the cord, while he and Edjop still had the mikes.

This tug of war in front of thousands of restless and agitated students may have created what would later become an open rift between the radical and the moderate student groups.

Freddie Salanga would later defend Edjop's action. Edjop, he said, did not mean to look arrogantly selfish. But he sensed that things were getting out of control; he wanted the rally to end quickly. "Our main concern then were the convent school girls," Freddie recalled, laughing. "We had given our word to the nuns in Maryknoll, Saint Scholastica's, Saint Theresa's, and other schools that we would be responsible for their students, and that the rally would be peaceful. So Edjop didn't give the mikes to Gary Olivar. He wanted to give the order to disperse. *'Umuwi na tayo!* Let's go home!' "

Joy Jopson confirms this: "Edjop simply could not bear the thought of anybody getting hurt in a demonstration he had helped organize."

But the radicals saw Edjop's action as a hostile act against them and their cause. From where they stood that afternoon, Edjop looked like an "enemy of the revolution."

Students unaligned with either the radicals or the moderates—who probably didn't even know that such a division existed—felt that Edjop, in refusing to pass the mike, was actually denying a fellow student's right to speak. He seemed to be behaving like the school administrators and government officials denounced for trying to suppress student activism.

"Certainly there can be no justification for the action of the militants," continued Lacaba's account. "The NUSP leaders had every right to pack up and leave, since their permit gave them only up to six o'clock to demonstrate and they had declared their demonstration formally closed; and since it was their organization that had paid for the use of the microphones and loudspeakers, they had every right to keep these instruments to themselves. Yet, by refusing to at least lend their mikes to the radicals, the NUSP leaders gave the impression of being finicky; they

acted like an old maid aunt determined not to surrender her
Edwardian finery to a hippie niece, knowing that it would be
used for more audacious purposes than she had ever intended
for it. The radicals would surely demand more than a nonpartisan Constitutional Convention; they would speak of more fundamental, doubtless violent, changes; and it was precisely the
prospect of violence that the NUSP feared. The quarrel over the
mikes revealed the class distinctions in the demonstration: on
the one hand the exclusive-school kids of the NUSP, bred in
comfort, decent, respectful, and timorous; and on the other
hand, the public-school firebrands of groups like the KM and
the SDK, familiar with privation, rowdy, irreverent, trouble-
some. Naturally, the nice dissenters wanted to dissociate themselves from anything that smelled disreputable, and besides the
mikes belonged to them."

What Edjop did may not have been politically sound. But he
was hardly the shrewd, sophisticated political leader that the
radicals thought him to be. At that moment of confrontation,
he was simply the leader of a bloc of the student movement,
whose only sure way of distinguishing himself from the radicals
was the fact that they were for violence and he was not.

In any case, Edjop probably had no idea what the little cha-
rade involving two microphones would lead to. The radical who
grabbed the mikes instantly lambasted him and the other moderate student leaders as "counter-revolutionaries who want to
end the demonstration."

As the loudspeakers blared out attacks against him, Edjop had
already gone down to the crowd and was running from one
group to the other, giving the command for the NUSP members
(most especially the convent-school girls) to disperse. A number,
including Edjop's sisters, obeyed his command. But for the rest,
there was not enough time. *"Rebolusyon! Rebolusyon!"* went the
crowd, as the radical firebrand, a labor leader, went on to de-
nounce "fascism and imperialism."

"Passions were high, exacerbated by the quarrel over the
mikes," wrote Lacaba, "and the President had the bad luck of
coming out of Congress at this particular point."

It is not clear how the melee really started. The students burned a paper effigy of Marcos as the president was coming out. According to Lacaba, there was also a cardboard coffin "representing the death of democracy at the hands of the goons-tabulary in the last elections" and "a cardboard crocodile, painted green, symbolizing congressmen greedy for allowances." The students reportedly hurled the coffin, and then the croco-dile, at Marcos. After that, according to Lacaba, "things got so confused that I cannot honestly say which came first: the pebbles flying or the cops charging."

Edjop was still trying frantically to get the NUSP people to disperse when the scuffle broke out. The riot police attacked with the ferocity of wild dogs. They made no distinctions be-tween moderates and radicals among the students, whom they whacked furiously with their rattan sticks. "The Metrocoms just started jumping us and smashing people's brains," Romy Chan recalls.

According to Jun Pau, there were young men with crew cuts and black boots who mingled with the demonstrators. "When the riot started," he recalls, "these guys started kicking and hit-ting the students. They were infiltrators." Edros saw a company-size contingent near the Post Office building.

"Putang-ina! Putang-ina!" Dicky Castro heard Edjop mutter an-grily. It was the first time he had ever heard the NUSP president use invectives.

The students counter-attacked with bottles and stones. By then they, too, had forgotten tags and labels. "When the cops started hitting our fellow students," Dicky recalls, "we just didn't care anymore what camp one belonged to. We just hurled any stone, any bottle, we could get our hands on, at the police." Freddie Salanga, normally gentle and mild-mannered, was seen with a stick, looking mean and agitated. "He was ready to club the first policeman who came his way," says Dicky. "Good thing nobody did."

Edjop's four sisters had just gotten inside their car, parked nearby, when they saw the other students running in all direc-tion. "A policeman chased one student toward our car," Marie relates. "The boy was pinned down to the windshield and beaten mercilessly by the police. We watched the brutality happening right in front of us, and we were all screaming, '*Tama na!* Stop it!'"

Policemen cornered one CEGP member at the Intramuros wall. The student pointed to the press card on his chest, yelling, "Press! Press!" Unimpressed, the cops whacked him repeatedly in the face. The student lost all his front teeth. "That day," recalls Edros, who was a buddy of the unfortunate CEGP member, "a new student was recruited into the KM."

As the skirmish intensified, Edjop, Dicky, and Freddie retreated, taking with them any student whom they could still save from the raging battle. Edjop was pretty agile for a short guy. But Freddie could not run as fast as his friend, so Edjop had to hold him by the arm, while trying to protect him from the stones and bottles that flew overhead.

They reached a restaurant where other students and a few media people had taken refuge. Reporters immediately tried to get a statement from the NUSP president. But Edjop, still in some sort of shock, was speechless. "Edjop was really affected by the incident," says Dicky Castro. "He was really hurt." But though Edjop was emotional, he remained cool, according to Freddie: "He was the one who kept telling us to calm down, as we made plans to help the other students still in the streets."

At one point, Dicky recalls, he also heard Edjop mutter privately to himself, "What a shameless thing they did. It was our rally, and they started the trouble."

Edjop and his group moved to the Ateneo campus on Padre Faura, not too far from Congress. There they monitored the skirmishes and assisted students hurt in the riot. Edjop dropped by the family supermarket to check on his sisters. Having confirmed that they were safe, he immediately rejoined the other NUSP members.

Meanwhile, in the streets of Manila, the battle raged. "In the parliament of the streets, debate takes the form of confrontation," Lacaba wrote, recounting how the battle shifted from one setting to another—from the front of Congress, Burgos Drive, the Muni Golf Course to Luneta—with the students gaining the advantage at one time, and the police at another. "There were about seven waves of attack and retreat by both sides, each attack preceded by a tense noisy lull, during which there would be sporadic stoning, by both cops and demonstrators."

The students, armed with rocks and bottles, put up a bold challenge, which sometimes bordered on the senseless, as they stoned the limousine and driver of one senator. But it was the police who had a bloody, bone-cracking field day, beating up poorly-defended youths. Pete Lacaba's report spoke of a student crumpling to the ground while being whacked, right in front of Congress, by about ten policemen for everyone to see; a police assault on a jeepney filled with students; a student clinging desperately to a traffic sign while being clubbed by three policemen, until he and the signpost collapsed.

An episode in Lacaba's book provides a clue to why the radical students were so daring. Two girls and a boy had been clubbed by the cops. "The two girls were cursing through their tears; the boy was calm, consoling them in his fashion. 'This is just part of the class struggle,' he said, and one girl sobbed, 'I know, I know. *Pero putangna nila, me araw din sila!* Those sons-of-bitches will have their day!"

"It was," Lacaba wrote, "impossible to remain detached and uninvolved now, to be a spectator forever."

9
Meeting with Marcos

The January 26 battle lasted until late in the evening, leaving scores of youths beaten and wounded. The next few days saw a barrage of statements and counter-statements on the incident. The Manila Police Department asserted that its riot squads "acted swiftly at a particular time when the life of the President of the Republic—and that of the First Lady—was being endangered by the vicious and unscrupulous elements among the student demonstrators." Marcos himself declared, "Students have a legitimate right to manifest their grievances in public, and we shall support their just demands, but we do not consider violence a legitimate instrument of democratic dissent, and we expect the students to cooperate with government in making sure that their demonstrations are not marred by violence."

On the other hand, government officials, including Senators Benigno Aquino Jr., Gil Puyat, and Salvador Laurel, while critical of the student militants, condemned the police's unwarranted use of violence in breaking up the rally. The UP faculty also denounced "the use of brutal force by state authorities" and supported "unqualifiedly the students' exercise of democratic rights in their struggle for revolutionary change."

Of all reactions to the incident, the NUSP statement was the most controversial. While the organization condemned "police brutality," it also asserted that there were other groups in the demonstration which did not belong to the NUSP. Furthermore, the manifesto stressed, "the NUSP had already sung the national anthem and dispersed when the riot started." Other youth groups interpreted this to mean that the NUSP leadership under Edjop was dissociating itself from the other groups at the demonstration, and were indirectly condemning the violence, not only of the police, but also of the militants.

A typical reaction among the radicals, and of those who began to sympathize with their cause after the January 26 incident, was

72

that of Ceres Alabado. Ms. Alabado, a writer of children's stories, is now a board member of the Edgar Jopson Memorial Foundation. At that time she was scornful of the moderates' response to the January 26 incident. In her eyewitness account of the First Quarter Storm, *I See Red in a Circle,* she calls the NUSP a "yellow scalawag" whose leaders tried to wash their hands of the demonstration bloodshed.

The NUSP statement, Freddie Salanga would later explain, made official the split in the student movement. "From hindsight, I'd say that our reaction to what happened on January 26 was wrong," Freddie commented. "Rather than help forge unity in the student movement, we—the NUSP and the Ateneans—decided to detach ourselves from the rest. In effect, we declared, '*Hindi kami kasali diyan! Gawa iyan ng mga radikal!* We have nothing to do with what happened! The radicals were responsible for it!' And this was a divisive position. It was wrong. We thought we could drag the entire Catholic school bloc away from the radicals and we were successful for a time. But in doing so, we only helped divide the student movement when unity was of the utmost importance."

Apparently, Edjop made the same realization. A news item in the *Manila Times* on February 7, 1970, quoted him as saying: "It is unfortunate that some newspaper reports gave the impression that I was putting the blame on the KM for the January 26 riot. . . . I appeal to all youth and student groups not to allow unfortunate incidents like this to divide us at a time when a solid united front is most urgent and important."

But neither his clarification nor his call for unity healed or concealed the deepening rift. Suddenly Edjop found himself caught in hostilities. "He was getting clobbered by everybody," says Romy Chan.

Edjop was still bent on pursuing his own brand of activism. In the aftermath of the January 26 confrontation, when the radicals' call for youth militance became louder, he and other student leaders of the moderate bloc agreed to a dialogue with President Marcos on January 30.

A few months earlier, during the bicentennial anniversary of the Ateneo, Edjop and other members of the Ateneo student council had visited Malacañang at the invitation of the First Lady, Imelda Marcos. "It was a social visit," recalls Romy Chan. "Imelda showed us around the Palace."

But the January 30 meeting was different. "We had just gone through a sudden awakening," says Chan, who remembers Edjop telling him just before the dialogue: "This time, we are going to Malacañang for a different purpose."

The dialogue was supposed to start at around two in the afternoon of January 30. But Marcos kept the student leaders waiting for about an hour and a half. According to Freddie Salanga, Edjop was about to walk out when then Executive Secretary Ernesto Maceda walked in with the president. As was his style, Marcos was "arrogant and intimidating," said Freddie. Marcos gave the impression that he had a lot of things to do and the students were keeping him from his business as president.

Salanga would later describe the meeting in an article for *Panorama Magazine,* October 10, 1982: "It was mid-afternoon by the time the President got to see [Edjop] in the latter's study, a small room easily jam-packed as much by reporters and student leaders as by curious Malacañang personnel and hangers-on out to catch a glimpse of the boy who had led what was, till then, the bloodiest student demonstration in history. There the demands of the 26th were threshed out, Edjop's normally deep baritone quivering at first but then slowly gaining confidence as the President began to nod his head at a number of points he was raising. As the tension eased in the room people began to notice how like a boy indeed he was, his feet barely touching the polished floor as he sat on a stiff high-backed chair by the left-hand side of the President's table. To the President's right was an equally small person, Portia Ilagan, who then headed the National Students League, an organization of students from state colleges and universities. To many in that room it must have seemed highly improbable that these two could have actually marshalled thousands of students, but that was the stark fact."

While the meeting went on, students were massing right outside Malacañang Palace. The NUSP, the National Students League and other moderate groups had come early, taking their positions at Freedom Park. The KM, SDK, and other radical groups had held their own rally in front of Congress, but at around five they marched to Malacañang.

"It was growing dark," reporter Pete Lacaba would later write, "and the lamps on the Malacañang gates had not been turned on. There was a shout of *'Sindihan ang ilaw! Sindihan ang ilaw!'* [Turn on the lights!] Malacañang obliged, the lights went on, and then crash! a rock blasted out one of the lamps. One by one; the lights were put out by stones or sticks."

As Dicky Castro tells it, in the darkness that followed, rocks were hurled from inside the Palace at the students mobilized outside, and the youths reacted by hurling them back. That, he says, was when the Palace guards attacked.

Meanwhile, inside Malacañang, another confrontation was brewing. "The question of whether the President was going to endorse the demand for nonpartisan elections to the Constitutional Convention was getting pretty near to some kind of resolution," continues Freddie's account of the dialogue, "when Edjop finally came up with the surprise demand of the afternoon. He wanted an assurance that the President would not seek a third term by circumventing the Constitution."

"I am constitutionally bound not to run for a third term," was the President's calm reply.

But Edjop was "adamant," said Freddie. "Mr. President, we want you to sign a document pledging that you will not run for a third term," demanded the young Jopson.

"That was when, so most everyone agrees, the President blew his top," wrote Freddie.

"Who are you to tell me what do!" Marcos shot back, followed by his famous mocking remark about Edjop: "You're only a son of a grocer!"

Portia Ilagan, in an effort to break the tension, cracked, "*Tingling! Ops, break muna!* Break!"

At this point, says Freddie Salanga, Marcos simply shrugged and smiled sarcastically.

Jun Pau remembers that Edjop was nervous during the meeting. "His voice was louder than usual," he recalls. "When Marcos snapped, we were silent and stunned. After all, it was the President of the Republic who had just barked. If he had had a gun with him then, I think he would have probably shot all of us right there and then."

Before the dialogue could proceed, a Palace aide came in with a report on the melee outside the Malacañang gates. The dialogue abruptly ended. At a little past six, Edjop and the other student representatives were seen to the door, but a battle was already raging right outside the Palace. "Jopson and company," Lacaba wrote, "fled back into the Palace, taken aback by the fury that had broken out at the gates. They were graciously shown the back door, ferried across the river, and allowed to go home safely, presumably to watch television. They missed out on all the action."

Edjop may have missed all the excitement—but his car parked right outside the gates did not. Some of the more fired-up radicals, aware that the vehicle belonged to the leader of the moderates—"the clerico-fascist reactionary" who, four days before, had tried to deny one of their leaders the right to address a rally—smashed the windows of Edjop's American Rambler.

The militants were prepared for bigger onslaughts. They commandeered a firetruck protecting the Palace, and sent it crashing through Gate 4 of Malacañang. With the palace gates opened, the radicals attacked. "Once inside the gate," Lacaba wrote, "the rebels stoned the buildings and set fire to the truck and to a government car that happened to be parked nearby."

But according to Edros, who covered the event for his school paper, most of the students were surprised to suddenly find themselves inside the Palace. "I don't think the students really had any intention of assaulting the Palace. After they had broken in, many of them simply milled around not knowing what to do. The soldiers didn't have a hard time dispersing them."

"Before they could wreak more havoc, however, the Presidential Guard Battalion came out in force," Lacaba's account continues. "They fired into the air and, when the rebs held their ground, fired tear gas bombs at them. The rebs retreated; the few who were slow on their feet, or were blinded by the tear gas, got caught on the Palace grounds and were beaten up with rifle butts and billy clubs and good old-fashioned fists and feet."

The Battle of Mendiola lasted until the wee hours of January 31, boiling over to Azcarraga (now Recto Avenue), España and Divisoria. When it was over, four students were dead.

During most of that night, Edjop was in his house with NUSP officers and leaders of other moderate groups, monitoring developments and drawing up plans to assist the students caught in the fighting. "I think Edjop was scared then," said Freddie Salanga. "But as usual he didn't show it. As usual, he was the one who helped us calm down. We were the ones who were agitated."

Eighteen years later, during a reunion at Freddie Salanga's house a few months before Freddie's death, Edjop's NUSP friends would look back to that historic day and year. At first, they disagree on whether Marcos had provoked the 1970 riots. Jun Pau believes that Marcos used "the chaotic atmosphere as an excuse to declare martial law." Romy Chan thinks "the Reds, more than anyone else, were responsible for the violence. They had more to gain from the trouble than Marcos." "Well, let's just say it was a combination of the Reds and Marcos," says Jun Pau. "*Talagang sinundot nila ang mga pangyayari.* They really stirred things up."

10
Socdem

Among those in Edjop's house on the night of January 30 was a medical student named Romeo "Archie" Intengan. Intengan, who later joined the Jesuit order, would be accused of leading the April 6 Movement responsible for a series of bombings in Metro Manila in the late seventies. He had been (and still is) a staunch anti-Communist, and on that night, according to Freddie Salanga, he told Edjop, "We have to do something to stop the Communists. These are classic tactics that they are using."

"We listened to him since he was older and was respected in socdem [social democratic] circles," Freddie recalled. "We wanted to rally all the non-Communists by pushing the issue of a nonpartisan Constitutional Convention. While the radicals were shouting 'Revolution!', we were saying, 'Constitutional Convention!' Our gut reactions then were very basic: 'The radicals are here! It's us against them!' "

Edjop was not a social democrat. In fact, some socdems, like Jose Alcuaz of the *Kapulungan ng mga Sandigang Pilipino* (Assembly of Philippine Organizations or KASAPI), thought Edjop was "a bit conservative," because of the latter's faith in reformism and his non-ideological approach to politics. But Edjop became close to many socdem leaders, many of them former Ateneans like Raul Manglapus of the Christian Socialist Movement, Jeremias Montemayor of the Federation of Free Farmers (FFF) and Johnny Tan of the Federation of Free Workers (FFW). They were, according to Freddie, "authority figures" whom Edjop looked up to.

The social democrats were then the most organized segment in the moderate bloc, with their own alternative political vision and program. On the surface, one would not see much difference between the socdem and the natdem, or national democratic, positions on issues. Filipino socdems also considered themselves radicals, but they sought to distinguish themselves from the KM and other natdem groups by calling themselves "democratic socialists" or the "democratic left." Like the natdems, they were committed to overhauling Philippine society, but they put much emphasis on the "Christian" and "humanist" dimensions of the liberation process.

Though they did not always use the terms and formulations of the national democrats—who saw the "three basic ills" of Philippine society as "imperialism, feudalism, and bureaucrat capitalism"—the socdems also opposed foreign domination, mentioning not only the United States but also Japan and China as the meddlesome forces in the Philippines. They condemned the elitist character of the Philippine political and economic system, denouncing the exploitation of workers by foreign and local capitalists and the landlessness of the majority of Filipino peasants.

Towards a Filipino Social Revolution (1972), a compilation of articles explaining the position of a socdem organization called Ladasdiwa, enumerates the aims of the Philippine social democratic movement: to organize and empower the Filipino masses; and to create a new order through a "Filipino social revolution."

Like the natdems, the socdems criticize the "reformist view," which is described in the book as being "ignorant of the presence of vertical power structures in society." The book adds: "Reformists have a wrong analysis of the Philippine problem, mistakenly contending that the revolution must begin 'from the top'; hence they "naively appeal to the ruling elite to have a 'change of heart'. . . . [Reformists] cannot comprehend the realities of class conflict—that the ruling elite is formed by material class conditions that yield privileges, attitudes of mind, and vested economic interest of a dominant class in society. . . . The ruling elite will do anything in their power, legally or illegally, to secure and increase their already tremendous political power and economic wealth."

The statement implies a position almost as radical as that of the natdems. But Lakasdiwa stresses "Christian humanism" as the core of the socdem world-view, as opposed to "dialectical historical materialism" or "Marxism," which the socdems regard as a "godless ideology." Lakasdiwa describes Marxism as an "extreme reaction to the violent inequalities" in Philippine society, adding: "Communism stresses the paramount view of society over the individual. The common good is more important than the individual good. Society is not made for individual man; rather, man is made for society. Thus, individual freedoms and even family relationships may be sacrificed for the sake of the common good . . . Communism espouses a totalitarian form of government that resorts to coercion to achieve its ends . . ."

As articulated by Lakasdiwa, social democracy in the Philippine context advocates a "New Nationalism" that "does not hark back to the glories of the past, but rather looks forward towards the modernization and the future of the country; it no longer shadow-boxes with past colonial masters and buried ghosts like 'clerico-fascists' of Spanish colonial times, but rather opposes any neocolonial ventures perpetuated by American business corporations, Chinese retailers or Japanese entrepreneurs. . . . Moreover, in the Asian region, the nations of the Third World would especially be wary of any form of imperialism, from the West or from the East, from Uncle Sam or Chairman Mao."

Lakasdiwa further contends that "the People must seize political power," and this must be done through "social organization." The road to genuine social change should not be a choice between violence and nonviolence, for no particular mode of struggle is the correct path to follow. The means must not be "absolutized"; instead, the forces of change "must utilize the most effective means for achieving People's Power."

The Lakasdiwa formulation implies the socdems' openness to armed struggle as one of many means in fighting for reforms. But, according to Gerry Esguerra, the question of violence was, in fact, the crux of the socdem-natdem rift.

"We recognized armed struggle as a valid option," Esguerra explains. "We respected people who chose that road. But on our part, we preferred to give peaceful struggle a try. We believed it could work so long as the people were organized. The radicals considered this useless or counterrevolutionary. But for us, it was worth pushing for.

"More importantly, we could not accept the cost, in terms of human lives, of the alternative that the radicals were presenting. We believed it was too bloody a process in trying to achieve change. At that time, we only had Russia, China, and Vietnam as examples of the kind of revolution and society that the radicals were pushing for, and these weren't exactly acceptable models for an alternative society. We thought of how many people had to die in these countries just to get where they were then— and we couldn't imagine such a bloodbath happening in our country.

"No, for us, it wasn't worth it. We preferred to work peacefully for reforms. The reforms may be slow, or may seem like palliatives at times, but so long as things were moving forward, so long as we are getting more people organized, then we were willing to work for social change without using the gun."

11
Versus the Radicals

The rift between the moderates and the radicals heightened after the First Quarter Storm. In streets and on campuses, each tried to launch bigger mobilizations, and bigger and broader school and community organizations.

What began as a simple intramural contest for Ateneans like Freddie Salanga and Edjop had turned into a deep political involvement, where concepts like "love of country" and "nationalism" became serious issues. Amid the raging word war, Edjop and the core leaders of the NUSP turned to Salanga, who became the one-man think tank of the moderate student bloc, plotting strategies and drafting counter-statements against groups like the KM and the SDK.

It was, at times, a juvenile rivalry. Ging Raterta of the NUSP complains of one of the radicals' tactics: they would dominate rallies by rushing to the front with their red banners.

At other times, the competition became comic. The rift was apparently known to some law enforcers, who became more selective when attacking demonstrations. Salanga related an anecdote about a rally attended by both radical and moderate students. When the police began dispersing the rallyists, a student belonging to the moderate bloc held up the NUSP banner to a charging cop, shouting, "*NUSP ako!* I'm with the NUSP!" The policeman spared the student, saying, "*Aha, moderate tabi ka!* Get out of the way!" He then beat the first KM militant he saw.

As Romy Chan sees it, "Edjop and the moderates snatched the ball away from the leftist students. We just kept on running with the ball. Where were we going? We didn't know. But the leftists wanted that ball very badly. They were out of the limelight. Jopson and the NUSP were in the limelight. Jopson made news, he made waves. The leftists? Once in a while, but only as critics of Jopson. Center stage was for Jopson. The leftists were only foils or accessories."

To the natdems, this is an inaccurate assessment. While they agree that, after the First Quarter Storm, many still looked disapprovingly on the KM and its brand of activism, a growing number of youths, they say, were being drawn to the natdem movement. They affirm that, by the end of the First Quarter Storm, the national democratic youth movement had come of age— 1970 was KM's year.

Former KM members claim that, immediately after the January 26 and 30 demonstrations, young people flocked to KM headquarters to join or to ask how they could form chapters in communities. "It was a rather easy time to organize," says Boni Ilagan, who chaired the KM's UP chapter. "Young people themselves were coming to us."

According to Baltazar Pinguel, who became national spokesman in 1970, the KM had as many as 75,000 members nationwide after the First Quarter Storm. Manila was the center of KM activity, but there were chapters in different regions from Northern Luzon to Mindanao. Pinguel jokes that, in Manila, there was practically a chapter on every street, "*sa bawat kilometro, may KM,* in every kilometer was a KM chapter," referring to the fact that on every national road each kilometer is marked with a milestone with the capitalized abbreviation for kilometer: KM.

Young people joined because their friends did; or because joining was new and fashionable; or out of curiosity. The KM was so popular to a large segment of the youth that some business interests rode on the fad. One ad for a popular soap product went: "*Lahat tayo'y anakpawis, pero hindi kailangang maging amoy pawis.*"

Still, Bal Pinguel asserts, "Serious-minded people were attracted to the KM." He himself was still in high school when he heard about the October 24 Movement. "The organization was in the papers for a week and I never forgot about it. I never forgot about the KM." When he enrolled at the UP, he signed up with the nearest chapter. Bonifacio Ilagan first heard of the KM at the UP Los Baños, where it was constantly under attack. That the organization was the underdog and under fire made him more keen on casting his lot with it. He signed up after transferring to UP Diliman.

In KM ranks were the best and the worst, the most and the least committed, young people ever assembled together. They wore revolutionary pins or insignias, and military fatigue jackets which signified the activist's readiness to do battle.

There were the student intellectuals—Rafael Baylosis, Nilo Tayag, Monico Atienza, Ninotchka Rosca, Rodolfo Salas who engaged in polemical brawls at the state university cafeterias.

There were the romantics, who read and idolized the revolutionaries of Cuba, Russia, and China. Bal Pinguel admits to being of this type. He often wore a red T-shirt, a black leather jacket, black pants, and John Lennon eyeglasses—the attire of a Bolshevik agitator in the movie *Dr. Zhivago.* "Martial law put an end to that, when I and that kind of getup became illegal."

There were the activists of "proletarian origins," the sons and daughters of ordinary farmers and workers, who came from distant barrios or lived in Manila's urban poor communities, and were attracted to the radical affirmations about the "struggle for land reform and workers' rights." Charlie Palma, before joining KM, was already manning the barricades in the Quezon City slum district of Tatalon, where he and the other residents resisted the Araneta-Tuazon group. He later became chairman of KM-Tatalon, helping organize the community of 6,000 families.

To be sure, the KM had its share of bad eggs. Also in its ranks were fraternity bro's who had gotten tired of campus rumbles, and who now found street battles with the police more exciting. There were the rebellious brats who shouted slogans without understanding their meaning. They were the "stereotype radicals portrayed in the movies," says Raul, a moderate who later joined the Communist Party. He remembers a KM member who "had a ready answer to any question." Says Raul: "Everything was clear to him. Whenever I raised questions about the political line of the KM, he would tell me, 'Oh, you're just confused.' "

KM activists were often dauntless, many of them cocksure of the "correctness" of their cause. When asked in an interview with *Now Magazine* (September 30, 1970) about the chances of the national democratic struggle, UP Student Council Chairman and KM activist Ericson Baculinao said: "It cannot be overcome, because it is strictly scientific. . . . these theories are invincible, you see. The principle of relying on the Philippine masses—the mass line—and the people's war. Now, its victory may be delayed, but it is inevitable, society will change."

Though sympathetic to the national democratic cause, Pete Lacaba remained critical of the Chinese cultural revolution's strong influence on the KM. "KM members talked about nationalism but didn't even know how to use Filipino images and references. For instance, they would quote a Chinese saying used by Mao, about hitting one's foot with a stone, unaware that there is a similar Pilipino saying about hitting one's head with a stone: *Para mong pinukpok ng bato ang sarili mong ulo.*"

But the most undesirable elements, KM members later found out, were also among those who were most diligent as activists. According to one former activist, one out of about 20 members who joined the KM in 1970 turned out to be a government agent. "This was not surprising," says Bal Pinguel. "We were running an open organization."

KM boasted a strict education program, where applicants went through "intensive intellectual discussions" three times a week, with fixed curricula and regular assignments. "Everybody was required to speak up, to discuss ideas," adds Boni Ilagan.

Members had to be conscientious students of Philippine history, serious in their role of advancing the "Second Propaganda Movement." The 1896 Philippine Revolution, to them, was not just an event they read about in college history books, but a cause they were championing and continuing. "We became very conscious about what happened then in that part of our history," explains Linda Taruc Co. "How the revolution was lost, and why, and what must be done."

Activists read the works of Rizal, Bonifacio, Mabini, Jacinto, and, of course, those of Joma Sison, Claro M. Recto, Lorenzo Tañada, and Renato Constantino. The list included foreign writers—Karl Marx, Lenin, Mao Zedong, C. Wright Mills, David Guest, Maurice Cornforth, and Felix Greene. As Monico Atienza, KM secretary-general in 1970, puts it: "It became natural for us to also learn from the experiences of other movements in other countries."

Mao Zedong's "Little Red Book"—which Boni Ilagan describes as "cute and very handy"—was the KM activists' Bible, and it was the fad always to carry it around. At the start of every meeting, a passage from Mao was read and discussed by the members—similar to Bible study sessions nowadays.

In solving organizational, ideological, and even personal problems, the "great little book" was consulted. It was not unusual for ordinary activists to have memorized entire passages from the Chinese leader's work. Members who disagreed with a certain policy or line were diagnosed as "confused" and were asked to read and study a particular chapter from the Red Book.

There were also CSC—"criticism-self-criticism"—sessions, which each collective religiously conducted among its members at every meeting, regarding every action and for every issue. "This may seem so rigid and dogmatic now," says Boni Ilagan, "but, back then, the practice helped set the right attitude."

But the KM also sought to transcend its own radical subculture. The activists preached the "mass line," an orientation derived "from the masses and for the masses." They subscribed to the precept "theory-practice-theory" in order to reconcile what they learned from books and discussions with concrete realities.

These were accepted principles in the KM since its formation in 1964. But the activists, at first, were clumsy and mechanical in applying them. As one former activist tells the story, then KM chairman Joma Sison once organized an "exposure trip" to a remote barrio in Laguna. Among the "exposurees" were top KM cadres, including Ninotchka Rosca. They knew no one in the area and soon found themselves seeking shelter in a deserted house. Struck suddenly by a consuming passion to do "peasant work," they all started digging in the ricefields for no clear reason other than to try to experience the kind of work farmers did. It must have been quite a sight, the young Sison in barong Tagalog, and Ninotchka Rosca in a pink long-sleeved mini-skirt dress, in the middle of a rice paddy, tilling soil.

By 1970, the activists had become more systematic. With more established contacts among peasants and workers, the organization launched a "learn from the people" campaign. All members were required to "integrate with the people" in urban poor communities, factories, strike areas and barrios, where they "learned from and served the masses."

Not everyone took this campaign seriously or appreciated the experience with ordinary peasants and workers. There were activists with romantic notions about plunging into the arduous but noble world of the struggle. At rallies, they spoke like valiant warriors, ready to lead the assault on Malacañang Palace. But many of them eventually marched back to their homes in the cities, their illusions shattered by their inability to cope with the real conditions of the people.

In the countryside, with the people they were supposed to be fighting for, they behaved like messiahs, unable to reconcile Mao's Red Book with the *masa's* own logic and way of life. One well-known firebrand during the First Quarter Storm reportedly treated peasants like servants, making them walk long distances to fetch water with which he washed his feet.

But, even then, a core of devoted and mature activists was being molded by the experience, young men and women who were able to blend "theory" and "practice," thus acquiring a well-grounded, deeper affinity with the masa. The peasant and the worker, to them, evolved from a vague concept in the slogans they mouthed during demonstrations, to real people with strengths and weaknesses. They learned to focus on the masa's strengths, imbibing the tremendous resilience ordinary peasants and workers had in the face of adversity, and were thus prepared for the coming "protracted struggle."

Natdems of this mold earned the respect of many activists in the moderate bloc. Raul, who spent 16 years in a Catholic school, was a member of a socdem organization but became a national democrat after the declaration of martial law. "Even when I was still with the moderates, I already had a lot of respect for the natdems. *Pag sinabing KM, ibig sabihin, lubog sa masa.* A KM activist, it was assumed, integrated with the masses. This was my impression too."

But other moderates continued to see the radicals in a negative light. To them, the natdems were scheming political manipulators who launched noisy self-righteous campaigns, which were often destructive and counter-productive.

In February 1970, the NUSP launched a P30,000 fund drive for the restoration of lamps and other tourist facilities at the Rizal Park, which radical students destroyed in a demonstration. "Luneta is a park which belongs to the Filipino people and should not have been made the object of wanton destruction," Edjop said in an interview with the *Manila Times* (February 22, 1970). The *Times* also reported: "The NUSP challenged civic-minded citizens, including the student 'militant groups,' to show their sincerity by helping repair Luneta Park."

Edjop himself became a victim of what moderates call "leftist arrogance." Says Romy Chan: "The radicals were probably saying, "This guy Jopson, these stupid clerico-fascists, what do they know?" They really hated our guts." Bal Pinguel of the KM admits that their contempt for Edjop and the moderates "reached a point where we would curse and spit at him."

Adel Musidora (an alias), also a former KM activist, and now chairman of the *Artista at Manunulat ng Sambayanan* (Artists and Writers of the People or ARMAS), a member-organization of the National Democratic Front, explains that Edjop was an "effective mass leader," and it was precisely for this reason that he was attacked: "We condemned him for attracting people whom we thought should have been on our side."

"I never met him personally at that time," Musidora adds. "We were never introduced. But, I think, if we had been introduced then, I would have snubbed him and I would not even have shaken his hands." (A few years later, Adel Musidora, now an NDF cadre, would recognize and accept not only the friendship but also the leadership of Edjop, his political officer.)

Some natdems were less rigid in their views of Edjop. One former KM activist admits: "Many in our ranks began to recognize Edjop's sincerity. We didn't like his politics, but as far as the leaders of the national democratic youth organizations were concerned, he was not an enemy of the people."

But to the rank-and-file radicals, Edjop was still far from being a model in political involvement of the youth. In fact, to them, he could never be anything more than a talented, perhaps sincere, but nevertheless irrelevant figure in the history of the student movement, one who was unfortunate not to have been on the "right side" of the fence.

Lacaba relates this incident in an article in the *Philippines Free Press* (March 28, 1970): "Nelson Navarro of the Movement for a Democratic Philippines was with the group that came from Quezon City, and he immediately pointed out the new recruits: the Ligang Atenista and the KKK Ateneo. We've got three busloads of Ateneans joining us for the first time, mostly high school boys," Nelson chortled. 'They're not Jopson's boys, you can be sure of that.' "

Radical activists painted *"Jopson, Kleriko-Pasista!"* or *"Jopson, Reaksiyonaryo!"* along with *"Mabuhay ang* KM!" and *"Isulong ang Rebolusyon! "* on the walls of the streets of Manila. To them, Edjop was a "clerico-fascist," one who used faith and religion to deceive and exploit the people, thus leading them away from the revolution. It was a term usually reserved for priests and nuns, but the radicals thought it was fitting for "the Jesuit boy" from Ateneo.

Some radicals, not contented with militant graffiti or fiery speeches, resorted to more violent measures. In some of the KM-led marches that passed through Earnshaw Boulevard in March 1970, radicals threw rocks and Molotov cocktails at the Jopson Supermarket. Once, Josefa Jopson received a threatening call from someone she believed was a KM activist.

"Tell your son to be careful! We are going to burn your store!" the supposed militant warned.

"Do you know what you're doing?" Edjop's mother said, emotional, but calm. "If you burn our store, we can still recover, for we have insurance. But what about our neighbors, the poor people who live around our building? If they suffer and die because of what you plan to do, can your consciences live with it? Go ahead and burn us, if you like!"

The caller was speechless for a second; then he hung up. Nothing happened to the supermarket.

Edjop's family, of course, was furious. "Why do they do those things, when you all want change?" a frantic Marie asked her brother.

"I really hated the KM activists then," she recalls. "Here was my brother, whom I loved and admired so much, and they were calling him some sort of fascist. I had always thought of a fascist as the military, or the police who beat up defenseless students at the January 26 rally. I couldn't understand why they called Ed that, when he was so gentle and mild-mannered.

"They attacked my brother without any valid explanation. They called him 'clerico-fascist' but they didn't bother to define the term, the way they didn't define their other 'isms.' To make matters worse, I didn't even like the way the militants looked. My brother was clean-cut and respectable. On the other hand, the radicals had long hair and always said vulgar words. *Ang moda sa kanila, hindi maligo.* It was a fad for them not to take baths."

The attacks should have been enough reason for Edjop to cut himself off completely from the radicals, to be hostile toward them. But strangely enough, Edjop never shared his socdem colleagues' contempt for the militants, nor did he ever lose his cool in the face of the abuse heaped upon him.

"Why don't you defend yourself? Why don't you clear your image?" Inday once asked him.

"There are so many things to be done, why should I waste time reacting to such things?" Edjop replied. "So long as I know the truth about myself, nothing should faze me. Why should I be bothered by what they say or do?"

His own colleagues in the moderate camp attest that not once did they hear Edjop lose control, curse, or make angry statements about hitting back. "I don't think Edjop considered the attacks as attacks on his person," says Edros. "At that time, we were more worried about coming out with statements to answer the charges of the radicals. We didn't say, We have to fight back,' but rather, 'What do we say?' "

Alex Aquino, then of the Ateneo, attributes Edjop's sobriety amid all the attacks to "his ability to see beyond the petty bickerings and not take the attacks too hard to the point of being petty about them." Salanga sometimes interpreted Edjop's calmness in the face of harsh criticism as "cold-bloodedness." But he added that Edjop was mature enough to make a statement like, "The issues are beyond us. They are beyond personalities. We are all transitory figures at this time."

According to Cha Nolasco, the attacks only challenged Edjop to ask: "Why are they calling me a clerico-fascist? What really are our differences?" She adds that the radicals, in calling Edjop a "clerico-fascist," were overrating him. "They were glamorizing Edjop, giving him credit for things he did not do. Because Edjop then still did not have a fixed position from which he would not budge. *Naghahanap pa siya.* He was still searching for answers."

In fact, according to Alex Aquino, the January 26 and 30 demonstrations led many Catholic school students like Edjop to examine their political standpoint:

"We came face to face with violence from the state. We got to know the capacity of the state to defend itself and to promote the kind of system it wants. At the same time, we were faced with a student movement that was bursting with energy, that was growing and moving so fast. And yet we didn't know where to go.

"Many of us felt trapped, not being able to sympathize with the national democrats, but at the same time aware of the ferocity of the Marcos government. *Parang sinabi namin, 'Hintay muna, mas mabigat pa pala itong kalaban natin kaysa mga radikal.* It seems that Marcos is a tougher enemy than the radicals.' I would go to the extent of saying that some kind of schizophrenia plagued the moderate student movement then."

Edjop, said Freddie Salanga, "could have escaped the condemnation by joining the bandwagon, to make things easier for himself." But at a time when the moderates were searching for direction, Edjop hung on. He did not, says Cha Nolasco, accept "ready-made formulas like the other radical activists."

Salanga described Edjop then as a "tabula rasa"—a blank page. "His consciousness was unstructured. He was willing to learn and was never afraid to acknowledge that he could have been mistaken. The radicals were condemning him, saying Edjop was leading the students away from the mainstream, and maybe he was. But the guy had intellectual honesty. At that point he could not accept a student movement that was radical, or that would even entertain revolutionary ideas. But if he held out for a long time, it was only because he wanted to test if his ideas, no matter how unstructured, were correct."

In his search for direction, Edjop, together with other core leaders of the NUSP, pored over books and other reading materials on the social sciences, held endless discussions among themselves, and went on "exposure trips." They also invited "authority figures" like the FFF's Jerry Montemayor and the FFW's Johnny Tan to speak before them. Edjop himself held informal dialogues with some natdem leaders like Chito Sta. Romana of La Salle and with fellow Ateneans identified with the radicals like Ferdie Arceo and Eman Lacaba.

At this time Freddie Salanga was, in a sense, Edjop's mentor. The closest of friends, they had often talked politics, and it was Salanga who provided Edjop with Marxist literature to read. This makes Salanga partly responsible for Edjop's later conversion to the national democratic revolutionary movement. But Salanga had not planned on molding his friend into a full-fledged revolutionary, revealing, with a boisterous laugh, that he gave Edjop those books so he would "learn more about the enemy."

The moderate student movement in the early 1970s, Cha Nolasco admits, "never got its act together." The natdems, on the other hand, made a lasting impact on their generation. "Though we did not agree with the ideology of the Reds," says Ging Raterta, "we owe the development of a politicized youth to them. Even the term *First Quarter Storm* was coined by the radicals. The moderates tried to hold back this storm, while the Reds were, definitely, pushing it."

The radicals, says Cha Nolasco, "knew where they were going, while we [the moderates] were still in search of a vision. In fact, many of us didn't even know why we were called moderates. We had begun to see the problems of society as being rooted in structures. But we were still groping for a framework."

Edjop, she adds, "led an open and honest search for a vision to start a movement. The whole search was some sort of crisis for Edjop and the rest of us. We didn't go into it as if we had all the time to find the answers. There was a very strong sense of urgency to learn and study, to know where we should go."

12
Bantay

Edjop graduated from college in April 1970, finishing his five-year management engineering course, cum laude, in only four years. Father Raul J. Bonoan, one of his professors at the Ateneo, recalled the occasion in a homily he wrote a year after Edjop's death.

"In 1966, Edjop was the high school valedictorian. In 1970 when he graduated cum laude from college, he was not the valedictorian, but when his name was called, the crowd broke into the loudest and longest applause of the evening. Indeed, as he walked up the stage, he represented everything the Ateneo could hope for: brilliance of mind, academic excellence, fresh and vibrant leadership that made him a national figure at the age of 22."

"We thought that when he graduated from college, he had also graduated from activism," recalls Mrs. Jopson. "*Hindi pala.* It was not to be so."

The summer after he finished college, Edjop was once again in the thick of things. On May 22, 1970, two barrios in Bantay, Ilocos Sur, were razed to the ground, killing an old woman and leaving scores of residents homeless. The burning and the massacre were reportedly on the orders of Vincent "Bingbong" Crisologo, son of Floro Crisologo, the local political warlord, who had lost heavily in the last congressional elections in that district.

News of the incident, which seemed to epitomize the violent state of Philippine politics, shocked the whole country. For an increasingly politicized studentry, it was another demonstration of how ordinary folk could become victims in the political conflicts of the elite.

A campaign to assist victims in the Bantay barrios of Ora East and Ora West was launched by various groups and personalities, including Joaquin "Chino" Roces, publisher of the *Manila Times.*

The NUSP, under Edjop's leadership, volunteered to go to the devastated barrios to help bring the survivors to safety in Manila. The national government sent a Philippine Constabulary escort for the NUSP students. Edjop refused any help from the military, but the PC team accompanied them anyway.

Edjop and 50 other NUSP members went to the site of the tragedy. The people had dispersed after the burning and were living on the outskirts of the town, hungry and afraid. The students made arrangements for them to meet in a clearing in the center of one of the barrios.

The buses which they brought could not enter the area, and the students had to walk about half a kilometer to the rendezvous. They walked in twos, with Edjop in front. When they reached the site where the 200 Ora residents had assembled, there was an emotional meeting between the young idealistic students from Manila and the destitute peasants.

A farmer, seeing the short fellow leading the pack of students, immediately embraced Edjop. And the young Jopson, Salanga would later recall, was speechless. The experience, Beng Jopson remembered later, had a tremendous effect on her brother; it made Edjop re-examine his position on the peaceful road to change.

"*Nakakatindig ng balahibo*. It gave me goose pimples," Cha Nolasco says of the meeting. The peasants welcomed them "as saviors," according to Jun Pau. Says Edros: "There was a lot of crying and hugging. Although we couldn't understand Ilocano, we understood the pain they felt. The barrio was nothing but black ash and burned wood. The residents set up a camp in a nearby lot filled with bamboo trees. They looked haggard, and obviously hadn't had any sleep and little to eat."

At almost the same moment that the students made contact with the peasants, then Defense Secretary Juan Ponce Enrile arrived in a helicopter. He offered to take some of the victims to Manila. But the people refused—they would go only with the students.

The Bantay victims were brought to the Ateneo campus, where

they were billeted in the classrooms. They had a dialogue with Marcos who made the usual promises about seeking justice for the peasants.

On the way down to Manila, during one of their stops for lunch, Edjop got into a shouting match with a young lieutenant, the commanding officer of the PC escort team. Salanga distinctly remembers hearing the young lieutenant asserting, "Not all military men are bad." The young lieutenant was Lieutenant Victor Corpus, who, about a year later, would defect to the New People's Army, becoming one of the most wanted rebel leaders in the country.

In June 1970 Edjop entered the UP College of Law. Meanwhile, the NUSP, under his leadership, got more and more involved with victims of repression and exploitation—farmers from Sampaloc, Quezon, whose land had been illegally taken by a bank; employees of government agencies, protesting corruption and mismanagement; workers on strike in different factories in Manila. Once, says Cha Nolasco, employees of the National Police Commission (NAPOLCOM) even turned to the students for assistance.

"Everyday, we just got sucked into one event after another," says Romy Chan. "There were so many causes stumbling one after another. There was, we discovered, no shortage of injustice in the world. We did not completely understand what was going on, or what we were doing. But we had a sense of purpose, of idealism. We tried to do 20 things at the same time, educating ourselves and trying to educate and organize other people. On the Ateneo campus, with its country club atmosphere, we were like babes in the woods, so naive and innocent. It became exciting for us to step into the real world, to understand that there was, after all, poverty and injustice in the Philippines."

Apprehensive that the left would "use big gatherings for their own purposes"—which, the moderates believed, was what had happened in the January 26 and 30 demonstrations—the NUSP, according to Jun Pau, decided against big assemblies and concentrated on smaller mass action on specific issues.

The NUSP formed an anti-graft brigade, which investigated

and exposed corrupt government officials and personnel. Says Cha Nolasco: "While the radical clamor to 'finish the unfinished revolution' was ringing in our ears, Edjop and the moderates asked that the financial books of government institutions be opened for public scrutiny."

The NUSP launched a successful campaign for the ouster of the head of the National Cottage Industry Administration (NACIDA) after the students, together with NACIDA employees, documented and exposed cases of corruption against her. The students also launched a 40-day live-in picket with workers in front of Congress, to push for an increase in the minimum wage. The radicals condemned these efforts as "palliatives" that did not address the roots of the country's problems. But, says Cha Nolasco, "taking up the cudgels for oppressed people" contributed to Edjop's education.

Cha has fond memories of her crusading days with Edjop. He had, she says, "a heart of gold." His NUSP friends called him "Charlie Brown," after the wide-eyed comic-strip kid who was always thinking of ways to improve the work and constantly in search of ideas.

"Little things made him giggle," recalls Cha Nolasco. " *'Sige, gawin natin, iyan.* Yes, let's do that,' he would eagerly say about a new plan or project, so naive in his sincerity. He felt strongly about social issues. In many ways, he was like a child. *Parang hindi makakamatay ng langaw.* He couldn't have hurt a fly."

Inday heard the same comment from one of Edjop's classmates, who told her, "Your brother will not last long in the political arena. He is too sincere. *Tinototoo niya, at hindi dapat ganoon.* He shouldn't take things too seriously."

Sometimes, Edjop went with friends on out-of-town trips, to relax and momentarily forget the campaigns they were involved in. Once they went to Cavite, where his buddies planned Edjop's initiation into manhood.

"We rented a cottage in some resort and hired a girl for Edjop," relates Jun Pau. "It took us some time and effort to convince him to go into the cottage with the girl. He eventually did, and we took our positions outside the cottage, to eavesdrop. But all Edjop did the whole time was talk to the girl, asking questions about her background and why she took that kind of occupation. We couldn't believe it."

On the way back to Manila, the boys violated some minor traffic regulation and were ordered to pull over by a policeman. "Edjop was so scared of being recognized that he grabbed my eyeglasses and put them on," Jun Pau continues. "But in his nervousness, he fumbled and wore the glasses upside down."

In December 1970, Edjop became the first re-elected president of the NUSP. This time, he won by a more comfortable margin. The congress theme—"Towards a United Front of Peasants, Workers and Students"—reveals much about the way student politics was taking shape.

Edjop's second term as NUSP president was, however, not as exciting as the first, according to Salanga. "There was no more fire on his second year in office. The novelty of the NUSP had died down. It was not that popular anymore. At that point, we were just trying to salvage what we could. There had been a decline in our membership. The student councils were no longer that solid. The stigma of being a moderate group was already very clear. The momentum of the moderate student movement was gone. The radicals already had the momentum."

On June 12, 1970, KM Chairman Nilo Tayag was arrested in San Pablo, Laguna. Immediately the militants cried out: "*Palayain si Nilo Tayag!* Free Nilo Tayag!" Tayag had been a legend, adored by thousands of radical activists who would later seriously study his article, "On Commitment," written in prison. Recognized as a modern-day Emilio Jacinto, he was the symbol of the revolutionary youth.

In December of the same year, the Manila Jaycees named Edjop one of The Outstanding Young Men (TOYM) of the year, for "community service through student activism." Among his co-winners were then Senator John Osmeña and newspaperman Jose Burgos Jr.

Edjop, according to Salanga, felt "no real joy in receiving the award" and had thought of declining it. "He was being honored for being a leader of a student movement that was actually divided," said Salanga. "That was the painful thing about it. This was already very clear then. The TOYM award was actually the prize of the Establishment to Edjop for staying faithful to the Establishment."

But Edjop was prevailed upon by friends to accept the award as a "practical move." The TOYM award, Romy Chan asserted, could boost Edjop's and the NUSP's "credibility to business and other influential sectors." This, to a certain extent, was an accurate assessment. Businessmen and politicians started offering Edjop help in different ways: money, plane tickets for NUSP sorties, contacts. According to Salanga, then Vice-President Fernando Lopez himself once asked for a meeting with Edjop.

On the other hand, the radicals hated Edjop even more. On the night of the TOYM awards held at the Manila Hilton Hotel, the KM and the NUSP-left-wing picketed the ceremonies, distributing leaflets and shouting slogans against Edjop. Salanga would later note that Edjop was "ambivalent" about the demonstration. In his acceptance speech, Edjop said:

"I can only accept this award if it goes beyond my name and my person. For neither I nor any single student activist can claim a monopoly of leadership or a monopoly of action. The award must go to the outstanding young men and women of the National Union of Students of the Philippines, and it must even go beyond them to the other outstanding young men and women of the student movement.

"This award must go to their outstanding commitment to dissent against the present social order. It must come as an acknowledgment of their emergence as a potent force for change in this society.

"Solutions to our problems may divide us, but these should never override the unifying need for these solutions. It is this need that unites us in the student movement; it is this need that unites us ultimately with other progressive sectors in our society. . . ."

13
Joy

Edjop's romance with Joy was almost as stormy as the January 26 and 30 confrontations.

Everybody, including his sisters, knew that Edjop had his eye on Joy. But this was not clear to Joy. "*Ang labo-labo niya noon.* He just wasn't clear about what I was to him," she recalls. Yes, they went out, she says, an amused nostalgic look on her face. "Ed was also fun to be with." They went to movies, ate out, watched basketball games—"the usual stuff."

But Edjop was so busy that they rarely saw each other. Ed's sisters usually had to set their dates. Worse, Ed was often late or stood her up. This, according to Inday, was because her brother didn't have second thoughts about breaking an appointment with Joy in order to attend a meeting or fulfill some speaking engagement. "So I just didn't expect anything anymore," Joy says.

She had Ed's sisters and friends on her side, and they resorted to "radical" tactics to arrange a date with the moderate leader. They would secretly tell Joy to wait at a certain place and then trick Edjop into going there.

"For a long time, I didn't really know if we had a relationship or not. Ed just didn't say or ask anything about it. Of course, I already had a crush on him, but he never talked about us. I didn't know where I stood with him."

Joy was also a student council officer as internal vice-president of the St. Theresa's College Council. In this capacity she some-times attended NUSP meetings or soirees, where she would see Ed. One time she attended an NUSP meeting escorted by a friend, an Atenean who was a notorious playboy. "Naku, Edjop, you better act fast," the NUSP president's friends teased. "If you want Joy, you better make your move now."

Edjop apparently took the advice. He paid Joy a visit on her birthday. To his surprise the other guy was already there ahead of him. *"Aalis lang ho ako sandali,"* Edjop excused himself. "I just have something to attend to." He parked his car some distance away from Joy's residence; when the other guy left, he returned to the house.

"We began to go out more often after that," Joy laughs.

Politics, Joy knew then, was an essential part of Ed's life. It was a fact she had to accept. At that time she was, as she puts it, "quite apolitical." As a student council officer she was more concerned with internal campus affairs—"student discipline, academic affairs, and things like that" rather than with national issues, although she did join the January 26 demonstration and other activities sponsored by the NUSP.

With a nationally known student leader for a suitor, however, she couldn't be uninvolved in and uninformed about what was happening. So, before Ed came to visit, Joy would studiously read the newspapers, to prepare herself for the serious topics that Edjop might bring up.

It was on Valentine's Day 1970 that Edjop "made his move."

"On that day, he asked me out," Joy recalls. "It was one of the few times he himself set a date. We went to Fort Santiago, where the NUSP was sponsoring the cultural show of some minorities. His friends asked him to fetch a pig which was going to be used for the performance. To my surprise, Ed said he couldn't do it, since he couldn't leave me.

"We stayed for the show and afterwards went with some friends to the Antipolo Hotel. When we got out of the car, he held my hand. His sisters Sucel and Beng, who were also there, saw us and announced to the whole group, 'Look who's here and they're holding hands.' I was a little embarrassed and I tried to hide both our hands.

"We went by the poolside and talked—it was then that he actually proposed. He said that he had wanted to propose for a long time, but that he wasn't sure if I'd accept him. *Sigurista talaga iyon, e.* He didn't want to take any chances. Well, I asked him if, with all his involvements, he thought it was practical for us to have a serious relationship. He said he wanted someone with whom he could share his work and his dreams. We liked each other, that was already clear. But could the relationship really work? We both didn't know . . ."

So, the bond they formed that day was, she says, "an open-ended type of thing"—as open-ended and uncertain as Edjop's own political vision and involvement.

Two years later, while on a study tour in Beijing, Edjop and Joy would have a falling out. One afternoon after their quarrel, he invited her for a walk around Tiananmen Square, where Joy suggested that they break up. "Maybe it would be better for you if you did enter the priesthood," she said. There was no way their relationship could work, she then thought.

"But in our conversation in Beijing, Ed affirmed that he loved me and wanted me to be his wife and for us to have a family. He then took my hand and said, 'I want a woman who can make me feel strong when I am feeling weak . . .

"But I still could not fully accept his commitment to the people. I also felt the same way about the plight of the workers and peasants, and the need for change. But, with Ed, it was different. He was bent on being part of the struggle for change. He was really serious about it. The problem is, I had doubts if I could make such a sacrifice, if I could take the committed and complicated kind of life I knew we would have to lead. . . .

"I guess I was like any college girl then, who dreamt that the guy I would marry would give me the stars and the moon. But Ed was so engrossed in his work that I felt he was neglecting me. If I were to list his priorities at that time, his involvement came first, followed by his studies. I was a poor third. . . .

"So, one time, I decided to set my own priorities, putting God on top, and then Ed. It seemed fair, and the Christian thing to do. For a time, I became indifferent to Ed. God, not Ed, was the center of my life. For a time, this attitude gave me some peace of mind. I felt there was meaning in my life as a Christian even without Ed. . . .

"But then, during one retreat, I came to a realization. I thought of Ed whom I loved so much, and who offered so much of himself for the sake of other people. Meanwhile, there I was feeling sorry for myself, thinking about how much I was being neglected by him.

"I knew Ed didn't have to be that involved. It would have been a lot simpler for him to forget his involvements and spend more time with me. That would have been more convenient for him— and for me.

"But I asked myself, 'Who of the two of us was the real Christian? Was it not he who was giving so much, and was willing to lose so much for the sake of others?' This made me realize the value of this man whom I loved and who also loved me in his own way. From that realization I learned to accept Ed, as a person, and as a man committed to a cause for ordinary people."

14
Con-Con

After the First Quarter Storm, Edjop and his fellow moderates continued to cling to the idea of a nonpartisan Constitutional Convention as the "last hope for democracy" in the country.

The NUSP became active in the Citizens National Electoral Assembly (CNEA), a mass citizen movement for clean and honest elections. Edjop served as national vice-chairman and secretary-general of this national organization, which included prominent citizens like lawyer Charito Planas, banker Chester Babst and civic leader Leticia Perez de Guzman. One of Edjop's former colleagues in the CNEA remembers that the organization had "one clear position: that if everything which we were afraid would happen did happen, then our entire system of freedom would collapse, our whole way of life would be lost."

Student council leaders were inducted as pollwatchers in the elections. Edjop led teams of volunteers to political hot spots, including Ilocos Sur. In Danao City, Edjop met the local warlord, Ramon Durano, face to face.

"Durano had about ten armed bodyguards with him," Dicky Castro recalls. "There were three of us. Edjop carried himself like a little boy, a young student, with a lot of idealism. On the other hand, Durano, I think, thought of Edjop like a son. Edjop knew that Durano was a crook and a big political lord. But by calmly sticking to the principles of clean and honest elections, Edjop was able to gain concessions from him. Edjop was a good salesman. He knew how to gently and indirectly push a warlord into a corner. Durano himself accepted the CNEA organization inside Danao City."

In December 1970, Edjop led two busloads of NUSP volunteers to Vigan. Freddie Salanga relates the experience in *Now Magazine* (December 15, 1970):

"We were out in Pampanga in the middle of the night, and some two hours away from Manila, but they were still at it: sing-

ing lustily and long. Even Edgar Jopson was singing. I was on
the road with them, the first batch of NUSP volunteers who had
offered to police the polls in the first district of Ilocos Sur. Bong
Montes was with the second batch, and between the two they
had over a hundred students, male and female. They were willing and they were eager. Of such stuff are Children's Crusades
made. . . .

"Ed Jopson expected only forty volunteers to show up at the
NUSP office for the 9:00 [a.m.] briefing. Ninety-six stout hearts,
who had nothing else to do on Election Day but to be on the
loose in Vigan, reported. Some left home under bogus alibis as
to where they were going; they would not have been permitted
at the mere whisper of the word 'Vigan.' "

The students were embarking on a dangerous mission. Ilocos
Sur, during election time, was like a war zone. The Bantay incident had occurred just a few months earlier, and now Edjop and
the NUSP-CNEA student volunteers were on their way back to
a land where ballots mixed with blood and bullets.

In Ilocos they heard about, or witnessed for themselves, political violence of different forms and degrees. Some of them were
harassed or physically driven off from polling places by the
goons of local warlords. There was rampant cheating, and there
were shooting incidents which left a number of people killed. A
bridge was dismantled, reportedly by soldiers, isolating eight
towns from Vigan.

Edjop and the other NUSP officers coordinated with local
government officials, including Defense Secretary Juan Ponce
Enrile, and the military officers. But they felt helpless in the face
of the traditional guns, goons, and gold of Philippine elections.
In the end they had to hurriedly leave for Manila to escape the
election rampage.

According to Inday, in one convent they stayed in, they had
to literally crawl to the bus, to avoid being spotted by goons hot
on the trail of pollwatchers from the big city.

Wrote Freddie Salanga: "The last entry on a note pad reads:
'Group decides to go home.'. . . . Edjop was shepherding the rest

of the volunteers into a final debriefing, but they were all sprawled in the foyer of St. Paul's College, dirty, sleepy, haggard, sluggish, and mostly dazed, even stunned at all they had gone through, all that seemingly boundless energy their bodies had yielded, all that strain from the fear and excitement of the last three days. But more important, they were alive, yes, still alive."

Back in Manila, Edjop and the other students worked day and night, setting up more pollwatching teams in different provinces, raising funds for their operations, working out schedules. The pressure must have begun to take its toll on Edjop. During one scheduled meeting at his house, he yelled at colleagues who had fallen asleep, "If you don't feel like having a meeting, then just leave!" A heated argument ensued between Edjop and another NUSP member, but the conflict was settled quickly, with an apology from Edjop.

Such moments were rare, according to government official Gerry Esguerra, then an Atenean and a socdem organizer: "Edjop was, more often than not, cool and always in control. He knew how to pace himself."

During the campaign, Edjop spoke at numerous symposia and debates on the Con-Con issue, and at one such gathering in La Consolacion College, he found himself in a heated exchange with the National Press Club president, Antonio Zumel.

"I granted Ed good intentions," Tony Zumel, now an NDF representative, says. "But I didn't like his politics. I felt that he served as an obstacle to genuine change, in trying to make the people believe in illusions."

At the symposium, Tony told Edjop: "You are making people expect much from the Con-Con when you know that they have nothing to expect from such a body."

"We are not putting all our hopes in the Con-Con," Edjop responded. "We just think that we should give it a chance."

After the forum, Edjop approached Zumel to ask if the NUSP could hold a press conference at the NPC building, then known as a hangout of radical groups. (After being dispersed at rallies, students often retreated to the NPC compound.) Zumel assured him that they would be welcome. However, Tony relates, "I never did see him come to the Press Club. Maybe he just felt awkward seeing all those ND [national democratic] people at the club. But he seemed like a nice guy. Even when he noticed my partiality for the national democrats, he was still very polite."

In the middle of the campaign, as the predominance of candidates from the wealthy classes became clearer, Edjop and the moderates modified their call for a nonpartisan assembly. "Edjop admitted in the later stages of the campaign the inadequacies of our perspective," Freddie Salanga would later recall. "By then, we had realized that even with a nonpartisan Con-Con more people from the upper stratum of society would get elected and not necessarily more from farmers and workers. Thus, we started emphasizing the truly representative aspect rather than nonpartisanship."

Even then, Edjop and his colleagues already had a feeling that the Con-Con, despite the promises of President Marcos and other traditional political leaders, was going to be neither representative nor nonpartisan.

As Freddie Salanga wrote in *Now Magazine* (December 15, 1970):

"Senate President Puyat's son ran for the Convention. NP President Roy's son also ran. So [did] Speaker Laurel's brother. LP [Liberal Party] Secretary-General Ninoy Aquino openly proclaimed support for his candidates in Tarlac. And, of course, President Marcos' own 'Dirty Dozen' were very much in the news, despite expected protestations that such a group did not exist.

"Jopson must surely have known this, too. But this didn't stop him. He was made national vice-chairman of CNEA and he quickly went around organizing schools, colleges and universities throughout the country. He set up a massive political education program to prepare students for their eventual politicalization of the masses. He encouraged and supported rallies and registration drives in most parts of the country."

When the elections came to an end, it was clear to Edjop and the moderates that the Con-Con in which they had placed so much hope had turned out to be another spurious congregation of the elite. According to Freddie Salanga, the November 1970 delegate elections yielded a number of 'conscience candidates,' notably from Manila and Rizal (among them were former UP Student Council Chairman Voltaire Garcia; Antonio Araneta Jr; and future NDF lawyer Romeo Capulong).

"But the overall results were, to [Edjop], far from encouraging," Salanga wrote. "Shortly after all the delegates-elect had been proclaimed, a slightly disillusioned Edjop dropped a bomb with a list purportedly showing sons, fathers, brothers, sisters and in-laws of congressmen, senators, governors and Cabinet members elected in spite of the nonpartisan ban."

On June 1, 1971, the opening day of the Constitutional Convention, the NUSP, together with radical groups, held a joint demonstration outside the Manila Hotel, where the convention was to be held. Their joint objective was the opening session, according to Salanga—"the radicals to express their disgust, the moderates their disappointment."

The NUSP contributed 200 caskets to the rally. They were meant to symbolize the "moral death" of the convention delegates.

A former Con-Con delegate would later admit: "The first month of the convention—which was, by the way, described by President Marcos in his address as the greatest act of freedom— was spent in boring speeches. Of course, a couple of things were immediately acted upon, like the huge P3,000 monthly allowance and P100 daily per diem for each delegate. In 1971, when the peso was still decently equated with the dollar, those were fantastic figures."

The Con-Con eventually became mired in controversy. A major scandal, exposed by a delegate, involved government maneuverings to influence certain proposed constitutional provisions which would have allowed Marcos to seek a third term.

The fraud and violence during the campaign, and the disappointing election results, heightened Edjop's frustration with the Constitutional Convention—and, presumably, weakened his faith in parliamentary reforms.

15
The Moderates

Edjop, according to Freddie Salanga, always had a "grudging admiration" for the national democratic movement, which by 1970 was undoubtedly bigger and more consolidated than any of the formations of the moderates. As Edjop and his closest NUSP associates contemplated their long-term political involvement, they felt a need for a movement of their own. In late 1971, they formed *Buklod Kalayaan* (Freedom Organization).

Romy Chan says they envisioned a movement patterned after the organization of the national democrats. Buklod was supposed to be the youth and student sectoral organization of the movement for reforms, a movement which already included the Federation of Free Farmers (FFF) representing the peasants and the Federation of Free Workers (FFW) representing the workers.

"We wanted to form a movement with a more cohesive direction and a core of committed leaders," explains Jun Pau. "The NUSP was not the ideal structure, since the leadership changed every year and it was limited to students. We wanted a movement with a long-term objective. We wanted to develop our own ideology."

"To be frank about it, Buklod was a reaction to everything that was happening," says Edros del Rosario. "We felt the NUSP could not react properly to the threats from different forces—the left, primarily, and the so-called Establishment. We began to think about our own political agenda. We were, of course, for a parliamentary form of struggle, where we would strive to win enough seats in Congress, in the Constitutional Convention or in whatever venue. We planned Buklod to evolve into a political party."

Buklod, he adds, had the support of student council leaders and NUSP members in key cities and provinces like Davao, Cebu, and Zamboanga. The group claimed "a substantial number of members, though we were never able to put up a formal organizational structure."

The Buklod members, most of whom were in their late teens or early twenties, rented a small apartment in Quezon City (near the Jopson residence) which they used as the Buklod Kalayaan headquarters.

"We practically left our families," says Romy Chan. "Almost everybody lived in the office. Edjop, I think, was happy to know that there was this group behind him, who would stick it out with him.... though we didn't really know how far we were going to go."

Meanwhile, Edjop pursued the objective set during the last NUSP congress, to "forge a united front of peasants, workers and students." According to Ricky Nolasco of Lakasdiwa, another socdem formation, it became a fad among moderate students to go on exposure trips and to integrate with workers and peasants.

The NUSP declared April 6, 1970, "Lobby Day" for the raising of the minimum wage to P10 for non-agricultural workers and P8 for agricultural workers. In a statement published by the *Manila Times* (April 3, 1970), Edjop affirmed the NUSP's support for labor, proclaiming "our common battle for just, human living in the Philippines where unjust and inhuman living is common practice and has already benumbed the conscience of our leaders."

The following year, in 1971, Edjop helped set up the *Kilusan ng Bayang Pilipino* (Movement of the New Filipino or KIBAPI), an alliance of different sectoral groups such as the NUSP, the FFF, the FFW, Lakasdiwa, and the Philippine Congress of Trade Unions (Philcontu). It was, according to a former member of Lakasdiwa, an attempt to consolidate all the moderate organizations.

But in a period of rapid polarization, the word "moderate" hardly described the calls and demands of some of these groups. A distinct change could be noted in Edjop's own pronouncements.

In a KIBAPI-sponsored rally on August 2, 1971, he called on the students to "continue the struggle for social justice, hand in hand with the farmers and workers," stressing that "the role of the student in the revolutionary movement is mainly supportive, and that the students must respect the genuine aspirations of the labor and peasant groups."

Two people made a strong impression on Edjop at this time: Edmundo Nolasco of Philcontu and Jeremias Montemayor of the FFF. (Nolasco and Edjop's father were old friends, having fought side by side in Bataan during the Second World War.) Both Nolasco and Montemayor were former Ateneans, and both were respected authority figures in moderate circles, where they were considered genuine and sincere men of the masses. In his ongoing search for an alternative, Edjop turned to Nolasco and Montemayor for leadership.

Of all the parties, organizations, and movements they worked with, Edjop and his colleagues became closest to the FFF. "The FFF, to us, represented an alternative to communism," says Romy Chan. "It put forward a theological approach to justice on this earth, consistent with Christian values. We tried to fit into the role of being the student arm of the FFF. We seriously underwent political indoctrination under FFF leaders like Charlie Avila and Edicio de la Torre."

In May 1971, Edjop and other student volunteers from the NUSP helped set up the Philcontu youth arm. Aside from industrial workers in Manila and its outskirts, students integrated with farm laborers in big plantations in Mindanao and Negros.

It was on one such trip to Negros, that Edjop met a 36-year-old priest who, like him, was also going through a process of discernment.

Luis Jalandoni belonged to a prominent Negros family, owners of one of the biggest sugar estates on the island. As a priest and social action director for the diocese of Bacolod, he came in close contact with peasant settlers struggling against land-grabbing and with sugar workers and *sacadas* demanding higher wages and better living conditions. These battles were often met with force by the landlords. Not a few sugar workers were hurt or killed in clashes at the picketlines.

Through it all Jalandoni remained a reformist and could not accept the violent option in the fight for change. But one incident changed his mind.

In 1971, sugar workers went on strike in a town called Bais. Jalandoni went there from Bacolod to support the sugar workers who, after being driven from their homes by the landlord, had set up camp along the road. Security guards armed with shotguns tried to dismantle the huts they had made. The workers resisted and the landlord's men opened fire.

Jalandoni dove into a canal with the other sugar workers. But the guards kept on coming after them, and Jalandoni and the other workers had to run and jump from one canal to another, until they reached the sugar cane fields. Hiding in the fields with the workers, Jalandoni thought, "My God, the sugar workers and peasants also need their own armed force in order to counter the violence being used against them."

Several strikers were wounded and Jalandoni helped bring them to the hospital. "On the way, I reflected on the experience," he says. "The sugar industry seemed very peaceful when you look at the fields. But it hid a lot of violence. When the workers rose up to demand their rights, the violent nature of the sugar industry was exposed. The workers were demanding only two pesos a day. It was so little compared with the tremendous profits the landlords were making."

These realizations led Jalandoni to a more radical outlook. It also resulted in his being estranged from his own family and friends. At many parties and family gatherings he attended, he got into angry debates with his relatives. There came a time when he just stopped attending social gatherings.

"I became more and more out of place at social gatherings of the landowners. But then I became more and more at home at social gatherings, festivities of the sugar workers and peasants, who invited me to their birthday parties or the wakes and burials of their loved ones. I lost a lot of my friends from the landowning class but gained a lot of friends among the sugar workers and peasant settlers in the mountains and at the picketlines."

Edjop met Jalandoni at a multisectoral meeting in the Bacolod diocese, to discuss a conflict with Negros landlord Armando Gustilo.

"When Edjop came to the meeting," Jalandoni recalls, "he made a lot of strong suggestions on what we could do about the problem with Gustilo. He said that we should take the provincial commander to task. He was very eager and projected a powerful personality. But he made these suggestions without knowing the real conditions in Negros. We had to explain to him how things were on the island."

Jalandoni would have a different impression of Edjop when they met again three years later.

16
China

On August 21, 1971, the Liberal Party *miting de avance* on Plaza Miranda was rocked by two grenade explosions that left 9 persons dead and 97 others, including a number of the LP senatorial candidates, wounded. Marcos put the blame on the Communists. A few days later, he suspended the writ of habeas corpus.

Talk of martial law swept the capital. Many leaders of the KM and other radical groups went underground, and the rest braced themselves for a general crackdown. Two well-known student leaders, Chito Sta. Romana of La Salle and Ericson Baculinao of the University of the Philippines, were on a cultural tour of the People's Republic of China when the writ was suspended. They were on a list of youth leaders for whom a warrant of arrest had been issued, and they found themselves stranded in China. They wouldn't be able to come home until fifteen years later, after the fall of Marcos.

In August 1972, one year after the suspension of the writ of habeas corpus, Edjop led an NUSP delegation on a goodwill tour of the People's Republic of China, on the invitation of the Chinese Friendship Association. The trip, says Cha Nolasco, was still part of Edjop's search for answers; he wanted to get a glimpse of the society and the revolution that the radicals extolled so much.

The students visited universities, factories, and farm communities. They had discussions on various topics with Chinese students and teachers. At these meetings, recalls Deng Samonte (who later became Edjop's brother-in-law), Edjop was "like a child who wanted to learn everything, at once, about China, when we were going to be there for only one month. He asked so many questions on everything that the Chinese showed or discussed with us. Some of us already teased him, '*Ano ba naman, Ed, ang dami mo namang tanong.* You're asking too many questions.' "

In China Edjop talked with exiled student leader Chito Sta. Romana about the situation in China and in the Philippines.

Chito recalls his last meeting with Edjop: "He began to have doubts about the Constitutional Convention as a peaceful means to achieve changes in the Philippines. He began to turn to approaches that were not constrained by the Constitutional Convention, by reformism, or the parliamentary struggle. He then told me of his plans to join PAFLU [Philippine Association of Free Labor Unions]. He said he wanted to integrate with the workers."

Chito believes that, even then, Edjop's faith in the reformist struggle was already "shattered to pieces."

In fact, one of Edjop's speeches before the NUSP's hosts were hardly the words of a reformist:

"We are here to learn [from you] how to make education a tool in serving the masses, the workers, and farmers. In the Philippines, being a semi-colonial and semi-feudal society, education is an important concern in our struggle for national liberation . . .

"We realize that we still have a long way to go in changing our educational system. But we're determined to carry out the great proletarian cultural revolution in our country. We cannot do it alone. We must be one with the workers and farmers in bringing this about in the soonest time possible . . ."

Among those who went with Edjop was Joy, who was taken aback by some of her boyfriend's pronouncements.

"When we go back to the Philippines, we will seriously be involved in the struggle of the masses, the peasants, and the workers," Edjop, at one point, declared.

"You talk as if I shouldn't be involved in planning our future," Joy later told him. "What about our relationship? I also have marriage in mind."

On the other hand, Edjop also was piqued by some of the questions his girlfriend posed to their host. During a discussion about development under the socialist system, Joy asked, "But are we sure the Chinese are happy?"

Edjop threw a piercing glance at her. "He was obviously embarrassed by what I said," Joy recalls, laughing. "But I really suspected that our interpreters were screening some of the answers.

"But in many ways," she adds, "the tour was also an eye-opener for both of us. We saw socialism in practice, and it seemed to be working. The Chinese had obviously solved the problem of poverty. The workers really had good living and working conditions. We even ate with some of them in their houses, and it was really different from the conditions of our workers in the Philippines. Ed was obviously impressed, and I think the tour was a major factor that convinced him to join the national democratic movement."

Edjop was not able to finish the tour. Joy was scheduled to leave for home ahead of the group because of a commitment in Manila. As his way of making peace with Joy, he had agreed to accompany her on the flight back home. "Looking back, I shouldn't have asked that from him. Our hosts had scheduled a tour of Sian, where part of the Long March took place. I knew that, of all the places in China, he wanted to see that the most. Then, of course, he also wanted to learn more about China and socialism. Later, I felt guilty . . ."

But Edjop's trip to China, say Joy and his former comrades, was a turning point in his political conversion.

"After the trip, Ed became more interested in the national democratic alternative," says Joy. "But for me, I couldn't accept many of the precepts of the radical outlook, especially the concept of class struggle. I believed that each individual was entitled to his or her own salvation. Ed would tell me that armed struggle was valid as a last resort. But even as a last resort, I could not accept it because it would be bloody . . ."

Dicky Castro, then in charge of the NUSP organization in the Visayas, says that when the NUSP delegation returned from China, Edjop gave him instructions to take a more reconciliatory posture in dealing with the radicals.

"Concretely, he was telling the NUSP organization in the Visayas to avoid competing with the radicals in student council elections," recalls Dicky. "I was surprised by this, since I still assumed that Edjop was determined to keep the radicals from taking over the NUSP. But looking back, I think Edjop's attitude towards the natdems had already changed. The radicals, he knew, helped raise the political consciousness of the students, which was what Edjop also wanted."

"By then," Freddie Salanga would reveal later," Edjop himself told me, '*Alam mo, mukhang mali tayo.* I think we had been mistaken.' He already had doubts about the direction we were taking."

Developments soon after he returned from China left Edjop with even fewer options.

On September 21, 1972, Marcos declared martial law. Hundreds, including prominent figures like Benigno Aquino Jr., Jose Diokno, and Gerry Roxas were arrested. In two years, more than 50,000 would be detained.

The Congress was padlocked, and so were all major newspapers and broadcast stations. On campuses known to be centers of activism, such as UP and Lyceum, the military set up checkpoints and sent agents to monitor activities. KM, SDK, and other opposition organizations were outlawed; activists went underground.

Marcos argued that a growing threat from the left and the right, including an assassination plot against him, made the imposition of martial law a historic necessity. He proclaimed the start of a new era, a "Democratic Revolution from the Center," that would defeat the oligarchy and the Communists, and build a "New Society."

It was, undoubtedly, a brilliant coup that met no effective resistance from any opposition force. Marcos was now the most powerful man in the land, backed by a military that virtually served as his private security force.

Fear instantly gripped the capital. "*Nakakasindak*"—"shocking"—was how one activist describes the situation. "*Parang pinag-sasampal kami ni Makoy at sinabing, 'Mga putangina ninyo, wala naman pala kayong binatbat, e.*' It's as if Marcos slapped us all in the face and said, 'You sons-of-bitches are no match for me after all.' "

To natdems, it was the beginning of a new phase in the revolution, and a new life for them, collectively and individually. As many of them declared, "*Wala nang atrasan.* There's no turning back."

On the night of September 22, Marie and Adel Jopson, fearful for Ed's safety, climbed to the roof of their house on Paraiso Street, and kept an all-night lookout for military men who might come to take their brother away.

"We knew Ed had done nothing wrong," Marie recalls. "But we had heard about so many people being picked up. At least, we could warn him in case the military came."

But Marie and Adel had nothing to worry about, for Edjop was not on the military's list. Not yet.

At two o'clock in the morning of September 22, the PAFLU office in Tondo was raided. At eight o'clock Edjop drove to the house of Ed Nolasco in Quezon City. The old man was out, but his son Ricky was home.

"I was still sleeping when Ed came and said, '*Ricky, martial law na.*'"

A few minutes later, the elder Nolasco arrived, and Edjop informed him of developments.

—"You better lie low for a while," Edjop advised the labor leader, whom he figured, correctly, was on the military's list. (In fact, an Arrest, Search and Seizure Order, or ASSO, had been issued for the PAFLU leader. He was eventually picked up in 1975.)

Nolasco was sporting a beard, and Edjop suggested that he shave it off. He then drove the elderly man to another house where he could be safe.

Edjop then went to see Jeremias Montemayor, to get his views on the new situation and on what they could, and should, do. Gerry Esguerra says Edjop "didn't get the answers he wanted to hear."

According to Esguerra, Montemayor said things like: "These are dangerous times. We should first stay on the sidelines and see how the contradictions will resolve themselves. *Sila-sila lang ang nagbabanggaan. Walang pakinabang ang masa dito, kaya huwag na na tayong makisali diyan.* The elites are fighting among themselves. We gain nothing by joining the fray, so we better not get involved."

In October, Montemayor came out in support of Marcos' "land reform" program, supposedly the centerpiece of the "New Society." Immediately after that, Edjop aired his disenchantment to Esguerra, saying, "What has happened to this idol of yours? Look at what he has done."

By then, Esguerra had also grown disillusioned with the peasant leader, and all he could say to his friend was, "What can I do? I also thought that he was for real. I was wrong."

Edjop and Esguerra eventually broke their ties with Montemayor. By then, a disgruntled Edjop had become more cynical of the movement for peaceful reform—and its ability to meet the challenge of a new, deadlier storm.

17
Career Choice

A cum laude graduate of one of the most prestigious universities in the country, Edjop first worked as an ordinary clerk for a labor federation. Instead of roosting on the Escolta or Ayala Avenue, the Blue Eagle flew from Loyola Heights and landed in Tondo.

It was not the normal career path for the Jesuit alumnus billed "most likely to succeed," who had received the most resounding applause on graduation day. But in many ways, Edjop's decision was not rare, not in a time when young people thought the business of changing society more fulfilling, more exciting, than the world of corporate business.

"One just didn't make career plans during such an exciting period," recalls Cha Nolasco. " 'I don't remember any of us having goals like making our first million in five years. We felt the world was open to us, and felt strongly about doing something for our people and our society."

Edjop was expected to take over the family business. But he begged off from the responsibility, saying, "Mommy, Daddy, I have other plans now. Besides, I have ten sisters. Please just ask one of them to help look after the store. There are other people who need me."

Other job opportunities came Edjop's way, even without his asking for them. The United Nations offered him a position in an international youth organization based in Switzerland. Another international institution asked him to take a post in Indonesia.

Mr. Jopson endorsed these offers to his son, but Edjop stuck to his plans. "*Daddy naman, mga taga-ibang bansa pa ang makikinabang sa akin.* I'll end up being useful to people of other countries," he said.

Edjop tried law school at the UP. But even this failed to suit his needs and desires. He came home from Diliman one afternoon, fuming with frustration. He went straight to his sister Marie's room, slammed the door shut and angrily hurled his thick law books at the bed.

Surprised by her older brother's vehemence, Marie asked, "What's wrong with you? Did you get into a fight with anybody?"

"*Ay, naku!*" he sighed. "I don't think I can take any more of law school."

"I thought you said you could help more people as a lawyer?"

"It's impossible! The laws that we work so hard to study and understand are laws for the rich, not for ordinary people. *Mga batas lang ng mayayaman!* "

He quit law school after two years, having had "enough training to understand the workings of the legal system to understand how the law is used against the workers, and how the workers can also use it in their struggles."

Edjop knew that, as in the student movement, labels and charges—"reactionary," "revolutionary," "subversive," "genuine," "yellow"—were also bandied about fiercely in the peasant and labor movements. He did not engage in any name-calling. But he had learned not to take at face value the pronouncements of any leader or organization claiming to have the interests of the masa at heart.

A conversation he had with Ed Nolasco, right before he decided to join PAFLU—which the natdems had tagged a "yellow" federation—revealed the caution Edjop took in choosing a vehicle for "mass work." Edjop had gone to visit Nolasco at the PAFLU office in Tecson, Tondo. As they walked from the office to Nolasco's house in Quezon City, the labor leader told him that PAFLU president Cipriano Cid was hiring young organizers. Edjop was welcome to join.

"You say you want to help the workers?" Nolasco said. "You can do this as an organizer for a federation."

But Edjop was undecided. "I don't know, Ka Ed. I might make another mistake. *Baka dilawan na naman ang mapasukan ko.* I might be getting into another yellow organization. My credibility will suffer even more."

"Why don't you give it a try?" the elder man said. "You'll never know unless you try."

Edjop took Nolasco's advice. The next day, he reported for work. His first assignment, as a member of the PAFLU staff, was to deliver a union proposal to the owner of a company called Pioneer Briefs. The Chinese businessman had refused to talk to Edjop, and would not even let him step inside the factory compound.

Enraged by such arrogance, Edjop pounded furiously on the steel gate of the compound, shouting, "*E bakit ayaw ninyo akong harapin, e tao din naman ako!* Why do you refuse to face me, when I am also a human being!"

The Chinese called for the police, who chased the young troublemaker all the way back to the PAFLU office. Fortunately, Feliciano Rubio, PAFLU's vice-president for education, knew the policemen.

"Why do you want to arrest Edgar Jopson?" Rubio demanded. The cops told him Edjop had created such a racket, yelling and pounding on the door of the Chinese businessman's compound.

"What is the door made of, anyway?" Rubio asked.

"Steel, sir," was the reply.

"Well, no wonder he had to pound on it. *Masama kung bala ang ipinangkatok niya.* It would have been wrong if he had knocked on the gate with bullets. Why should you arrest him when all he wanted to do was deliver a letter to management?"

The police left Edjop alone.

"So you're Edjop," Cid greeted his new organizer. "For a man your size, you sure make a lot of noise."

Edjop had a falling out with his father soon after he joined PAFLU. Hernan Jopson still wanted his son to take over the store. Edjop had told Felicing Villados, then president of Elizalde Rope Employees Union and one of his closest friends in PAFLU, that he would agree to run the supermarket only if his father agreed to share the profits with the employees—a condition, Edjop knew very well, that his father would have rejected.

Ultimately, Hernan Jopson learned to live with his son's decision. Their relationship remained warm, as Edjop regularly came home for visits. His parents and sisters loved and respected him, despite the different, and unglamorous, lifestyle he led. As far as they were concerned, Ed was doing something noble.

But something about his being the scion of a supermarket magnate and, at the same time, a man espousing workers' rights, did not sit well with Edjop.

He knew about the gripes the employees had against his father—the company's non-compliance with the minimum wage and the policy of not paying for overtime. He knew that the employees at the Jopson's Supermarket were not unionized. According to Felicing, Edjop "simply could not live with that."

One day Edjop asked Ed Nolasco's help in setting up a union at the supermarket. On Good Friday in 1973, the two of them met with 16 employees whom Edjop considered potential union leaders. On that Good Friday Edjop was risking a death from which resurrection was uncertain—his family could disown him.

Edjop himself could have organized the employees. But he didn't want to be accused of putting up a "company union." He left the organizing to Nolasco, who helped the workers draft a collective bargaining proposal.

Hernan Jopson rejected the major union demands, and the employees filed a suit against the supermarket. Amid the dispute, Mr. Jopson turned to his son for assistance, complaining: "The workers like to make demands but don't know how to face up to their responsibilities. They forget that they also have an obligation to their employer."

"You have lawyers to advise you on these matters, Daddy," Edjop answered. "Please consult them and not me."

"Why not you?"

"Because I am with labor."

"You are still a Jopson," the father snapped. "Whatever you do, wherever you go, you cannot change who you are."

"I was hurt by his answer," Mr. Jopson recalls. "It was as if he had become ashamed of what we had worked hard for. He knew how we built that store. He knew the sweat and toil that went into it. But it seemed that, because he was with labor, he was rejecting all of that, as though he was breaking off all ties with his own family."

Father and son did not speak to one another for almost a month. Meanwhile, the union won its suit against the Jopsons, and this may have made Hernan Jopson more bitter. Edjop tried to resume a normal relationship with his father. He came home to visit regularly, trying to get his father to talk to him again. But the old man simply ignored him.

"He told me how sad it felt when he came home and only his mother and sisters greeted him," Felicing's wife Fe recalls. *"Nakapanghihina daw ng loob.* He really felt down."

Edjop went to visit his parents' house less often. When he spoke to Fe of his dilemma, the old woman advised him: "Your father is an old man, and old people react that way. They get angry and bear grudges. They have a lot of pride. Don't expect him to give way so easily. You must be patient. Just keep trying to talk to him, to get him to open up. Greet him and say hello, even if he doesn't say anything. Don't get tired of doing this— *huwag kang magsasawa.* Don't think that your father enjoys shutting you out. He is suffering as much as you are."

With a nostalgic smile, Felicing recalls: "Ed easily grasped the consciousness of the workers and the masses. But until that disagreement with his father, he understood very little about the consciousness of parents and elders."

Edjop followed Fe's advice. When his father was confined in the hospital for a minor illness, he came to visit the old man. By then, his father, too, had grown weary of the strained relationship. Edjop apologized for his attitude and the pain it had caused his father. Nothing more had to be said as father and son embraced.

18
Candidate Member

Ramil was one of the few Ateneans who joined the Kabataang Makabayan in 1970, at the height of the First Quarter Storm. He knew Edjop, and had discussed many an issue with him in school. Unlike the other radicals, he did not consider Edjop an enemy. But at the same time he didn't think much of Edjop's politics. Though impressed with his fellow Ateneans' abilities as a leader, he thought the name "Edgar Jopson" would simply fade away from the dusty pages of the Manila media. The man would retire comfortably, with memories of his public prominence and influence. This, at least, was what Ramil expected— even more so under martial law conditions.

But sometime in early 1973, Ramil was surprised to hear that Edjop had joined PAFLU. Ramil was tasked to help rebuild the revolutionary labor movement, which had been left in a shambles by the martial law crackdown. *Katipunan ng mga Samahang Manggagawa* (Association of Workers' Organizations or KASAMA), the natdem workers' organization, had been paralyzed— *dapa,* as cadres would say. Its activists had been arrested or deployed to other regions, after it became too "hot" for them to operate in Manila.

Edjop, Ramil learned, had become a respected leader in PAFLU. Ramil thought it wise to make contact with the former student leader. He didn't expect much from a man known for his staunch reformist views. "We were still a bit suspicious of him," he recalls. "We didn't really know what he had been doing since he left the NUSP. The thought that he had become a military agent did occur to us." At best, he hoped to find an ally with whom the underground could work on an issue-to-issue basis.

Ramil got more than what he expected. When he called up Edjop at the Paraiso house, he was surprised by Edjop's warm response. Edjop invited him over to the house for a chat, during

126

which Ramil revealed he was involved in labor organizing, along with other former KM activists. He did not introduce himself as a member of the Communist Party, but he believes that "Edjop knew it all along, that's why he invited me over."

Somehow, being in Edjop's big house and fully-furnished den eased Ramil's suspicions. He was "amazed that Edjop had actually turned his back on a luxurious life, to become a labor organizer."

The two of them talked about developments in the country since the declaration of martial law.

"He told me how disappointed he was that many of his colleagues in the NUSP had become 'soft'. *Nanamlay na*. He also shared some of his experiences in the labor movement, which he said was filled with corrupt leaders, who, more often than not, sold out the workers to management."

Edjop told Ramil that he respected Cid, explaining, "Without the old man, PAFLU would have been plagued with splits and dissensions."

It was a fruitful conversation for both. Ramil got more insights into the mainstream of the labor movement, and Edjop into the national democratic movement's analysis of the current situation.

Sometime after that meeting, Ramil got another surprise. Edjop expressed a desire to join the Communist Party.

Still cautious about revealing the extent of his involvement, Ramil simply said that he might know some people who could help Edjop with his request. He promised to get in touch with him soon.

A branch or a section of the party would have normally decided on any application for membership. But Edjop's was considered a "special case."

As Marcel, a Manila-based cadre, explains, "Edjop was a known political figure with defined views." Thus, whether or not he would be accepted in the party was a "major question" for a higher organ to decide. "I doubt if there had ever been a similar case."

The issue was passed on to the Manila-Rizal Regional Party Committee (KR-MR) where the "special case" of applicant Edgar Jopson became the topic of a minor debate.

"Edgar Jopson, an institution of reformism in the country. Now, he wants to join the Communist Party?"

This, some of the members of the KR-MR found unimaginable, and highly suspicious, says Marcel. Not a few eyebrows were raised. Many asked, "How can a political personality, condemned publicly by radical activists as an 'enemy of the revolution,' now wish to join the revolutionary movement?"

Others, those who had never shared their comrades' antagonism towards the former NUSP president, found his desire to be a Party member "flattering." For they had always seen the young Jopson as "sincere" in wanting to "serve the people," enough "to eventually realize the futility of the reformist path, and accept the national democratic line."

No one in the Manila-Rizal Committee accused or suspected Edjop of being a military agent. As Marcel says, "He was hated as a symbol of reformism. But I felt he was sincere about his views."

But it was precisely Edjop's sincerity that the objectors were questioning. They expressed doubts that he had really given up on reformism. They suspected that Edjop's real objective in entering the Party was "to discredit the revolutionary movement in the interest of advancing the cause of reformism," and that he simply pretended to believe in the revolution so that, as a Party insider, he could gain more ammunition with which to snipe at the movement's most glaring weaknesses. Some called this supposed scheme the "Ateneo project."

To resolve the issue, two comrades, Ramil and Marcel, were tasked to interview Edjop and submit their recommendations to the KR-MR.

Another meeting was set in Edjop's house. To Edjop, Marcel stressed the need for both sides to "lay down all their cards"— the party would tell Edjop what they thought about his application for membership, and Edjop must state honestly his reasons for wanting to join the movement.

The Communists had with them a highly lethal card. As a bonus "question"—and also to make the interview more interesting—Marcel casually pulled out his .45 caliber pistol, and laid it on the table, right in front of the applicant.

"Iniistiluhan ko lang naman siya," Marcel recalls, laughing. "I just wanted to see his reaction." But Edjop was unimpressed. *"Bale wala lang naman sa kanya,"* Marcel chuckles. "He took it as matter of course."

Ramil and Marcel focused on two basic questions: When and why did Edjop abandon the reformist position? What convinced him of the validity, and necessity, of armed revolution?

"Edjop mentioned two major factors that had shattered his illusions about reformism," Marcel relates. "The first blow was the Constitutional Convention, which became dominated by the elite. The next was martial law. Before that, he hoped that, through reforms, the situation of the people could still improve. But he knew this was impossible under martial law. He could no longer see how he could push for change under a dictatorship.

"Then he told us about his trip to China, where, he said, he saw some promise in Marxism and socialism. He said many of his biases against the left were clarified in China. He had read some Marxist literature, but he admitted that he still did not have a complete grasp of the ideology. But he had learned enough to conclude that the Marxist viewpoint offered a more scientific framework for viewing society. He had also read *Philippine Society and Revolution* and found it reflective of the Philippine situation and the process that could change it."

The interview was cordial, though Marcel had the impression that Edjop was "a bit tense." The applicant was formal and soft-spoken, but also "very careful of what he said and how he said it—*ingat sa mga binibitawang salita.*"

"He was sure of what he was doing," Marcel recalls. "But he was not sure we would credit what he was saying and take all his statements at face value. So he took pains to explain, to show that he was serious about joining the party—that it was a major decision, as far as he was concerned.

After a few more sessions, the cadres were convinced that the "party must open its doors" to Edjop. They made this recommendation to the Manila-Rizal Committee, explaining that the applicant was obviously "serious and sincere, a mature political person."

A few days later, Edjop was informed that the party had decided to accept him as a candidate member. This meant that he would be allowed to be part of a collective while under observation.

Another meeting was set in Edjop's house, this time to formally welcome Edjop as a comrade in the Communist Party. Ramil and Marcel served as witnesses. They asked Edjop if he had any questions before the oath-taking. Edjop had none. The simple ceremony proceeded.

With his left hand clenched and raised, Edjop solemnly recited the pledge which he would live up to, until his death:

"Sumusumpa akong tutupdin ang lahat ng tungkulin at pananagutan ko, sa abot ng aking makakaya, patataasin ang aking proletaryong rebolusyonaryong kamulatan, paglilingkurang lagi ang mamamayan at magiging malapit sa kanila, pananatilihing mataas ang dangal at prestihiyo ng Partido, pangangalagaan ang kaligtasan ng Partido at ng lahat ng kasama ko, buhay ko man ay ialay ... Kung kinakailangan, buong katapatang pupunahin ko ang kahinaan ko at ng aking mga kasama, upang mapahusay ang paggawa at istilo ng paggawa, batay sa tumpak na makauring paninindigan at upang mabuo ang pagkakaisa at lakas, at isulong ang kapakanan ng Partido at ng masa."

["I swear to fulfill all responsibilities and obligations, to the best of my ability, to raise my proletarian consciousness, to always serve the people and be always close to them, to maintain the honor and prestige of the Party, to look after the safety of the Party and of my comrades, even at the cost of my own life ... If necessary, I shall courageously criticize my own weaknesses and those of my comrades, to improve my work and style of work, based on the correct class standpoint and to maintain unity and strength, and advance the welfare of the Party and the people."]

Edjop's friends question Ka Marcel's account of Edjop's conversion.

"I tend to doubt that Edjop joined the CPP in early 1973," says Edros. "If he became disillusioned with the moderates, it could not have happened in 1972. At that time we were still intact as a group [Buklod Kalayaan]. I think Edjop was still very happy with our activities then.

"A few months after martial law was declared, we realized that we were not targets of arrests," Edros relates. "We started functioning as if nothing much had changed. Of course, we were more careful. But we were quite happy that somehow none of us had landed in jail. During that time, we could account for practically all of Edjop's time. We were together even when we went to sleep.

"There were no signs that Edjop had begun to accept armed struggle. At that time, he was still against the left. *Galit pa siya sa Kaliwa.* And I don't think it was any pretense on his part. He didn't express it through any direct statements. But there were no perceptual changes in the way he acted and talked. Like us, he was still on the lookout that we might be infiltrated by the left."

"Besides," Romy Chan adds, "I would say that the left still would not trust Edjop then."

"You don't just join the CPP," continues Edros. "You have to prove yourself, you have to join peripheral organizations before you are taken in. He was the symbol of the moderates. It would have been hard for him to suddenly change sides. It should have been a long-drawn-out process for Edjop to join them."

"Edjop was still very active then in the labor movement," adds Jun Pau.

"And PAFLU was also particularly careful about being infiltrated by the Reds," says Edros.

"He was married in 1974," says Jun Pau. "He could not have been a Party member before his marriage. He was also taking up law at the UP. At that time, who would dare operate aboveground, if you're a Communist?"

"I think some of the Reds are trying to change history," quips Ging Raterta. But Edros clarifies: "I'm not saying that the CPP people are lying. But knowing how loose their organization was, none of them probably had a direct knowledge of when Edjop was integrated into the movement. It was probably an honest mistake. Maybe they don't know who really brought Edjop in. Maybe they were talking about a casual meeting with Edjop. I don't think Edjop would have deliberately withheld anything new in his mind. It would have been difficult for him to hide from us that he was already a CPP member."

To Edjop's friends, the issue remains controversial. But there are other factors which they may have failed to consider.

"I see no reason for us to tamper with dates," says Arvin, who was a member of a moderate student organization before he joined the CPP in 1972. According to him, as early as late 1972, Edjop already let ND activists use his house for meetings.

Arvin relates his own recruitment into the party: "When a friend told me that some CPP cadres wanted to talk to me, I thought that these party members would come from some cave in the mountains. I was surprised to find out that they were actually people whom I'd been working with for so long, some of them were even friends of mine. Many people have the wrong notion that CPP members are so detached from the rest of society. But, in fact, they are immersed in the population."

Despite what Edros said about Edjop's openness, Edjop may have kept his membership in the CPP a secret, not because he didn't trust his friends, but for other considerations.

"Party members do not broadcast the fact that they are with the movement," Arvin explains. "Occasionally, we have had to evade questions on that. One reason is security, the CPP being an outlawed organization. Another is the still prevalent bias of the population against communists. Comrades find themselves cut off from relatives and friends when they are found out as party members. Some of us have found ourselves being cornered with categorical questions and have opted to tell white lies. We don't want that—but we simply have no choice.

"What many of us try to do is to gradually diminish these biases in some of our friends, at least to a measure of open-mindedness, before we reveal our membership in the party. In many cases, this has proven to be the more prudent thing to do."

Inday herself came to know less about her brother when he joined the movement. "I told Ed how bad I felt that we didn't seem as close as before," Inday says. Ed replied: "Yes, I know it is difficult. But many people know how close we have always been. Those trying to get me might do so, by hurting you. It is better that you don't know anything about my work. *Mas mabuti nang wala kang alam.* This is for your own protection. I hope you understand."

Edjop proposed marriage to Joy in early 1973. "Before he gave me a chance to answer him," Joy relates, "Ed revealed that he was already a member of the CPP. He wanted me to know that before I decided to accept his proposal. I guess I wasn't that surprised. He had gotten more involved since leaving school. When we were already married, there were things he asked me to keep secret, including our address and the people who went to our house."

Contrary to what Jun Pau thought, not all CPP cadres went into hiding, or to the mountains, when martial law was declared. Many of them worked in legal institutions in the city, while secretly serving the movement.

"Since most of us from the moderate camp were not pinpointed as active members of the movement, it became easier for us to go around and work in the city," says Raul. "This is not to say that nobody among us went to the countryside. But we became most effective in urban work, partly because of our middle-class background, which facilitated our movements in the city. There was the need to develop Manila, to revive the protest movement in the capital. Those of us left in the city had to take up that responsibility."

According to Marcel, Edjop's first task as a kasama was to develop contacts in PAFLU and the unions under it—an assignment best performed by a cadre with a legal personality. Edjop facilitated the recruitment of two other kasamas into the PAFLU staff. The two comrades, Elisa and Frank, were also members of Edjop's first collective.

Thus, although he still maintained links with his friends—who, as Edros says, could account for all his time—Edjop, as an employee of PAFLU, performed the tasks of a cadre. He was still *legal*, and even assumed a high profile as a labor organizer. But he met secretly with kasamas of his underground collective, who, conveniently, were also his colleagues at work.

Many of the PAFLU leaders, as Edros rightly pointed out, were cautious about "Red infiltration." But Cipriano Cid was also a staunch opponent of the dictatorship. With the climate of fear under martial law, he welcomed young people, like Edjop and his comrades, who were willing to risk their necks to serve the labor movement.

That Edjop joined the revolutionary movement at all is a mystery. There were other moderate leaders, like Manny Yap and Edicio de la Torre, who went over to the radicals. But, as his friends say, Edjop was the symbol of the moderates. He was the last person society expected would join the "other side."

On December 31, 1973, the Buklod Kalayaan headquarters was raided. Romy Chan, Edros, and 20 other members were arrested and detained. As a result, the group broke up, and that, says Edros, was when "Edjop started floating by himself."

"He had no more mass base and no group to support him," says Edros. "He went into hiding knowing that, since we were in jail, he could also be a target of arrest. I think, the month after our arrest, Edjop was busy trying to keep himself scarce. When things cooled down, he surfaced only to realize that he had no more group. *Kalat-kalat na kami.* We were scattered. The others who were in the periphery were also gone. I don't know what really happened to him."

Cha Nolasco, who was also a member of Buklod Kalayaan, does not find Edjop's conversion surprising. "It would have been unnatural for Edjop not to have gone underground," she says, adding, "He was dogged in his desire to work and be one with the people, to play a role in social change. I was not surprised by what he did."

Ed Nolasco, Edjop's mentor in the labor movement, felt the same way. "In the student movement, words like 'imperialism' are merely words. In the labor movement, Edjop saw how foreigners really controlled our economy, and how this made the lives of workers miserable. To go underground, to pursue a more revolutionary program, was a natural consequence for Edjop."

"*Medyo mainit,* a young man in a hurry," is how Nolasco describes Edjop: "He wanted reforms at once. *Gusto niya, madalian. Gusto niya agad, aksiyon.*"

"Many moderates realized that there was no future in the moderate camp," says Freddie Salanga. "As an Atenean, Edjop saw that the other guys—the natdems—were just as sincere as he was. With his support group gone, Edjop wanted to find another group where he could still be effective in the movement for change. He could have joined FFF, but he became disillusioned with the FFF leaders who went over to Marcos. The fact that he remained open to the radicals proved that he never took personally their attacks against him."

"There were a lot of people who ended up like Edjop," says Ging Raterta. "They felt that they had to go on. But what alternative did they have? The Reds. *Obligado na silang sumali doon.* But they did not necessarily accept their ideology or program. I would even say that the Reds drew much of their strength from the moderates who went over to them. But these moderates did not necessarily have a change of heart in their beliefs. But the Reds had the only vehicle for continuing their work. The situation forced the moderates to adopt the methods of the Reds. A lot of moderates were killed. There was a very thin line between being violent and nonviolent."

"We are not saying that these were the only factors that made Edjop join them," says Romy Chan. "But that could have been a starting point. He might have ended up asking, 'I'm on the run. Where will I go? *Lahat ng kasama ko, nakulong.* All my colleagues are in jail.' But, obviously, we can never tell what process he really went through."

In a way, Arvin agrees. "I think his own pronouncements on

the matter should be respected," he says. This, perhaps, is what Salanga does when he says, "I think Edjop realized that the CPP was the only effective force left that could fight Marcos."

At that time, the national democratic movement was far from being a formidable force, as cadres readily admit. "Edjop entered the party at a time when it was being tested intensely," says Marcel. "The movement was still in danger of being crushed, the future of the Philippine revolution hung in the balance. Those were the darkest days of the party. It was a very tight, very unglamorous period, not a time for an opportunist to join the revolution. *Iyong pinakadeterminado lang talaga ang papasok.* Only the most determined would dare enter."

It was, Salanga affirms, a qualification that Edjop definitely had:

"Edjop was the kind of fellow who would live through a decision. It took him a long time to decide to join the natdems, mainly because he had to accept [the national democratic line] first. His was always a total conversion. *Ang pagbabago sa kanyang pananaw, pagbabago rin sa buhay niya.* A change in his views meant a change in his lifestyle.

"There was never any dichotomy in his beliefs and his way of life. He was different from other people, other activists like myself, in whom there was some sort of intellectual conceit. We could make an intellectual decision, without making the necessary conversion in our own lives. *Kay Edjop, walang ganoon. Buongbuo siya parati.* I will always remember him as a solid guy, a strong man."

19
Union Man

Recalling her first meeting with Edjop still makes Elisa burst out laughing. When they met, Edjop was wearing a plain polo shirt, maong pants and sandals. *"Nakamedyas siya!"* she chortles, describing how Edjop wore socks with his sandals. But after one look at her new comrade in proletarian garb, she concluded, *"Okey ito. Hindi tipong burgis.* He's okay. Not the bourgeois type."

Elisa had been with the moderates in the 1960s and, like Edjop, had had her share of brickbats from the radicals. But by 1970 she was with the natdem movement, and Edjop was bearing the brunt of the radical tirade. Elisa had reacted to the assaults on Edjop. "He can be won over," she asserted to comrades. "I should know. I was also like him before."

But the attacks, the stoning of the supermarket, the angry slogans on the walls—these went on, "spontaneous outbursts of *aktibistas* who didn't know any better." To all these, Elisa simply shook her head, disappointed. Still, she believed Edjop could "someday be one of us." Thus, when Ramil introduced Edjop to her as the new member of the special group on trade unions (SGTU), Elisa was not the least surprised. "I also did not feel guilty," she chuckles.

There were two other former moderates, Frank and Dino, in Edjop's first collective. This, Elisa says, made Edjop's integration into the group smoother, since they shared common experiences in the reformist bloc. Ka Lem, as Edjop was now called, had no problem adjusting to his new comrades.

It was as a humble student in the fine points of working-class politics that he launched his career as a *rebolusyonaryo*. As Frank puts it, Edjop and his comrades were *bagitos* in the labor movement.

A mountain of difficulties lay before them. As a result of martial law, the workers' movement was going through a period of repression—and caution. No confrontational tactics were being employed, no demonstration of militance that would have been swiftly crushed by the authorities.

To the national democrats, the working class, as the "most advanced productive and political force in the Philippines and the world," is the "leading force" in the revolution. At the time Edjop entered the party, however, the entire underground trade union (TU) network of the "leading force" had been nearly crippled; a captured leading party cadre had collaborated with the military and exposed most of the organizers in the different unions.

At the end of the crackdown, the "vanguard party of the working class" had less than 60 cadres left for trade union work in Manila. Many of these organizers were former student activists who, according to Ramil, didn't even know what CBA (Collective Bargaining Agreement) stood for. They were courageous aktibistas committed to the "proletarian revolution," but they tried to apply in trade union work the tactics they had learned in the streets—rabble-rousing marches and demonstrations.

They knew little about organizing unions, and less about facing management at the negotiating table. In bargaining with management, they mouthed slogans and trite formulations, instead of presenting solid arguments on behalf of the workers.

On the other hand, the mainstream labor movement was then dominated by federations which the underground movement classified as either "CIA-supported" or "Marcos-controlled." PAFLU itself was far from the "genuinely militant" federation that the revolutionaries held up as an ideal. Despite the respect they had for Cid as an individual, they saw the federation as some sort of fiefdom, with Cid as its revered leader and with officials who lorded it over the member unions. PAFLU was viewed as *dilawan*—a yellow federation—with organizers and lawyers notorious for "selling" cases or making secret agreements with management. While these "labor dealers" mouthed platitudes about their commitment to the welfare of the manggagawa, many of them got rich from "sweetheart contracts" with the capitalists. They were generous with handouts and, says Dino, good at "demagogic propaganda."

"Pag nag-strike tayo, babaha dito ng beer," a PAFLU organizer, relates Dino, once announced to workers in Benguet, promising that their affiliates in San Miguel would support them by sending cases and cases of beer.

Political issues were never discussed at union meetings, except when the organizers and leaders—some of whom also moonlighted as wards of politicians—needed the workers' votes for the coming elections. But on the whole, the union and federation bosses were concerned mainly with what the underground called "purely economistic" issues.

Nevertheless, it was to federations such as PAFLU that many workers turned for leadership, if only to get wage increases, however slight, and other benefits.

PAFLU President Cid instructed his deputies to give Edjop the "most difficult assignments." The old man liked Edjop. He was impressed by the young man's potential as a labor leader, by his commitment and drive to serve the working man. In the two years that they worked together, Cid, according to former PAFLU staffers, treated Edjop like a son. By giving the young labor leader the toughest assignments, the old man hoped to toughen Edjop, and teach him the nitty-gritty of labor politics.

Edjop also admired Cid, and looked up to him as an institution in the labor movement, like Amado Hernandez and Felixberto Olalia. But, although Cid may have had more to share with Edjop, time was running out for the veteran union man. What Edjop had to learn to make his mark in PAFLU and the trade union movement, he had to pick up from his own experiences and those of the workers he came in contact with.

Edjop's first major assignment was to help the workers of the Elizalde Rope Company draw up a CBA proposal. Management claimed the company was losing money and could not give the raise being demanded by the workers. Edjop and Elisa teamed up and made use of all available data on the case—financial statements, statistics on production output, and standards of living of the workers, etc.—to look for loopholes in the company's claims.

In their investigations, they found out that the company was, in fact, in the red. "It was true, the company was losing money," Elisa says. "How the hell were we supposed to argue the case? Even the workers admitted that, based on the orders and the volume of production, the company was going down. No matter how we juggled the figures this fact was still clear. We just couldn't use the usual arguments in collective bargaining."

They broke the news during a union meeting. The workers raised questions and arguments about their conclusions. But Elisa and Edjop stuck to their findings. Then the union president, Felicing Villados, better known as Ka Felicing, stood up to speak.

"When the prices of raw materials go up, the company absorbs the increase," the dark-skinned and slender labor leader began in stinging Pilipino. "When power and water rates are hiked, the company also absorbs them. When the administrators ask for a raise in their representational allowances and other expenses, the company somehow finds a way to give them what they ask.

"But now, we, the workers, whose wages have been frozen for such a long time, are asking for a raise. How come the company won't absorb the increase we are demanding? What we are asking for is so little compared to the expenses that they have coped with in the past—when, in truth, we actually deserve more than we are getting now!

"Every year, when the company loses money, we get nothing but dirt. When it is earning, all the profits go to the capitalists. *Palagi na lang bang latak ang matatanggap namin?* Will we always get leftovers?

"Why do you see this case from management's view first, before viewing it from our side? Why must the welfare of the capitalists come first before ours? *Tingnan ninyo muna ang posisyon namin bago ang sa kanila!* Examine our position first, before you examine theirs!"

Ka Felicing's words, says Elisa, were the "most important lecture in trade unionism" she and Edjop ever heard. "Here was a man who had not studied theories about exploitation and surplus value as we had—who was not even a kasama—presenting simple but sound arguments from the the workers' standpoint."

Edjop subsequently got involved in the struggles of more than 100 unions—Royal Undergarments, Philippine Leather, Franklin Baker, Atlantic Gulf, Benguet Consolidated. As one cadre puts it, the years he spent in factories, picketlines and workers' communities molded him as a revolutionary "more than all the Marxist books he had read, and more than all the party Ed [education] sessions he had attended."

By the time his stint as a labor organizer ended, Edjop's political standpoint and style were, in his comrades' words, "proletaryadong-proletaryado"—unquestionably proletarian.

"The interests of the workers always came first," Elisa explains. "A company did not have to be earning for it to give the workers just and proper wages. The workers must always receive what is rightfully theirs."

This became the core principle of "genuine trade unionism," a term which, says Frank, they coined during the early years of martial law. GTU, as it is now popularly known, became a working class battlecry. Edjop, according to Frank, was the best articulator of the concept, as he wrote countless papers and manifestoes explaining GTU. These were then distributed in factories and communities.

"I never noticed Edjop lose interest in the work," recalls Frank. "He loved the work, he enjoyed it."

Timoteo "Boy" Aranuez, former president of GATCORD, recalls Edjop's participation in the case of the South Eastern Timber Corporation (SETIC), a big logging company in Quezon.

"The logging site was several hours away by bus from Manila," says Aranuez. "One had to walk a distance, then ride a *banca* [a small boat made of bamboo], to reach it. Nobody in PAFLU wanted to go there. But Edjop volunteered. He was able to organize the workers, who eventually won benefits from the company."

"Edjop also became some sort of attraction to the workers, who were used to the politicking-style of other PAFLU leaders," says Frank. "Ed not only spoke about the economic conditions of the workers, but also linked these to the political situation. The workers were always interested in the discussions."

He adds that, whenever other PAFLU leaders paid a visit to an affiliate union, they expected to be given honoraria and to be treated to a feast. But Edjop and the other youth organizers neither accepted money nor expected to be treated in any special manner. "This created some problems in the beginning," explains Frank, "since the workers had been used to that practice for years."

Some of the traditional PAFLU leaders were cynical of Edjop and the newcomers. "I think many of these leaders were envious of Ed," Ed Nolasco would later recall. "Ed had a clean record. The other leaders felt threatened because he was so straight."

Nolasco adds that, after Cid's arrest, Edjop was made a member of a triumvirate which took over the federation. PAFLU Vice-President Greg Abuy and another federation official were the other members of this leading body. But, according to Nolasco, it was Edjop who was practically running the federation. Nolasco recalls: "While the other leaders were hesitant or afraid to take any initiative, Edjop visited factories and talked to union leaders, not only in Manila, but all over the country. He held the federation together."

The Elizalde Rope case, where the union had to deal with a losing firm, was actually an exceptional one. In other companies, the exploitation was so blatant it wasn't hard for the unions to argue their case. Edjop once told his sister Marie about the conditions in a cigarette factory owned by a Chinese businessman. There were no windows in the factory, he said, and the doors were padlocked during working hours. The workers, who earned no more than seven pesos a day, had to bear with the heat and the fumes.

In some factories, workers who had been with the company for more than ten years were still considered casuals. Some were not paid for working overtime, while others were not paid the legal minimum wage. Many were not paid at all.

Despite the strictly-enforced strike ban, workers' protest actions, both organized and spontaneous, erupted in many business establishments throughout the country. Underground cadres were quick to consolidate these outbursts of defiance and build a support network in different factories. The Marcos policy of keeping labor repressed and cheap only made more attractive, to workers, the option presented by the revolutionaries.

What government authorities branded as "infiltration" was actually the clandestine efforts of city-based cadres who went to and lived in factories and urban poor communities, made contact with sympathizers and active supporters of the movement, and organized them into underground cells and committees. In time, the ranks of workers committed to the national democratic revolution began to swell. "At that time, it was not hard to sell the ND line to people who always wondered why, no matter how hard they worked, there was hardly any food on their table," recalls Dino.

"Suddenly, workers just didn't care anymore about the consequences of defying laws against strikes," says Frank. "They had nothing more to lose."

In one factory, workers held a sit-down strike. When confronted by the supervisors, they answered, "Well, we still haven't been paid. We're so hungry, we just don't have the energy to work." In another company, workers intentionally caused the machines to break down. One tactic—which, according to Dino, Edjop himself suggested—had workers ceasing operations to pray the rosary for about an hour or two. The company owners were so stunned, says Dino, that they immediately agreed to negotiate.

Edjop and the other TU cadres employed novel strategies in face-to-face encounters with management. In the past CBA meetings, only three to five people, including a representative from the federation and the top officials of the union, met with management. But Edjop marched to CBA sessions with no fewer than five other panelists, along with all the union board members, plus some workers. "Your group is so large," a management representative would complain. Edjop would casually reply: "Well, it's all right with us if you add members to your panel."

Edjop's well-rounded college training and experience in running the family supermarket made him familiar with the nuances of the business world, the tricks of the trade. As he himself said to Marie, the two years he spent in law school were enough for him to understand the ins and outs of the legal system, and how "it is used against the workers." At CBA meetings, Edjop usually let the union workers do the talking. But once he saw a worker running out of arguments, he did not hesitate to enter the discussion and defend the union position. He would go directly to the company data, which he memorized by heart, pounding gently on the table to stress a point, but always maintaining a dignified and diplomatic posture. Steadfast but cool, he smiled off the arguments of their opponents, before responding with a barrage of counter-arguments.

"Edjop was perfect at the negotiating table," Dino enthusiastically recalls. "For a small guy, he had a big voice and the bearing of a professional. *Tikas-propesyonal.* And, most important of all, he knew what he was talking about. He never tried to bluff his way through a point. No manager could talk circles around him. In fact, at times, it was Edjop who did the fancy talk, though he was always armed with hard facts."

Soon, company officials were requesting the old man Cid not to send Edjop to negotiations. "They complained about Ed's impassioned stance," says Elisa, laughing. "They said that Edjop spoke as if he was at a rally in Plaza Miranda. *Parang lagi raw siyang nasa Plaza Miranda.* But the real reason was Edjop's brilliance during negotiations. He was very tough. *Matinding pumukpok.* They also knew he could never be bought. He didn't have a price."

Some of the managers had heard of him as a national youth leader, and this, says Ka Frank, always made them think twice about trying to bribe him. With Edjop and the bagitos, no deal between union and management was made until the workers themselves approved the terms at a union meeting. Copies of the agreement were distributed to the union members, and the CBA itself was signed in front of the workers.

"This was new to us," says Ka Felicing. "In the past, organizers and union leaders made decisions all by themselves. But Ed insisted on consulting the workers. We held meetings before and after the negotiations, and the signing of the CBA. The workers were always aware of every position Ed took during negotiations.

"Ed advised us never to depend solely on organizers or even a federation. In CBA negotiations, workers themselves must take the lead. They must have the courage and consciousness to face up to the capitalists."

Edjop's collective helped put up federations of unions in specific industries, districts and corporations. One such alliance, where Edjop played an important role, was the National Union of Garment, Textile, Cordage and Allied Workers of the Philippines, or GATCORD.

In 1973 Edjop was involved with the workers of Gelmart, then the biggest garment firm in Asia, with over 10,000 workers. For 20 years, according to Dino, a "company union with leaders in the payroll of management" dominated the factory. The company was listed among the top 1,000 corporations in the country, but its workers were among the most exploited in the industry.

"All we got each year was a ten-centavo increase," says Eusebia Nolasco, a former Gelmart worker. "I had been with the company for ten years, but all I got was a ten-centavo raise.

"Edjop often visited us at our boarding houses, where we had our meetings. Most of the workers in Gelmart didn't know much about union work. I myself didn't understand it. I used to think that all I had to do was sign my name and I was already a union member. Ed taught us the importance of a union."

In 1974 the Gelmart employees elected union officers who were independent of management. Soon after that, union members demanded that they align themselves with a federation. On March 28, 1974, the new union officers called for a general meeting to vote on the proposal. But at around four in the afternoon on the day of the assembly, management, in order to pre-empt what would surely be a vote for more militance, locked the factory gates and called for overtime. The workers then scaled the walls and knocked down the door to break out of the factory. Outside, other workers and activists, including Edjop, joined the defiant employees. There were about 6,000 of them who marched from the factory, along the South Superhighway, to the Bicutan Plaza, where a demonstration was held and the Gelmart workers voted to join GATCORD.

The Gelmart management retaliated by suspending the union leaders. The workers protested and brought their case to the Department of Labor. New union certification elections were scheduled in May 1975. Aside from the GATCORD-affiliated union, five labor federations, including the Philippine Transport and General Workers Organization (PTGWO) of Roberto Oca and the Associated Labor Union (ALU) of Democrito Mendoza, were listed as among the contending federations.

In 1972 Edjop had had a brief stint with ALU, but had bolted out of the federation which, according to Ed Nolasco, Edjop accused of being "a creation of the CIA." The Gelmart elections were a major event in the history of the labor movement under martial law. The Marcos government had imposed a "one industry, one union" policy. Whichever federation won in Gelmart would have the right to represent the textile, garment, and cordage industry.

Edjop and the other workers and organizers campaigned tirelessly for the GATCORD union. But Oca and Mendoza were known to be cunning labor barons, with contacts in government and the military. According to a report in *Signs of the Times* (May 30, 1975), there were cases of harassment and intimidation of GATCORD workers and organizers. Some were offered bribes, others threatened with physical harm or the loss of their jobs.

GATCORD clearly had the majority's support, as proven by the march to Bicutan of over 6,000 workers. But their opponents could try to rig the elections. To protect the ballots, GATCORD got the support of friends and sympathizers from the church sector, many of them Edjop's friends. According to *Signs of the Times,* at least 110 priests and nuns were at the Gelmart factory on election day, May 24, 1975. With square pieces of paper, with the handwritten note "Itaguyod ang GATCORD" ("Support GATCORD") pinned or taped on their habits, they monitored election proceedings, guarded ballot boxes and reported anomalies.

It was the first time priests and nuns had gotten involved in union elections, and the other federations protested. But the presence of church members pre-empted any disruptive scheme other groups may have had. The elections pushed through, and the GATCORD union won more than 60 percent of the votes.

GATCORD was an affiliate of PAFLU, and the traditional PAFLU labor leaders expected to land top positions in the new alliance. Edjop and the other cadres in PAFLU thought they didn't have enough support within the federation to challenge the traditional leaders. They decided not to field any candidates in the federation elections, and asked the worker-activists not to nominate any of them.

But the cadres had underestimated the extent of the support they could muster among the unions. When a worker from Elizalde Rope nominated Edjop for vice-president for education and research, Edjop and his comrades were stunned. They found themselves in an awkward, yet opportune, situation. The traditional leaders of PAFLU, threatened by the bagitos, moved swiftly to block Edjop's nomination.

"Edgar Jopson is not a member of any union," one of the traditional leaders announced. "Therefore, he cannot be elected as an official of GATCORD."

As Dino recalls, at least three workers, from three different unions, immediately stood up and, almost simultaneously, declared:

"We hereby recognize Edgar Jopson as a member of Elizalde Rope Workers Union!"

"We hereby recognize Edgar Jopson as a member of Allied Threads Employees Union!"

"The Gelmart union declares Edgar Jopson as one of its members."

Other union leaders followed, and soon all the workers were clapping their hands and stomping their feet, cheering "We want Ed! We want Ed!"

It was a chance too important to pass up, and his comrades urged Edjop to take it. "Go for it," they said. "Accept the nomination. *Sunggaban mo na iyan.*"

But Edjop hesitated, and it was at that instance, says Dino, that he first saw him waver. The workers and his comrades milled around Edjop, pleading with him to accept the nomination. Some of his comrades were nearly in tears, overwhelmed by the outburst of support, and irked by Edjop's stubbornness.

"We were ecstatic that the union leaders had openly defied the traditional leaders, and were throwing their support behind Edjop—and there was Edjop unwilling to heed the cry of the workers."

"I'm not sure," Edjop said, confused. "I don't think it's the right thing to do. *Malabo, hindi ko kaya.* I don't think I should do it."

"He was not prepared for such a confrontation," says Dino. "We still considered some of the traditional leaders in PAFLU as allies, and Edjop did not want to sacrifice our relations with them for the sake of a post in GATCORD."

"In many ways, Edjop had always behaved that way," recalls Elisa. "If possible, he tried to avoid confrontation among comrades and allies. He always looked for a compromise. When things came to a head, he was always willing to give way. Edjop also did not want to give the impression that he was after any position in the federation. In fact, he was not after any position. He had always been conscious about being seen as a man with personal ambitions."

But the unions and his comrades pursued their demand for

Edjop to run. "The workers would not let him decline nor would we," says Elisa. "At that moment, we could only see the workers wanting a man they knew they could trust. I guess Edjop realized this in the end. He simply had to heed the workers' call."

In a meeting with comrades afterwards, Edjop would make a self-criticism, admitting weakness in his initial decision not to run.

Edjop accepted the nomination and won by an overwhelming majority.

20
Ka Fe and Ka Felicing

For about a year, Edjop and Joy lived with Ka Felicing and his wife Fe. A short scraggy-looking man with a dark complexion, Ka Felicing, then in his late forties, worked as a driver at the Elizalde Rope Company, where he earned a daily wage of eight pesos and forty centavos. After an unsuccessful campaign in 1968, Ka Felicing became president of the Elizalde Rope workers union in 1972. He met Edjop when Cipriano Cid assigned the young organizer to the Elizalde Rope Employees Union, a PAFLU affiliate.

Aside from being a housewife, Ka Fe was also involved in union work, attending meetings and helping organize the wives and families of other workers in the factory.

The couple lived with their seven children in a cramped wooden house in Meycauayan, Bulacan. The family stayed in two rooms. The space beneath the house had been converted into a basement room, and Edjop sometimes slept there. "It can't be called a room compared to what Edjop was used to," says Ka Felicing. At other times, Edjop slept on the kitchen floor or on a piece of galvanized sheet metal.

The house had none of the comforts Edjop knew on Paraiso— no maids to cook his meals, wash his clothes, and attend to his needs; no carpeted and fully-furnished room of his own; no plush toilets and air-conditioners. Water had to be fetched from an artesian well outside the house.

But the couple have fond memories of Edjop. Ka Felicing says the young man lived the life of a proletarian: *"Naging parang manggagawa talaga siya."*

In a videotaped interview, Ka Fe relates how Edjop would unceremoniously arrive in their house, take off his shoes, and sit on the floor to join their children in watching television. "He didn't make us feel that we had to entertain him or that he had to be treated like a special guest," she says.

Once he borrowed a T-shirt from Ka Felicing, who only had one with holes in it to lend. Edjop didn't mind. Another time he borrowed a pair of Ka Felicing's old house shorts, which he wore while washing one of two pairs of pants he owned. He also ironed his own clothes.

Edjop often worked in the kitchen at a beat-up wooden dining table, where he pored over books and documents concerning union and underground work. After finishing his work, he would get ready to sleep—right on the kitchen floor. He would ask for a sleeping mat. The couple could only lend him a worn-out *banig*. He never complained.

"He never even asked for a pillow," says Ka Felicing. "But we did give him a blanket—"

"So the mosquitoes wouldn't feast on him," the old woman adds. "But one time, I couldn't find any more extra blankets. I ended up giving him one of our curtains."

The couple laugh at the recollection.

Edjop used to catch *talangka* (small crabs) in a murky creek that ran behind the house; the creek also served as garbage dump. Ka Felicing remembers how excited Edjop was whenever he caught three or four of the little crabs. But the old man had to teach him how to eat talangka—Edjop used to just break off the legs, chuck what was left into his mouth and start chewing.

At one meal, Ka Felicing offered him a spoon to eat with. Edjop refused it and used his fingers. At first, he didn't know how to eat with his fingers, and Ka Felicing demonstrates how Edjop would scoop the food to his mouth with his palm. But Edjop, Ka Fe adds, was never choosy with food. "Whatever we served he ate," she says.

At first, the couple didn't know about Edjop's affluent background. He never talked to them about it, and they never suspected he was rich. If he had found out earlier, says Ka Felicing, he would have thought twice about letting Edjop live the way he did: *"Nahiya naman ako sa sarili ko."*

It was when Edjop took Ka Felicing to his house one day that

he and Ka Fe found out. But this never affected their relationship.

"I sometimes had to lend him money myself," the old man
relates, amused. "He used to come up to me and ask, Ka Felicing,
could you lend me two pesos for jeepney fare?' We were that
comfortable with each other. *Naging panatag ang kalooban ko sa
batang iyon.* I felt so comfortable with that boy."

The old man values the things he learned from the young
revolutionary. Edjop, he relates, taught him humility. Like other
union leaders, Ka Felicing was quick to claim credit for the
achievements of the union, and to see himself as the moving
force of the organization. But Edjop and the other aktibistas
emphasized "collective effort."

"Did you accomplish those things alone, Ka Felicing?" Edjop
once said. "Or were you not able to do them because of what
you learned from your fellow workers? You are not Superman."

"Ed would literally be pleading with me to understand his
point," Ka Felicing laughingly recalls. "He became intense as he
spoke, his saliva spurting out—*sumasabog na ang laway niya.* But
he never lost his cool. I never felt offended."

Edjop cautioned Ka Felicing not to explicitly show anger and
irritation during CBA meetings with management. "You can
make them feel that you are angry," he said. "But only in your
tone of voice, never in the expression of your face." Edjop himself was firm, but cool, when facing the capitalists. "Management
couldn't stand him," says Ka Felicing. "Ed really got the capitalists mad."

Edjop never revealed his underground affiliation to Ka Felicing. But the old man got hints. Once Edjop asked him if he
thought that raising workers' wages would help solve their
plight.

"No, of course not," the old man said. "Because history shows
that, even if wages are increased, workers remain poor. That is
the system."

"Then how can there be change? How do we change the
system?"

"Rebolusyon," the old man answered.

Edjop simply smiled. But after that conversation, Ka Felicing started receiving, from unidentified sources, leaflets and other reading materials about rebolusyon.

21
=== A Wedding in Navotas ===

Edjop proposed marriage to Joy in the summer of 1973. The wedding was set for January 26, 1974, the fourth anniversary of the start of the First Quarter Storm. In proposing, Edjop told Joy of his wish to "lead a very simple life." Joy did not object. By then, she had "accepted, and was willing to share in, his commitment to the people."

During one of their heart-to-heart talks by the murky creek behind the Villados home, Edjop asked Ka Felicing to be a *ninong*, a sponsor, at their wedding. "You can't ask me that, Ed," Ka Felicing said. "*Putsa!* You come from a rich family. I can't be your ninong."

"Well, if you won't become my ninong, then I guess I won't get married," Edjop kidded.

Ka Felicing finally agreed to be a sponsor at the wedding, but on one condition: "You must promise never to call me *Ninong*. You'll continue to call me *Ka Felicing*. I don't think I'd feel comfortable with you calling me *Ninong*."

The wedding almost did not happen. On December 31, 1973, a few weeks before Joy and Edjop were to be married, the military raided the Buklod Kalayaan headquarters. Several of Edjop's friends and colleagues, including Romy Chan and Ed del Rosario, were picked up and detained.

The incident stunned Edjop. "He said he didn't think he could get married while his friends languished in jail," Joy relates. Edjop thought of calling the wedding off. Joy protested. "I understood his feelings about what had happened to his friends. But it seemed like he wished that he had been arrested with them. I got angry with him for that. I asked him, 'Is going to prison a measure of one's commitment?'"

Edjop, however, seemed to have made a decision, and Joy resigned herself to the fact that she and Edjop would never be married. But a few days later Edjop came down with a fever and sent word that he wanted to see Joy. When she came to visit him, Edjop apologized for having thought of canceling the wedding.

For their eldest son's wedding, Hernan and Josefa Jopson had wanted to throw a big wedding celebration, perhaps a catered affair at a five-star hotel, with a hundred guests. But Edjop politely refused. He and Joy had planned a simple wedding to start a simple life.

They were married in St. Joseph's Church in Navotas. The reception was held in the social hall of the parish, where they served Filipino delicacies—*pansit Malabon, puto, balut, itlog na maalat* (salted eggs).

Edjop and Joy had sent out only 50 invitations, thinking that not many of the people they invited would bother to go all the way to Navotas. But about 300 people came. This became a problem—not enough food had been prepared for such a big gathering. Luckily, Joy recalls, "there were many restaurants in Navotas which served *pansit Malabon.*"

"Yellow, not red, was the wedding's motif," Joy would later recall with amusement. She did have a bouquet of red roses. And to add to the native flavor of the ceremony, there was a *salakot* (a traditional Filipino hat) on top of their wedding cake.

Some of Edjop's former classmates and family friends came to the celebration, dressed elegantly and riding fancy cars. This made Ka Felicing feel uneasy, as he drove an old beat-up jeep— which he had borrowed from his brother-in-law and which, to him, was already *"magara,"* though it was *"kakarag-karag"*—into the church parking lot. He wore an old-fashioned barong Tagalog, also borrowed, and black leather shoes, which he himself had cleaned and shined the night before.

Edjop immediately welcomed the old man and introduced him to his parents. "He introduced me as a top official of PAFLU, which wasn't true, for I was just a union president," Ka Felicing chuckles. Edjop's parents, he adds, were very warm, and he soon felt comfortable in the gathering.

Joy was late, held up in traffic. "For the first time in our relationship," she would later relate, smiling at the memory, "Ed had to do the waiting." Joy wore a jusi wedding gown, while Edjop was in a jusi barong.

Ateneo pre-novices, at Edjop's request, sang in the Mass. Joy chose the songs, which included "Sunrise, Sunset."

Monsignor Jose Mirasol, Edjop's uncle, was the main celebrant, with two chaplains from Student Catholic Action as cocelebrants. In the offertory, Ed Nolasco presented a hammer to symbolize the workers' movement, to represent Edjop. To represent Joy's commitment to community work, a nun, her colleague at the Catholic Action Center, presented a replica of a nipa hut.

It was a happy affair. Joy herself was "smiling all throughout," celebrating the start of a new life.

Edjop took the wedding seriously. A few days before the ceremony, he had gone to see a priest with questions about the ritual of matrimony. Eric, as this priest would later be known in the underground, was involved in Church social action work. He was known as a *progresibo* and a sympathizer of the revolution.

Edjop wanted to know "if the Church would accept the marriage of someone who believed in the armed struggle, in the revolution," Eric relates. "He didn't want a show wedding, held only for the sake of conventions. *Ayaw niya ng kasal-kasalan.* He wanted the whole affair to be relevant not only for him and Joy, but for all people who were going to attend it. By then, he disagreed with many of the teachings of the Church. But I told him that what is most important is a person's love for neighbor, his willingness to offer his whole self for God's people. These, I knew, Edjop always had. His bond with a woman who shared the same commitment would certainly be special in the eyes of God."

This may not make sense to those who have always believed that anyone who becomes a member of the Communist Party automatically renounces the faith. It's difficult to speculate on whether or not Edjop, after joining the Party, gave up his belief in God. His parents and Joy would assert that he never lost it. Some of his friends and former colleagues among the moderates, who were disappointed to learn of Edjop's political conversion, would probably say, "Yes, he had embraced a godless ideology." But Edjop's comrades in the movement simply shrug at the question, saying, "We don't know. We never talked about it."

Fr. Edicio de la Torre, an SVD priest who joined the Christians for National Liberation (a member-organization of the National Democratic Front), is just as uncertain about Edjop's religious beliefs as a cadre. They once met at an underground meeting, and during one of their informal chats Edjop suddenly fell silent and serious, took Edicio aside and said, "I would like to ask you a rather important personal question."

De la Torre is one of the most respected revolutionaries from the religious sector, and this may have prompted Edjop to turn to him and ask, "Do you know of Christians who joined the Communist Party? How did they resolve their belief in God?"

"I told him that I knew quite a few," Edicio recalls. "But, I said, for most of them their belief in God was not the principal question. When they were invited to the party, the CPP does not ask them first if they believe in God or not. For a lot of them, those who believed continued believing, and those who didn't believe did not find any reason to assert that.

"The most important question was: Were they willing to accept the responsibilities of leadership in the underground? This meant a tighter schedule, greater readiness to face risks and, most important of all, the painful and heavy responsibility of leading, setting directions, talking to a lot of people, shaping and uniting them to perform one united common task.

"Edjop did not pick up the question too much. But occasionally, I would catch him at other meetings, looking at me with a bit of question. I also gave him some materials to read.

"The whole issue of religious belief in a revolutionary movement, particularly in a Communist movement which includes atheists, is a very difficult question. A lot of books have been written about it. But it is ultimately a very personal question. I don't know how Edjop resolved it, or whether he felt any need to resolve it.

"People often ask me about friends and Christians who turn

Communist, asking, 'Have they stopped believing in God or not?' I tell them, I don't think so. A lot of people who react against easy 'god-talk' are reacting against people like Marcos who said, 'Before I declared martial law, I prayed very hard, consulted God, and God told me, 'It's okay to declare martial law.' Then there's President McKinley who went down on his knees, prayed very hard and asked, 'God, shall I colonize the Filipinos or shall I set them free?' And God told him, 'Yes, colonize them for their own sake.'

"That kind of easy usage of God and religion, for very reactionary political ends, is bound to create a lot of negative feeling and reaction.

"On the other hand, a lot of Christians have discovered a deeper faith in a God whom perhaps they don't mention so easily or casually every day, but whom they feel they serve and whose presence they feel when they are with people who undergo their liberating passion, death and resurrection on their way to what we call our common liberation.

"I would like to believe Edjop underwent such a passage. I would have wanted to talk to him later—if we ever got the chance—on how he resolved this question."

As Edjop and Joy knelt before the altar, he made the vow he would keep sacred till his death—just like the pledge he had made, almost a year before, when he entered the Communist Party.

As one cadre puts it, "Despite doubts some people may have about his beliefs, one thing is clear: Edjop never broke any of his commitments to his wife, to his cause and, most important of all, to his people."

22
On the Run

The day after his wedding, Edjop called his collective to a meeting at his parents' house in Quezon City. He and Joy were set to leave for Mindoro the next day, but he had insisted on reviewing the progress of the collective's work before going on a honeymoon.

In five days, as he had promised his group, Edjop and Joy were back from Mindoro. "We would have understood if they had stayed a little longer," Elisa says.

The newlyweds rented a room for P250 a month on the top floor of a two-story apartment in Sta. Ana, Manila. Their first home had no living room, and had only a dining table, some stools and Central Bank cash boxes for chairs.

Edjop was then earning about P400 a month at PAFLU. Joy was receiving P850 from her work at the Catholic Action Center. They were actually living on Joy's salary, although, she admits, they never really had any financial problems. Ed still received some support from his parents, who sometimes sent them money and groceries.

"But Ed and I really didn't need much then," says Joy. "Edjop had very simple tastes and needs. Sometimes I even felt guilty about buying things for myself, knowing how Ed got along without any new clothes."

Edjop also did not hesitate to give away some of his clothes and belongings to fellow organizers or workers in need. He cared so little about clothes, in fact, that Joy had to insist that he let her choose which shirts or pants he could give away, and which ones he must keep for himself.

"They didn't really have to make all those sacrifices," Elisa says of the couple's early life together. "We never suggested to him that, as a cadre, he had to maintain certain standards in his lifestyle or things like that. He was still operating legally, so he had no reason to live in what looked like a poorhouse.

"But, I think, to Ed, it was important to adjust to that kind of life. He was determined to continue as a cadre, and he knew the rigors of the life he may eventually have to lead. He was conscious of the remolding process he had to go through—and the discipline he must develop in himself."

On May 1, 1974, a loose alliance of unions and federations, called *Bukluran ng Manggagawang Pilipino* (Union of Filipino Workers)—Bukluran for short—was put up by workers affiliated with PAFLU and other independent federations. According to Dino, Edjop was among those who proposed the development of Bukluran as an alternative center for workers, with GTU, or genuine trade unionism, as its guiding principle.

In June 1974, Cipriano Cid died. A power struggle broke out between two rival traditional leaders, Onofre Guevara and Catalino Lozano, who contested the PAFLU presidency. Guevara, claiming to be the rightful heir to Cid's position (he even insisted that it was Cid's deathbed wish that Guevara should succeed the old man, according to Dino), took over the PAFLU headquarters in Tondo. Lozano put up his own headquarters. Both factions held separate conventions, the Guevara group in July and Lozano in September. The two groups were, from then on, dubbed PAFLU-July, headed by Guevara, and PAFLU-September, headed by Lozano.

To Edjop and his comrades, both were *dilawan,* yellow. Though they sided with the Lozano faction, which they considered "less corrupt," they began to focus their energies on Bukluran, as the new progressive labor center.

But something happened which derailed many of their plans.

Sometime in the late 1974, Mr. Jopson got a call from a certain Captain Esguerra, who asked about Edjop's whereabouts.

"He wanted me to bring my son to them," recalls Mr. Jopson. "They said they just wanted to talk to him. They were wondering why Ed was no longer attending his classes at the UP. They were worried that he had already gone over to the 'other side' because, the officer said, 'Getting Edjop would be a big propaganda gain for the Communists.'"

"I told them that my son wouldn't get involved in something before thinking about it first. That he was a mature boy.

"I said that if they wanted to talk to Ed, they could set a meeting with him at the house. I would even help them. They agreed."

To create the impression that he had nothing to hide, Edjop met with Captain Esguerra in the basement living room of the Jopson residence. Afterwards Edjop told his father of the captain's mission: "He wants me to work for them as an informer. They want me to reveal the names of my comrades. I told him that if they want to arrest people, they can sure do it without my help. I won't let them use me."

The military, Edjop said, threatened to arrest and detain him if he did not cooperate. "I think it's time for me to sidestep for a while," Edjop said. Sadly, Mr. Jopson agreed.

Subsequent investigation revealed that, in October 1974, a captured party member had collaborated with the military and exposed a number of underground cadres in the labor movement. Edjop had been introduced to that person at one underground meeting. There had been no need for them to be introduced, and it was a mistake Edjop truly regretted. He had later rebuked his comrades: "Why did you have to introduce me to that person?"

At the time of his meeting with Captain Esguerra, the military already knew that Edjop was a party member. Whey then did the military not arrest him right then and there? "They thought they could convince, or frighten, Edjop into working for them as an agent," explains Elisa. "They probably figured he was some naive former student leader who wanted to fight against Marcos but had unwittingly found himself dabbling in underground politics. They probably didn't think he was that serious, or committed, to the revolution."

In fact, Edjop was shaken by the incident. He had been betrayed by a comrade—this, says Elisa, Edjop found almost unbelievable. "He never thought a comrade could ever do something like that," says Elisa. "He had a very high regard for the movement and for the kasamas. He himself worked hard to maintain the prestige and reputation of the revolutionary movement. That's why he really felt betrayed—and, I think, a bit disillusioned."

But if he was flustered, Edjop did not let it show. As Elisa herself says: "He was not the type to lose control in crisis situations." Edjop calmly participated in collective discussions on security measures. His comrades agreed that, among them, Edjop was most vulnerable, because of his reputation and high profile in the labor movement. Edjop was advised to go "semi-UG."

They debated on whether they should all go into hiding. One side was for retaining their legal positions in the federation and continuing their work aboveground. The other side preferred not to take the risk that any of them would be arrested—all should go UG. The latter view prevailed.

"It was a very difficult decision for all of us," recalls Elisa. "After two years, we had grown to love our work. We had already adjusted to the pace and limitations of the labor movement. At the same time, our efforts in the past year had begun to bear fruit. Workers were getting organized. They were beginning to fight in a time of intense repression. We had been part of this process which, we knew, could pave the way for a formidable workers' movement. But because of what happened, we had to abandon our work. Just when we were making progress, we had to retreat. *Kung kailan puwede na kaming bumuwelo, saka pa kami aatras.*

"It was hardest on Edjop," Elisa adds. "Of us all, he had invested the most."

23
La Tondeña

Edjop and Joy moved to another apartment, and he asked her not to tell anyone their new address. He became more cautious in his movements, staying clear of places where he had often been seen in the past, and which the military might expect him to visit regularly. His visits to his parents' house became less frequent. Though saddened by this development, Hernan and Josefa Jopson understood the need to take precautions.

So as not to arouse the suspicion of other PAFLU staffers, who might wonder at Edjop's sudden disappearance, his comrades spread the word that Edjop was ill. To make the story more convincing, they actually had Edjop confined at the Mary Chiles Hospital, where some of his unsuspecting colleagues visited him.

Edjop was not totally unprepared for the sudden change. After more than a year working with other full-time comrades, he knew what to expect in the underground, or UG. Besides, though he took the necessary precautions, he was careful not to overemphasize the threats to his security. He was not driven to inaction.

In February 1975, Edjop's and Joy's first child, Liberato Labrador Celnan, or Nonoy, was born. For another year, Edjop was involved in trade union work. Though he and the other party cadres had pulled out of PAFLU, they maintained links with some unions and with individual workers.

It was a crucial period for the labor movement. Edjop had made contact with priests and nuns he had gotten acquainted with as a student leader; they were now active, one way or another, in the workers' struggle. By this time, the urban middle classes had begun to stir from the benumbing effects of martial law. This was true even in the sector which the radicals never imagined would one day be their ally—the Church.

The early years of martial rule saw the involvement of priests and nuns in "peoples' struggles." They gave aid to urban poor

163

communities, joined workers at picketlines, and helped out relatives of political detainees. They formed task forces and organizations, for general and specific issues—the Friends of the Workers Committee, the Friends of the Farmers Committee, the Friends of the Urban Poor Committee, and Task Force Detainees.

Edjop was known to church people not only as a student leader but, by the mid-seventies, also as an experienced labor organizer. In 1975 he was asked to help conduct a study on the conditions of industrial workers in Metro Manila, in the course of which he set up the Church Labor Center (CLC).

It was while on this assignment that Edjop and Father Luis Jalandoni met again. Jalandoni had been arrested in 1973 for organizing sugar workers in Negros, and was detained in Manila. Soon after his release, he joined the newly-formed CLC as head of the education department. Edjop was then head of the organization department. When they met again, Jalandoni noticed "how much Edjop had matured after only a few years."

In October 1975 came the La Tondeña strike, the first major workers' strike to be launched under martial law. The very first work stoppage under the regime had erupted in October 1972, when workers of the Apple Sidra Corporation went on a five-day sit-down strike; Edjop was also involved in that earlier protest action. But it is the La Tondeña strike that cadres and activists look back to as the first "explosion"—*unang putok*—that rocked the foundations of the dictatorship. What happened in that drab-looking factory near the Pasig River in Tondo, inspired many workers and activists during the dark years of martial law.

On October 10, 1975, the management of the La Tondeña Distillery, a company owned by the prestigious Palanca family, announced new "criteria for employment." Drafted by two former Armed Forces of the Philippines colonels who worked for the company as factory and personnel managers, the memorandum stated, among others, that an employee must pass an I.Q. test and secure clearances from the police, the National Bureau of Investigation, and the courts.

The La Tondeña workers were outraged, as the new policies threatened to dislodge many of them from their already unstable jobs. The *Kaisahan ng Malayang Manggagawa ng La Tondeña Inc.* (Union of Free Workers of La Tondeña) rejected the new guidelines, calling it a management ploy to retain the temporary status of most workers in the factory, and to get rid of the more militant union members.

"Some of the workers had been with the company for as long as ten years," explains Dino. "But they were still considered 'casual' employees. A military officer was supposed to give tests to all laborers, most of whom had not even reached high school. They naturally failed the exams—which was not really necessary, since their job was mostly washing and cleaning bottles."

But management was determined to impose the new policies. On October 15, union leaders received photocopies of an order from the Metrocom chief, General Prospero Olivas, "inviting" them to Camp Crame. Senator Jose Diokno, lawyer for the La Tondeña workers, asked General Olivas to state the reasons for the "invitation."

For the La Tondeña workers, the new set of guidelines was the last straw in a series of frustrations. For years they had demanded changes in company policies, including making regular employees out of around 600 "casual" or "contractual" workers. They also demanded a stop to the practice of arbitrarily dismissing "uncooperative" employees. Since 1971, they had sent countless petitions to the Department of Labor and the National Labor Relations Commission, but had gotten nothing more than empty promises. They even tried to present their case to President Marcos himself, to no avail. Now management, with a little help from the military, was adding more fuel to the fire.

The union voted to go on strike and turned to the Church Labor Center for advice. Edjop and Father Jalandoni met with the union leaders at the Apostolic Center in Sta. Ana.

Edjop had heard the same grievances many times before in a hundred other factories—no job security, extremely low wages, no vacation leave, no sick leave, no maternity leave for women. Furthermore, the La Tondeña workers were hired for only eight weeks, then dismissed; to be reinstated, they had to sign another eight-week contract.

But Edjop and his comrades knew only too well the possible cost that a full-blown strike would entail. The planned strike could crack wide open the iron curtain of fear and repression under martial law, but it could also lead to a bloody scenario of crushed skulls and battered bodies.

"In the beginning, we were against the strike," relates Elisa. "We didn't think that the workers, and the movement as a whole, were strong enough to withstand the expected reprisal. At that time, different forms of protest actions had been launched in various factories—sit-down strike, work slowdown, work stoppage and others. But there had never been an open, all-out strike."

The organizers decided to take advantage of a legal loophole to lend legitimacy to a strike. Under General Order Number 5 and Presidential Decree 21, strikes were prohibited in "vital industries." But, says Dino: "The government had not come out with concrete guidelines on what were vital industries. La Tondeña produced alcoholic drinks, so, obviously, it was not part of any industry which could directly affect the national economy."

Still, the organizers did not expect the martial law regime to be so reasonable. The strike ban was primarily imposed to keep labor repressed and cheap, and therefore attractive to local and foreign business interests. The ban also ensured political stability, under a climate of fear and intimidation. "We knew that a strike, if successful, could signal a resurgence on the labor front and the entire urban revolutionary movement. It could smash the terror effect of martial law. But a disaster, a massacre at the picketline, was a possibility too overwhelming for us to immediately endorse the idea."

In the event of a strike, neither Edjop nor the other leading cadres of the underground labor movement would pay the price. "This only made us more reluctant to support the plan of the La Tondeña workers," Elisa continues. "If we pushed through with it, everything had to be carefully planned, all precautions considered. We had to make many calculations. But since we were underground, we ourselves would not be at the frontline, and it was not for us to make such a decision when our necks were not at stake."

In five straight days of marathon meetings that lasted from late afternoon to late evening, the CLC organizers, led by Edjop and Father Jalandoni, and the La Tondeña workers argued their respective positions. "We suggested," Father Jalandoni recalls, "less dangerous alternatives—work slowdown, sit-down protest and others. But every time we made a proposal, the workers affirmed their decision—strike."

The cadres finally acceded to the plan. The next eight meetings were devoted to planning, setting policies, and preparing contingencies. "The main consideration," explains Elisa, "was how to make the strike bold enough to make an impact, but safe enough for the workers and activists at the picket line."

On the eve of the strike, Edjop and Father Jalandoni met with the La Tondeña workers for the last time. Again, Edjop went through the possible consequences of what they were about to do. By the time he finished speaking, the room was, says Father Jalandoni, so quiet "you could hear a pin drop."

"It seemed finally to dawn on the workers that they could be arrested, imprisoned and even killed in the strike. In that brief moment of silence, I felt the tension in everyone."

But then a young man, dark and hardened by years of work, stood up and said, "*Kailangang ituloy ang welga. Limang taong galit na nasa loob ng aking dibdib ang kailangang pumutok bukas.* We must go on with the strike. I have five years of frustration and bitterness inside me that must find release by tomorrow." A woman worker followed, declaring, "*Tama. Dapat natin itong ituloy. Kung hindi, walang kinabukasan ang ating mga anak.* That's right. We must go on with it. Otherwise, our children will have no future."

"Nothing more," says Father Jalandoni, "had to be said after that."

24
Another Storm

At exactly six-fifteen a.m. on October 24, 1975, a Saturday, the machines of La Tondeña ground to a halt. More than five hundred laborers, men and women, stopped working and began putting up barricades in different parts of the factory. Asia's biggest distillery was paralyzed. The first full-blown strike to defy the Marcos dictatorship had begun.

In mimeographed statements distributed to passers-by, the La Tondeña workers declared an "indefinite strike" which they vowed to continue "until our demands are met." The manifesto, according to Father Jalandoni, was drafted from the words and expressions which the workers themselves used in describing their plight.

"For years, we have been treated like rags which, after being used, are thrown away like garbage," said the manifesto. "For years, we have been treated like animals. In fact, Palanca treats his pet dog better than the workers. His dog has a big house. Palanca feeds it meat and calls a veterinarian whenever the dog gets sick."

The manifesto was capped by a slogan formulated during meetings with Edjop and Father Jalandoni: *"Sobra na! Magwewelga na kami!"* (It has gone too far! We're going on strike!) As the strike progressed, this would be modified into *"Tama na! Sobra na! Welga na!"* (We've had enough! Things have gone too far. It's time to strike!) It was this modified slogan that workers and their supporters from the church and urban communities chanted defiantly at the picket line. More than ten years later, the slogan would be transformed once again to *"Tama na! Sobra na! Palitan na!"* (We've had enough! Things have gone too far! It's time for a replacement!)—a slogan that a housewife running for president would adopt to rally the Filipino people in the final confrontation with Marcos.

But that would come much later. Marcos was still at the height of his power on that Saturday in October of 1975 when La Tondeña decided to go on strike. At around 9:00 a.m., supporters from the church and the surrounding urban poor communities began to arrive at the factory. Priests, nuns, and lay workers, including a number of foreign missionaries, brought food, helped walk the picket lines, and sang songs about the workers' conditions and their struggle for a better life. They distributed copies of a letter—which they had sent to company and government authorities—expressing their support for the strike.

"We support the collective action that the [La Tondeña] workers have undertaken to obtain justice and we very strongly propose that you take immediate action to assure that the rights of the workers are recognized," said the letter, signed by 93 church and lay leaders (one of whom, Sister Christine Tan, was to become a constitutional commissioner after the fall of Marcos).

Edjop and Father Jalandoni set up a monitoring center a few blocks away from the factory. As the most experienced labor organizer among the cadres, Edjop was made head of the central command, the main group which monitored developments in the strike and advised the workers and cadres at the picket line. Priests and nuns reported to Edjop by phone or through runners.

"For three days and nights, we had absolutely no sleep," Father Jalandoni relates. "It was exciting, tense, and demanding all at the same time. We knew we could be on the point of a breakthrough in the labor movement. But the risks were so real. The situation was so fluid, and changed almost every hour. Anything could happen any minute."

At a little past nine a.m., police and Metrocom troops arrived at the factory. The workers, priests, nuns, and other supporters instantly went on the alert. But, as a correspondent for *Signs of the Times* (October 31, 1975) wrote, "Instead of being cowed, the people shouted at the military men, asking them not to intervene."

At around ten a.m., a union delegation, accompanied by some priests and nuns, called on Archbishop Jaime Sin, who, according to *Signs of the Times,* "sympathized with them and promised to write a letter to President Marcos and to call up the Palanca family concerning their demands."

At ten-thirty, a priest and a nun went to see Antonio Palanca in his office, on the latter's invitation. They informed him of the workers' demand for direct negotiations with the Palancas. The workers had refused to talk to representatives from the Department of Labor or the factory management.

The first major sign of trouble came at noon, when soldiers in plainclothes entered the factory in search of union leaders. But the workers were ready for just this eventuality. Key union officers had disguised themselves as female employees, and when the soldiers demanded to know who the union leaders were, all the strikers raised their hands.

Frustrated, the soldiers threatened to force the workers out of the factory if the strike was not lifted by two-thirty that afternoon. The workers stood firm, and by the time the soldiers had left, more support from the neighboring communities and factories had arrived. It was, says Elisa, the "most well-supported strike" she had ever witnessed.

Management had cut off the power in the factory when the strike began. But the workers had gas lamps and flashlights. Bags of food and other supplies were continuously being brought into the factory. The laborers cooked their meals over the factory's acetylene burners.

At three p.m., three representatives from the Department of Labor arrived and asked the workers to lift the strike. The labor officials promised to do their best to convince the Palanca family to grant the strikers' demands. But the workers merely recounted their frustrating experiences in dealing with government.

At around seven p.m., soldiers returned, again with the intention of arresting union leaders. Failing in their mission, they threatened to arrest all the workers before ten-thirty that night. At around nine, they came back and ordered the strikers to disperse. The workers stood their ground.

The soldiers asked the priests and nuns at the picket line

about the demands of the strike. They were told to talk to the workers, and the workers repeated their demand to speak only with the Palancas.

A little later, Deputy Labor Secretary Amado Inciong arrived with four other government officials. Inciong told the workers that the company had offered to make some 400 casual employees permanent by Monday, October 27. The workers asked him to put his proposal in black and white, so the union could study it further.

The military returned for a third time while Inciong was still negotiating with the workers. They came in two Metrocom cars, one van, and one fire truck. Constabulary Intelligence Service (CIS) agents approached some women workers and tried to pressure them to go home. The women ignored them. After making the usual threats of arrest, the military left.

There were no more "visitors" after that. The rest of the first night of the strike passed without incident. But the workers and their supporters remained alert. So did Edjop and the other cadres at the command post.

The second day of the strike began pretty much like the first. The priests, nuns, and other sympathizers sang songs, gave speeches, and had discussions with the workers. More food and supplies came. Military and police agents continued to keep a close watch on the activities in the compound.

The day before, during confrontations with either the military or government authorities, the workers had asserted that La Tondeña was not part of a vital industry, and therefore the strike was legal. The argument apparently worked. Grudgingly admitting the vagueness of Government Order No. 5 and Presidential Decree 21, the authorities did not try to break up the strike for violating any labor law. But, as expected, the government tried to find another excuse to crack the whip.

At around ten-thirty p.m. on the second day of the strike, military officers in five military cars arrived. Loudspeakers blaring, they ordered the workers to go home before midnight—or else they would be arrested for violating the curfew.

The workers did not budge, but they relayed the warning to

the command post. Edjop, Father Jalandoni, and other cadres met at once. "In just a few minutes, Edjop was able to assess the situation, sketching possible scenarios," relates Father Jalandoni. "Though he was clearly concerned about the safety of the workers, he was totally in control as he led the discussion. I admired his grasp of tactical leadership. He was not one who would take hours to decide on things. He immediately got into the situation, and came up with very practical decisions. For three days and nights, he kept a clear mind. Edjop was very cool under fire."

The collective agreed to rally more support for the workers, and they drew up a list of all the people whom they knew to be sympathetic to the La Tondeña workers' cause. Starting at around eleven that night, Edjop and his comrades drove all over Manila, waking up priests and nuns and asking them to go to the strike area.

"Once, while in the car, Edjop mentioned how difficult it was to ask people to be at the picket line when we ourselves could not be there," Father Jalandoni recalls.

Many of those who were approached that night immediately got dressed and went directly to the strike area. One of them was Father Leopold Van Vugt, a Dutch priest assigned to Manila. Father Leopold had initial misgivings about Edjop's actions during the strike.

"Ed was very conscious about his own security," he relates. "Sometimes I got the impression that he was afraid. He stayed in the background during the strike and was never at the frontline. Yet he gave directives from the observation post. One would have thought that he was a coward. But later I realized this was not so. He was simply aware of his specific role at that time. He knew his responsibilities in the movement. Looking back, after all that has happened, I realize that Edjop was a courageous man."

At about one a.m., the military returned and repeated their warning. The anonymous correspondent for *Signs of the Times* gives a detailed account of what happened next:

"Shortly after the warning, soldiers entered the factory compound, with seven Metrocom buses and one Air Force bus. When the soldiers were about to enter the main building, the workers started singing the national anthem. The soldiers hesitated. They waited for the singing to stop before they finally entered the factory. They forced the workers out of the building and into the military buses. . . .

"Many workers, especially those in the Manual Washing Section, defied the Metrocom order to board the buses. With arms interlocked—some clung to whatever they could get their hands on—they resisted and had to be carried out of the factory and into the buses. It took some time before everybody could be hauled into the military vehicles. The last bus was filled only a few minutes before four a.m., the end of the curfew period."

The presence of priests and nuns in the factory deterred the military from employing rougher tactics in breaking up the strike. Still, the experience was as unpleasant for the church people as it was for the strikers they had tried to protect.

In a joint statement after the strike, the priests and nuns who were involved in the strike would recall: "When we approached one of the buses several women inside were crying hysterically. They told us that they had been forced into the bus, including one sick worker; some had been pushed or dragged, some were hurt, and they were afraid of what the guards would do to them next."

The church people asked the military to let them ride on the bus with the workers "to make sure that they would not be further mistreated or hurt." One priest argued with a certain Colonel Manuel: "Why can't you allow two or three religious inside the bus? This will also be of help to you, because our presence may help calm the people down." But the colonel could only reply: "That's against my orders."

Two nuns and a priest, a daring little Italian named Father Peter Geremia, decided to cling to the door and windows of one bus. Colonel Manuel, who would later tell some of the church people he was a devout Catholic, was "nearly in tears, confused," according to *Signs of the Times*. "He said that he 'could not understand why the religious wanted to support the masa in defiance of the military's orders.' " Another witness noted that "Colonel Manuel was visibly shaken, apparently embarrassed, and he did not allow the bus to proceed with the three religious hanging on."

But another officer ordered the driver to get the bus moving. The bus went about two blocks, with the priest and the two nuns still clinging to the door and window bars. Colonel James Barbers of the Manila Metropolitan Police then ordered the driver to stop and the soldiers to pull down the religious from the bus.

The workers were brought to Fort Bonifacio and booked for violating the curfew. But the military could not explain why the priests, the nuns, and all the other people who had poured out into the streets in support of the strike were not also arrested. (One cadre describes the outpouring of support as an "early version of the 1986 people power.")

"This proves that the real reason why the workers were arrested was not the violation of curfew," the church people said. "Incidentally, the workers were on strike even the previous night, but no one mentioned the curfew violation at that time."

General Prospero Olivas, then Metrocom chief, later claimed in a news story in the *Times Journal* that "utmost courtesy was extended by Metrocom troopers in apprehending the factory workers. . . . Except for a priest and two nuns who clung to the bus's protective screen as the vehicle sped off, there was no untoward incident. . . . The trio was apparently inciting the workers to defy the authorities when the order was being carried out at the La Tondeña compound."

Church people refuted this, saying, "We could not possibly be inciting the workers to defy the authorities because the workers were already held inside the bus at the complete mercy of the troopers."

Reports about the arrests reached Edjop and his comrades.

"That was the first time I saw Edjop become a bit agitated," Father Jalandoni says. "Several times, I heard him mutter *'pu-tang-ina'* or *'mga walanghiya.'*

Later, during an assessment meeting after the strike, several weaknesses in the tactics employed in the strike were pointed out. Father Jalandoni recalls the results of the assessment: "The military could have been delayed if the workers had set up more obstacles in the compound. The military cited curfew violation as a pretext for arresting the workers. Had we been able to delay them for an hour or two, the strike could have gone on until four a.m., when the curfew period ended."

Back in the factory, the church people held an outdoor mass with the workers' relatives and other supporters, who tearfully sang *"Bayan Ko."* According to Father Jalandoni, there were speeches which "exposed the connection between the capitalist owner of La Tondeña and the military." As one nun put it: *"Iyong alak at iyong militar, magkasabwat.* Booze and the military connive with each other."

But what seemed like a total defeat turned out to be a significant victory, not just for the La Tondeña workers, but for the entire labor movement as well. Before noon the next day, all arrested workers were released.

At ten a.m. on October 27, Don Antonio Palanca met with union leaders in the factory. Palanca agreed to hire as regular employees more than 300 "veteran" casual workers. As for the remaining 300 casuals, he promised to make them regular employees at a later date. He also promised to review the cases of those who had been arbitrarily laid off.

Most of the provisions in the controversial "criteria for employment" were scrapped. Though the workers still had to undergo physical examinations and to secure a clearance from the military and the courts, Palanca promised that "those found to be sick will not be dismissed, but be provided medical care."

The 44-hour strike was over. The La Tondeña workers had won. In a statement after the strike, they affirmed: "We achieved in our two-day strike what we were unable to obtain in almost five years [of appeals and negotiations] with the Department of Labor."

Workers, priests, nuns, cadres, and other supporters celebrated. A meeting was called to assess the conduct of the strike and share insights into the historic event. "Edjop facilitated the discussions, helping draw lessons from the experiences of those who participated in the strike," Father Jalandoni recalls. "He helped pinpoint weaknesses and strengths."

On the whole, the strike was seen as a big victory.

"The workers felt the tremendous power they had when they were united," Father Jalandoni continues. "During the strike, they were daring, but highly disciplined."

"Whenever there was a need to link arms, they really hung on to each other," Elisa says. "They were ready to fight and get hurt for their rights. The workers of La Tondeña taught us important lessons in the workers' struggle."

But the victory of the La Tondeña workers was far from final. On November 3, 1975, barely a week after the strike, Marcos issued Presidential Decree Number 823. All strikes in all industries, whether vital or non-vital, were banned. In reaction to the support church people gave the La Tondeña workers, all persons, organizations, or entities, Filipino or foreign, were prohibited from participating in trade union activities or giving any form of help to workers' groups.

The new law merely drew more flak, not only from the labor movement, but also from church and civic leaders. Archbishop Sin himself wrote Marcos a letter of protest, signed by other members of the clergy.

On November 25, 4,000 workers, students, intellectuals, priests, and nuns, led by the Bukluran ng Manggagawang Pilipino, held a protest mass at the Santa Cruz Church. The affair was called *Misa para sa mga Manggagawa*—mass for the workers—and was the biggest anti-dictatorship demonstration since the declaration of martial law.

On December 6, a bigger rally of more than 8,000 people was

launched, coinciding with the state visit of then U.S. President Gerald Ford. The demonstrators, chanting anti-Marcos slogans and the now popular *Tama na! Sobra na! Welga na!,* tried to march to Malacañang Palace, but were blocked by riot policemen on Bustillos Street in Sampaloc, near Jopson's Supermarket. The protesters staged the rally at Plaza Miranda instead.

"The march shattered the climate of fear," Father Jalandoni recalls. "As we marched through the center of Manila, people clapped their hands and expressed their support. The mass movement had been unleashed."

Edjop was often a member and, at times, the head of the group in charge of planning many of these demonstrations. As in the La Tondeña strike, his was a very delicate responsibility, as he and his comrades figured out ways for the mass movement to advance without provoking a violent backlash.

In February 1976, amid intensifying protests against the total strike ban, Marcos issued Presidential Decree 849, amending Presidential Decree 823. Strikes were now prohibited only in vital industries. But labor and pro-labor groups were quick to see a catch: the guidelines actually covered all industries. The protests intensified.

As Edjop and his comrades predicted, the La Tondeña strike sparked a resurgence in the workers' movement. From November to January 1976, more than 25 strikes, involving around 40,000 workers, erupted in factories in Metro Manila. This number rapidly increased for the rest of 1976. In the first two weeks of June 1976 alone, 20 strikes, all in "vital" industries, were launched by some 17,000 workers.

Amid the upsurge, the Bukluran ng Manggagawang Pilipino became the recognized center for the labor movement. Less than a year after it was founded in February 1976, Bukluran was reaching about 100,000 workers in 150 factories.

It wasn't long before Marcos reacted to the rising tide of dissent. A new wave of arrests and disappearances swept the metropolis. Labor and civic leaders, including the former president of the La Tondeña union, were picked up. Two Italian priests working among the urban poor in Tondo were apprehended and deported.

In January 1976, 39 student leaders of the University of the Philippines, including *Philippine Collegian* editor Ditto Sarmiento, were detained. (It was under Sarmiento, that the *Philippine Collegian* popularized the slogan *Kung hindi tayo kikibo, sino ang kikibo? Kung hindi tayo kikilos, sino ang kikilos? Kung hindi ngayon, kailan pa?*—adopted from a similar call by the Black Panthers.)

But a government crackdown at this time had less of an effect on the national democratic movement than it had in 1972. "We easily adjusted and shifted back to a less open mode of struggle," said Raul, who was involved in the series of demonstrations. "The main problem was how to consolidate the mass of new activists and cadres."

A Bukluran-sponsored demonstration, which was supposed to be held on January 25, 1976, was called off to avert a possible disastrous encounter with a regime on a rampage. In a statement, the Bukluran affirmed: "Let us not fall into the trap prepared for us by the military. For the moment, we are not prepared. Let us return to our communities and factories to continue our just struggle. Let us return to convey to our fellow workers and citizens the truth that we cannot rely on anybody else but ourselves. . . . We must remind the military: A tame lamb may also become violent."

The situation had also become too "hot" for Edjop and the other ND cadres working in legal institutions. Sometime in early 1976, Edjop went underground. He would never again be directly involved in the workers' movement in Manila. But he was not easily forgotten in the factories and communities he helped organize.

In February 1976, Ka Felicing and other union officers were arbitrarily dismissed by the Elizalde Rope management. In protest, more than 300 Elizalde Rope workers staged a spontaneous strike. Ka Felicing himself led the march to the office of the Department of Labor.

"Ed had already gone underground by then," he recalls. "But somehow, we felt that he was also in the crowd. He served as an inspiration to us during that time. We never forgot Edgar Jopson."

25
Middle Forces

In January 1975 Edjop, along with other White area cadres, was called to attend a top-level Party plenum in Nueva Ecija. By then he was known as Ka Gusting. It was one of his early visits to a guerrilla zone. Strict security precautions were observed. No one, not even wives and husbands, and some comrades in their respective collectives, knew about the trip.

The cadres packed their bags carefully, making sure that all items that could be considered "subversive" by military men manning checkpoints were well hidden—documents, books, notebooks, papers. Anticipating long, hard, and wet walks in the middle of the night, they brought raincoats, jackets, and flashlights. But these, too, had to be concealed. Only a few, those with combat experience, carried guns.

On the bus, during the trip from the city to the countryside, they looked clean and well pressed—*disente*—in their long-sleeved shirts, leather shoes, and dark glasses. No one must suspect that they were on their way to a guerrilla camp.

They travelled separately and in small groups. They took different routes, went on different buses to different towns, and from there took different paths in the long trek to the guerrilla zone. Some travelled for a day; others, for several days.

Edjop travelled via Pampanga, escorted by a guide and an NPA squad. There, during a stopover in a guerrilla camp, he met Bernabe Buscayno, the legendary Dante, commander-in-chief of the New People's Army.

"We met in a remote barrio," Dante recalls. "It was raining when he arrived. When he saw the Red fighters, and realized who I was, he was very happy and started embracing everyone.

"He asked a lot of questions, about the lives of the people in the barrio, about revolutionary land reform, about our experiences in the *hukbo*. He expressed a desire to join the people's army. Of course, the NPA is more than willing to have a very

180

intelligent cadre like Edjop. I told him that he was more than welcome, and he was very happy.

"He went with us for a few days, walking in rice and sugarcane fields, crossing rivers. I noticed that his skin was very smooth—*makinis ang balat niya*. He was obviously not used to the hard life of a guerrilla. But even so, Edjop was not deterred by tall grass and muddy trails. Once we came across a deep muddy portion of a trail, almost like a swamp.

" 'Stay clear of that, Ka Gusting,' I told him. 'You'll be buried alive in that mud. *Mababaon ka diyan.*'

"And he just answered, '*Katetakutan mo iyan e kung sa kaaway hindi ka natatakot?* Why should we be afraid of a little mud? We do not even show fear in the face of the enemy.' He went ahead and crossed in the mud.

"He went with us from barrio to barrio. He often talked to the peasants. He helped explain things to them, and he asked about their grievances."

After a few days, Edjop separated from Dante's group. He was escorted to another camp where the central committee meeting was to be held.

There, Edjop was welcomed by Amado Guerrero, a.k.a. Joma Sison, founder and chairman of the Communist Party of the Philippines. Nine years had passed since they first met at the Ateneo in 1966, when the KM leader's rhetoric about repression and revolution had failed to impress the bright-eyed freshman student councilor. Now they were meeting again as comrades, in a guerrilla camp near a river at the foot of the Sierra Madre Mountains in Nueva Ecija.

Jason Montana, a poet-priest who had joined the party, was also present at the meeting. He observed the way Ka Amado related to Ka Gusting: "Joma respected Edjop the way he respected Louie Jalandoni. Joma was often very talkative, even boisterous, with other comrades. But there was some degree of formality in the way he talked with Edjop, like he was respecting some space between them. *Parang may iginagalang siyang espasyo.*"

"We didn't talk anymore about our past squabbles in the student movement," Joma recalls the meeting with Edjop. "I assumed that he had had enough of that. *Alam mo naman ang mga bata, pag nagkita may kantiyawan at biruan.* We would have been wasting time, if I still let him go through that again."

They were there on business. The CPP chairman had requested the meeting to discuss Edjop's perspective in revolutionary work. Earlier, Edjop had volunteered to join one of the NPA armed expansion teams in the Cordillera mountains. Edjop, Joma recalls, was a "very modest person, sincere in wanting a lower and more dangerous task."

But the CPP chairman had something else in mind. Ka Gusting, he said, would be of greater use in the cities, doing united front (UF) work. Ka Gusting was asked to head the National Democratic Front's Preparatory Commission (NDF Prepcom).

Many cadres viewed countryside work, particularly in the New People's Army, as the ultimate sacrifice one could make for the revolution. It is hard to say if Edjop shared this romanticism. He had been excited, like a child, in asking Dante if he could join the NPA. But according to Frank, Edjop's comrade in the Special Group for Trade Unions, Edjop once asked him: "I wonder if I can make it in the countryside if there ever comes a time when I must work there? *Makayanan mo kaya?*"

There was a great need for cadres to help build and strengthen the revolutionary organization in the regions. The Cordilleras then was not the formidable bastion of the movement that it is today. In most regions, there were only skeletal organizations of cadres and guerrillas, who were almost always on the run.

"Edjop's reasons for volunteering, I think, were really very simple," says Mauro, who became Edjop's deputy in the NDF Prepcom. "There was a need for comrades in a particular place and he wanted to help fill it."

But after the deaths and arrests of many brilliant cadres, the party had become more careful in deploying to the countryside comrades who may have the spirit for guerrilla work, but not the necessary stamina and skills. Their talents could have been better utilized in other lines of work, they would not have fallen so early in the struggle.

After the La Tondeña strike and the workers' upsurge that followed it, Manila had become an important arena of political struggle. Edjop, Amado Guerrero knew, was an exceptional White area cadre, with a grasp of both united front and trade union work.

But Ka Gusting was not thrilled about his new assignment. "He didn't want to head the NDF Prepcom," recalls Jason Montana. "He said that he would rather do mass work in the provinces. I guess he didn't want to be stuck in the cities, where his work would have no direct involvement with the masa."

But Edjop was also, as his comrades would say, a "good soldier" who put the needs of the *rebolusyon* above his own personal preferences. He took over the NDF Preparatory Commission in August 1976.

By the mid-1970s, the revolutionary movement had recovered from the setbacks it had suffered in the early years of martial law.

In 1972, there were about 3,000 national democratic activists and party cadres, mostly concentrated in Manila and other major cities. The New People's Army numbered about 600 guerrillas, spread out in seven guerrilla fronts in Ifugao, Zambales, Pampanga, Bicol, Isabela, Quirino, and Panay Island.

Martial law nearly crushed the underground movement in the cities. After three years, dictatorial rule had been consolidated. At center stage was the military, which grew from 60,000 troops before martial law to more than 200,000 by 1975. The Armed Forces of the Philippines (AFP) got the lion's share of the national budget, from P800 million in 1972, to P3 billion in 1975.

Protests were banned or repressed. More than 50,000 people had been either imprisoned or killed. In 1975, an Amnesty International mission to the Philippines confirmed the military's use of torture on political prisoners, the majority of whom were natdem cadres and activists.

Responding to the call for organized retreat, hundreds of activists who had eluded arrest fanned out to the barrios and far-flung areas in the countryside, spreading, as one cadre put it, "the fire of revolution."

The temporary withdrawal of most cadres from the cities was complemented by an organizing and propaganda offensive in the rural areas. By 1976, the movement had about 2,000 activists and cadres spread out all over the archipelago. The number of NPA guerrilla fronts increased from seven to 23, reaching as far as Samar, Negros, and Mindanao. Despite the meteoric expansion of the AFP, the NPA grew to around 2,000 guerrillas.

But the movement still had a long way to go, as Mauro would later admit: "There were still gaps in between guerrilla areas in the countryside. There were still no line organizations in many areas, only elementary formations of basic mass organizations. *Naglalatag pa kami noon.* We were still laying down the foundation of the movement."

Expansion was the movement's major thrust, to open more guerrilla base areas and fronts, and organize more people. "But we had to make sure that one area did not get so far ahead of the rest," says Mauro. "Our expansion and growth had to be more or less even. This was to prevent the military from wiping out one region or front that had become too strong."

In the cities, the main concern was to revive the mass movement and create an atmosphere of protest and resistance against the regime. "We wanted to institutionalize open mass mobilizations, while at the same time cushioning them against repression," says Mauro.

In what activists called "lightning rallies," ten to twenty activists, their faces covered with handkerchiefs, massed up, unfurled banners and shouted or painted slogans on walls—all in a span of five to ten minutes. These were usually launched in busy areas in the city, near marketplaces, bus stops and commercial centers. Hundreds of activists got themselves arrested and detained during these snap demonstrations.

Later, with the success of protest actions led by the urban poor and the workers, such as the La Tondeña strike, bigger, open mobilizations were launched.

By then, to many in the middle classes, the promise of a new society under martial law had been exposed as a cruel and ugly joke. As an American journalist wrote in the *Philippine Times* (November 1-15, 1975), "The splashy rhetoric with which Marcos launched his one-man campaign to save the republic in September 1972 has given way to uncertainty, self-doubt and self-questioning."

In an open letter published in October 1975, Bishop Carmelo F. Morelos of Butuan City said, "In all candor and honesty, we must ask each other today: Has martial law brought about the conditions favorable to our development as a people? If there are achievements, were they brought about with justice, with truth, with Christian love? If so, let us praise God. If not, if there are failures, let us find out what is the responsibility of each of us for the failures."

A new consciousness—militantly opposed to dictatorship and committed to the struggles of the masa—blossomed among the church rank and file.

A nun's reflections on a strike at Solid Mills, which the military had violently dispersed, shows the political keenness with which many other church people began to view repression under martial law, and resistance to it: "Why was it that management never faced the workers? Why was it that when the workers tried to air their just demands peacefully to management, they found themselves face to face with the military instead? How did it happen that members of the Department of National Defense were defending an alien factory owner against a group of defenseless Filipinos?"

A priest in Leyte, reacting to the killing of a farmer by Philippine Constabulary soldiers, wrote: "Even granting the benefit of the doubt that the powers that be in Manila have good intentions of trying to overcome the abuses of the politicians and subversion through a centralized military regime, how can they expect to control the new abuses when the only ones wielding authority in the far-out areas are, for the most part, half-wits who feel they can assert their importance by brandishing an Armalite?"

The same priest wrote of his encounter with new friends, cadre organizers of the revolutionary movement: "For the past eight months or so, there have been young people, well-educated and very kind, that have been living in the forests and visiting the people regularly. By day, they would work with the people, clearing the land and planting their crops and during the evening they would sit around with the people and talk about the injustices of the present society—international, national and local. Since there is nothing else to do in the evening, the people would sit around them and listen. Many things they taught were very Christian, like telling the people to work together in groups, raise more pigs and chickens, share with the needy, the widows, the orphans, and others."

Priests-turned-revolutionaries, like Edicio de la Torre, helped build links between the underground movement and the Church. Others, like Zacharias Agatep and Nilo Valerio, joined the armed struggle.

In the cities, a new generation of student activists, mostly from the University of the Philippines, emerged. Politicized in a time of intense repression, they used clandestine but militant modes of resistance.

Professionals—doctors, teachers, businessmen—many of whom had been part of the student nationalist upsurge before martial law, contributed in one way or another to the revolutionary cause, providing material and other forms of support to the underground movement.

This was the situation in 1976 when Edjop was assigned to the NDF Prepcom. The first Preparatory Commission had been formed in April 1973. This, and a second body, disbanded when its members were captured or were killed or left the movement. Edjop was tasked to form the third Preparatory Commission which was to pave the way for the establishment of the NDF as the "broad united front of the national democratic revolution."

Under Edjop, the NDF Preparatory Commission's major task was to consolidate the different natdem groups, like the Kabataang Makabayan, Christians for National Liberation, *Kapisanan ng mga Gurong Makabayan* (Association of Nationalist Teachers or KAGUMA) for teachers, *Malayang Kilusan ng Bagong Kababaihan* (Free Movement of the New Woman or MAKIBAKA) for women and other mass organizations which were scattered or forced underground in 1972.

The commission took charge of secret collectives called "national democratic cells," composed of cadres, activists, and sympathizers who had been organized for various tasks and lines of work. Leading committees were established in different sectors. When Edjop took over the NDF Prepcom, there were around 400 natdem activists in Metro Manila.

The commission was also concerned with strengthening ties with church people, and individuals from the middle classes, who supported strikes and other protest actions of the workers and the urban poor. It established strategic and tactical alliances with other "progressive" forces and personalities.

Edjop stressed that the urban middle class, also known in the movement as "middle forces," should be mobilized in support of the basic sectors, and be organized on the basis not merely of their respective sectoral interests, but more, on the basis of the issues and struggles of workers, peasants, and the urban poor.

"Edjop's proposal was based on his own personal experiences as a student activist and a cadre," explains Tani, a member of the NDF Prepcom under Edjop. "His development as a revolutionary was due primarily to his own exposure to the plight and struggles of peasants and workers. He knew that other people who had the same background like himself could be moved to join the struggle by letting them witness and experience how the other half lived and struggled.

"The La Tondeña strike, I think, was an eye-opener for Edjop and the other comrades. There we saw priests, nuns, and ordinary people from affluent families joining in a fight that really had nothing to do with their own respective interests. This and other experiences were the key to their involvement."

Luis Jalandoni, who was also a member of the Prepcom before he left the country to serve as NDF international representative, considers Edjop's proposed approach to middle class organizing "one of his main contributions to united front work."

"This approach deepened the commitment of the middle

forces and integrated them with the workers and peasants. It had a positive lasting effect. Later, many church people and middle-class activists went beyond giving assistance to the basic sectors. Some of them became full-time organizers and leaders in the labor and peasant movements."

UF, or united front, work suited Edjop well. He was one of a number of ranking cadres, including Luis Jalandoni and Edicio de la Torre, who commanded the respect of church and middle-class personalities. His background—the brilliant Ateneo graduate who joined the labor movement, the celebrated student leader who dared confront Marcos—made him acceptable to allies. As Mauro says, "For church and other personalities, knowledge of the person they were dealing with counted a lot."

Eric, a former priest who had been involved with the social democrats (the same person whom Edjop consulted before his wedding), was also a member of the NDF Preparatory Commission. He worked closely with Edjop in maintaining ties with church activists and supporters.

"At first, the priests and nuns we talked with didn't know he was Edjop," says Eric. "But even if they didn't know who he was, Edjop's personality usually stood out in the discussion. The priests and nuns would find out about him later and exclaim, 'He's Edjop? No wonder he's brilliant. *Kaya pala mahusay.*' They were surprised and impressed. As we became more familiar with them, Edjop even cracked jokes with the nuns. They eventually became fond of him and were honored to have him for a friend and ally.

"That Edjop gave up all the privileges and conveniences of someone who came from a rich family, and that he devoted all his time to the cause of the workers, made church people admire and respect him. No one questioned his sincerity and commitment. He was seen as a genuine revolutionary, not an armchair activist good only at mouthing platitudes."

"Edjop went out of his way to show his appreciation for the support that particular priests or nuns gave us," recalls Luis Jalandoni. "He also produced results, and this made the church people even more willing to help and participate in whatever campaign Edjop was drawing them into. When we were working in the Church Labor Center, church people actually witnessed the work progressing. Labor organizers were being trained; workers learned from seminars, most of which Edjop planned and facilitated. After one session which Edjop facilitated, one priest told me, it's an enriching experience listening to Edjop and watching him work.' "

As much as possible, Edjop kept his underground affiliation a secret. Many of the priests and nuns he met and worked with at this time may have suspected his clandestine links. But they were not enraged, nor did they feel that they had been used, when they discovered Edjop's affiliation. They did not see him as a brash, unthinking Communist cadre, but as a refined young man who, as one priest put it, was "admirably committed to helping other people."

Father Leopold Van Vugt, who also worked in the Church Labor Center, recalls his friendship with Edjop:

" 'I first met Edjop in 1974, when we were conducting a survey of the situation of industrial workers in Metro Manila. I immediately liked him because he seemed very friendly. He used to come to our staff house to join us in our meals. He was often dressed like a schoolboy, and always carried a school bag. I think he found our way of living kind of funny. As missionaries we led very simple lives. Maybe Ed wondered why we were living the way we were. I think he was surprised at our commitment and the risks we sometimes took. He often kidded us about these things.

"In the beginning, I did not know that he was connected with the underground movement. He was rather secretive about his background and his involvement. He was very security-conscious and would not tell you what he thought you didn't need to know. It was only later that I discovered that he was with the underground movement. I told him that I was quite impressed, and he was delighted."

His energy and confidence sometimes came across as arrogance to some. Edjop, as Father Leopold observed, at times became too sure of himself.

"Ed really knew what he wanted, and he tried to get me interested in them, too. I found him very intelligent, precise, and articulate. Once he had set his mind on something, he would move heaven and earth to get the thing done. Whatever the cost, he would get things done. At times, he could be very demanding, and would appear like a demagogue.

"He often talked to me about the ultimate aim of the underground labor movement, which would be a general strike. We had long discussions, analyzing the situation and making certain projections on how things would develop. He always tried to listen to your opinion, in order to check the correctness of his own. But often I had the impression that he had his mind set on his position, so there was no use arguing. Indeed, sometimes, when he saw you disagreeing with him, he got impatient and even angry.

"But despite these flaws that I observed in him, I still consider Edjop a great leader, a man with a vision. He came in close contact with reality, and this helped him understand the oppressive structures of Philippine society under martial law. But the thing I admire most in him was his great faith in the Filipino masses."

26
Simple Living

Underground life, says Edicio de la Torre, has often been glamorized in book and film, when all it actually means is that cadres "meet in smaller rooms and look over their shoulders every so often." The common belief is that a person who has gone UG has gone to the mountains—"*namundok na*," as the expression goes—and joined the NPA.

The romantic image of the *rebolusyonaryo* is one who lives in a guerrilla camp in the heart of the jungle, moves from barrio to barrio, with a backpack and an M-16 rifle slung over the shoulder. He or she holds secret meetings, agitates peasants, and shoots it out with the military in vicious encounters. Dante's film-bio has all these ingredients.

Some of the details are true to some extent, but only for cadres in the CS, the countryside. In the cities, UG life loses much of its mystique.

A full-time revolutionary in the cities is called a White area cadre. A white area is generally defined as an urban or semi-urban community where state power is in full control. For the movement, no area can be as "White" as Manila, where, as an activist would tell you, the fascists have their "ABC"—Camps Aguinaldo, Bonifacio and Crame.

Cadres engaged in military work in the cities are called partisans, better known to the media and the public as "sparrows." But more often than not, White area cadres are unarmed. For White area cadres, the *rebolusyon* can be as hectic and as dangerous as it is for their comrades in the countryside. They may occupy responsible positions in the movement, as Edjop did; or they may belong to the staff of some Party committee. They may be in charge of a variety of tasks: preparing reports, writing manifestos, analyzing developments, formulating policies, giving guidance to lower collectives, soliciting funds, contacting allies. But unlike NPA guerrillas in the CS, or partisans in the

191

cities, they have to do "revolutionary work" without the protection that weapons can give.

Their only weapon is anonymity—the ability to blend with the crowd, to change colors like a chameleon, or to assume another form, as a caterpillar turns into a butterfly.

White area cadres could be the guys sitting beside you in a jeepney, or the young women munching Big Macs at McDonald's. They could be in T-shirt, maong pants, and rubber sandals, hair long and unkempt; or they could be in polo barong, black formal pants and leather shoes, hair tidy and gelled. Like salespersons or business executives, they may be walking around with attache cases. They may hold meetings in a restaurant or a UG house, staying away from places where other people may know them, or where there may be "spotters," intelligence agents on the lookout for subversive-looking characters. At the end of the day, they may go home to a UG house, which could be a cheap apartment in Tondo or a plush townhouse in Parañaque provided by a rich ally or sympathizer.

UG life in the seventies was a lot simpler—but also far more difficult. There were not as many colors, costumes, or lifestyles to choose from and use as cover. Cadres had to bear with two realities: they got very little support from allies and sympathizers; and the military was after them like a pack of wild dogs.

"Week after a week, a comrade was either caught or killed," says Marcel, a former member of the Manila-Rizal Party Committee. "There was really no underground network in Manila to speak of. There were only a number of stable UG safehouses. There were not many allies and sympathizers to seek help from. We were constantly on the move. We had very limited resources. I knew of some comrades who often didn't have any place to stay. They sometimes spent the night at funeral parlors."

The movement could afford to pay only the rent of a UG house. Other expenses, like food, medicine, and allowances, were left up to the cadres.

"We could really depend on no one but ourselves," says Raul, a member of a district Party committee in Manila. "We had to be resourceful to survive."

"Most of the activists who went underground were very young, most of them in their teens," says Pedring, a journalist who went underground in 1972. "The general attitude then was: 'Okay, we don't have much to start with. But we are going to fight and see the revolution through against all odds.' "

Real life, especially for those who came from well-off middle-class families, did not always match the gallantry of this pronouncement.

"After a few months in the UG, I found out that some of my comrades sometimes went home to have their laundry done or to have lunch or dinner with their families," says Raul.

One woman cadre, who used to be a student at an exclusive girls' school, was once asked by her comrades to do the marketing.

"*Pero hindi ako marunong mamalengke*," she said. "I don't know how to buy stuff in a public market. I wouldn't know the right kind of fish to buy."

"That's easy," one of her comrades said. "Just remember that fish whose eyes are red are no longer fresh."

But the former colegiala misunderstood the advice. She came home with a basketful of red-eyed fish.

Cadres who received little or no support from families or friends had a tougher time. Raul's brothers and sisters were shocked by his joining the Communist Party, and were reluctant to give any assistance. An underground house he once shared with comrades was a drab room, about three-by-two meters, with walls made of hollow blocks. There was an improvised divider between the kitchen and the living room. At night it was very cold; they had to rub their bodies with *alcanforado,* or camphorated oil, to keep warm.

In another house Raul stayed in, there were rats so big they scared cats away. The bathroom was directly linked to a pigpen. "*Talagang pumapasok ang etsas sa banyo namin.* Shit flowed directly into our bathroom."

Once they were neighbors with a family in which the husband regularly beat up the wife. "We wanted to help the woman. But we could not. We couldn't afford to expose ourselves."

Laura, a Party cultural worker who would later work with Edjop in Mindanao, went underground willingly, without any qualms about leaving the comforts of her middle-class home. Simple living and hard struggle, the way she experienced it, meant eating out of cheap tin plates which cost 25 centavos in Divisoria and picking cabbages which fell off trucks in the public market. There came a time when she and her comrades ate only banana-cue and Sarsi cola. Rarely did they have meat.

"We had to save money to spend for other things needed in our work," she recalls. "We were concerned only with producing results, with the number of people we could recruit and the reading materials we could come out with. We focused all our energies toward helping the movement get through that very difficult period right after the imposition of martial law.

"But I never complained or expressed any regrets about joining the movement. The sacrifices were necessary—they were part of what we were fighting for."

For other cadres, UG life was more bearable. They could rely on "pledges," money regularly received from family and friends, some of whom might be willing to take them in during times of difficulty.

Edjop enjoyed such advantages. His parents sent him money and clothes. He was assured of a constant supply of groceries from the family supermarket. He and Joy had savings, to use in times of a financial crunch, and former friends and classmates who, though disappointed with Edjop's political standpoint, were ready to come to his aid.

Still, the classic dictum of "simple living, hard struggle" became the guiding principle in Edjop's life as a cadre, and this he observed with discipline, determination and, his former comrades would even say, dogmatism.

"Edjop was very rigid," says Mauro, who served as Edjop's deputy in the NDF Preparatory Commission. "He wanted to lead some sort of a spartan lifestyle, and he expected his comrades to do the same."

According to Tani, formerly a member of the NDF Prepcom,

though they got their groceries free from Jopson's Supermarket, Edjop always insisted on getting only the cheapest items: "Ed wouldn't take fancy or expensive food items like meat loaf or ham."

In fact, according to Selmo, an underground activist who lived with Edjop when the latter was already head of the Manila-Rizal Party Executive Committee (KT-MR), their budget allowed them to have meat only two times a week.

"It was Edjop who set that policy," he adds. "Our basic diet was fish and vegetables. He was strict about our food budget. In other UG houses I stayed in, a kasama could prepare his own meals, if he wanted to. But Edjop would not allow this. We had to share whatever food or snack had been prepared. If a comrade did not like what was being served, then he could buy his own food, but he had to take it out of his own allowance.

"But despite the simplicity of our diet, it was pretty much balanced. *Hindi naman niya kami ginugutom.* He never starved us. In fact, for such a small guy, Edjop had one of the biggest appetites in our group. But he was never choosy when it came to food."

At that time, UG houses survived on an P800-P1,000 monthly budget, with each cadre receiving a daily food allowance of P5. A kasama also got an average monthly personal allowance of P300, depending on his or her operational expenses. Selmo, who had to do a lot of travelling in and out of the city, received a little more.

Like a housewife, Edjop closely monitored the prices of different food items. Sometimes, during meals, he would ramble about how much they had spent for their food that day, proudly pointing out how much money the collective had saved: "The vegetables cost eight pesos. Then the fish, three pesos ..."

"*Oo na.* Yes, kasama, we get the point. Just go ahead and finish your food. *Kumain ka na lang,*" his comrades would tell him, more amused than annoyed over their leader's litany of expenditures.

"I think he developed this habit from his experiences with the workers," says Eric. "Because they had very little money for food, workers were always conscious of the rise and fall of prices. Edjop saw how disciplined the workers were with their budget."

All the collective's expenses had to be based on a set budget. Edjop allowed little room for "liberal" spending.

"Each comrade was expected to account for every centavo spent for operations," says Mauro.

With an amused grin, Selmo relates, "When you borrowed from him, Edjop never forgot about it. He would always remind you about it, no matter how small the amount. Up to now, I still wonder how a man who came from a rich family could be such a cheapskate."

"If I were to use Edjop's behavior as the basis, then I know why his family became so prosperous," Remo, then a Manila-based cadre, quips.

Jackie, a former member of the NDF Prepcom secretariat, considers Edjop's attitude "positive at a time when the movement had nothing much to survive on."

Edjop was just as particular about the way comrades showed appreciation for any support they got from the masa. Once Edjop, Jackie, and another comrade met in a peasant's house in Central Luzon. The owner of the house served rice, boiled fish, and coffee with condensed milk. Jackie, who comes from a rich family (like Edjop, she is considered in the movement as "natbur," or belonging to the national bourgeois class), ate her share of the boiled fish "the way any burgis would"—that is, she didn't touch the head and the tail. Edjop noticed this and said, quite seriously, "You must eat all of it. The masa don't have much to eat, yet they share their food with us. The least we can do is show our appreciation for what they have offered us."

"*Sinimot ko lahat ang nasa plato ko,*" Jackie laughs. "I ate everything on my plate. Edjop felt strongly about such seemingly little things. But I didn't feel bad about what he said. He was right, after all. A cadre should never take for granted anything that the masa offer."

Jackie still tells this anecdote to her comrades, "especially those who don't eat everything on their plates."

Another time, four underground activists in the house of a worker were served four bananas. Edjop politely returned two of the bananas, saying two were enough for the four of them.

Nor did Edjop fail to show his appreciation for support from another comrade. Adel Musidora, a cultural cadre and writer, once donated P1,000 to Edjop's group.

"That really made Edjop very happy," Adel recalls. "He shook my hands with a lot of emotion, saying, '*Maraming salamat. Maraming salamat talaga.*' It was as if I had donated something worth more than a thousand pesos."

Edjop once criticized a comrade who used the gas stove to light a cigarette. He told the kasama to buy his own matches. He had also learned to smoke. But while his comrades puffed Marlboros and Philip Morrises, he settled for the cheaper, and throat-bruising, Champions.

One afternoon, while they were having a meeting, Edjop's comrades asked for a short merienda break. Edjop agreed and even volunteered to go out and buy some snacks. He came back with three sticks of "adidas," or barbecued chicken legs. "He could have just bought us some banana-cue, and it would have been just as cheap," recalls Tani, bursting into laughter.

On out-of-town trips, his comrades preferred not to go with Edjop, who tried hard to keep expenses at a minimum. "You ended up always eating at the cheapest restaurants and taking the cheapest means of transportation," says Mauro. "There was nothing basically wrong with that. But Edjop had a way of taking 'simple living and hard struggle' a little too far."

"We could say absolutely nothing against Edjop's own life-style," adds Tani. "Whatever policy he set, Edjop followed to the letter."

Edjop, who never did house chores when he was still living with his parents, strictly observed his schedule in washing dishes and cleaning the house. During one of his rare visits to his parents' house, Edjop surprised his sisters when he volunteered to do the dishes. "It was obvious that he was still not used to it," Inday recalls. "He practically hugged the plate as he wiped it."

Edjop became more familiar with laundry work. In fact, if there was anything he was particularly sensitive about, it was the cleanliness of his clothes. "His indicator for clean clothes was the smell," says Joy. "I wasn't so good at washing clothes since I never did the laundry when I was still living with my parents. So Ed preferred to wash his own clothes."

He never learned to cook, however. "He knew how to fry eggs and cook rice," says Joy, "but that was all. Before leaving the house I had to make sure there was something for him to eat."

Back then, UG houses were known for having bare interiors, with no chairs, appliances, or any fixtures. Edjop's group once occupied a big house in Bacoor, Cavite, which they rented at P500 a month. They always kept the windows on the ground floor closed. "We were worried that our neighbors might become suspicious," says Jackie. "After all, we were living in a big house which didn't even have tables and chairs. All we had then was a ping-pong table in the living room."

But the house in Bacoor was an exception. In the movement, Edjop became known for keeping a well-furnished UG house, complete with chairs, a sofa, a television set, a refrigerator and a stove. Comrades from other units who visited with them were often surprised to see a UG house complete with all the comforts of home.

Remo, who was used to UG houses that "looked more like warehouses," thought Edjop had been using Party funds for such luxuries. But most of the things in the house actually belonged to Edjop and Joy. "They had acquired one item after another after they got married," says Remo. "When Ed went underground, he brought most of their belongings to the UG house."

Edjop usually went around in a plain T-shirt, maong, and rubber shoes. When he had a meeting in a decent public place, he wore a checkered shirt-jack, formal pants and leather shoes. "He actually wore the same pair of pants he had in his college days," recalls Jackie. "We used to joke how Edjop was way ahead of his time. Back in the sixties, when the fad was bell-bottomed pants, he wore tapered pants, made of double-knit or some ma-

terial long out of fashion. By the mid-seventies bell-bottomed
pants were *baduy*, and tapered pants became the fad."

"He dressed so simply that you easily forgot what he actually
had on," quips Tani. "He was often that drab-looking and
colorless."

"He may have joined the radicals," says Alicia, then an underground student activist. "But he was still a moderate in the way
he dressed. By the way he looked, one wouldn't suspect that
Edjop was out to change society."

Joy felt the same way, and she sometimes insisted that Ed let
her pick the clothes he was to wear: "The color combinations of
the clothes he chose to wear were often terrible. They really
turned me off."

Waging revolution was tough, and the movement demanded
much self-sacrifice from a cadre. But in many ways Edjop made
demands on the movement as much as the movement made
demands on him. "I don't think it was so much the movement's
rigorous adherence to certain rules that made Edjop want to
adopt a spartan lifestyle," says Mauro. "His upbringing, before
he got into the movement, had a lot to do with it. The movement
merely beefed up the values he already had. Edjop was really
cut out for UG life. He was already that way even before he
entered the movement."

Joy agrees: "Even if Edjop had not become part of the movement, I think we would still have led a simple married life. That
was how Ed himself would have wanted it to be."

Members of the NDF Preparatory Commission—code-named
"Makati Commercial Center" or MCC—lived together from
1976 to 1979. In those three years they occupied six different
UG houses, in different locations, including Caloocan, Parañaque, and even as far as Bacoor, Cavite.

They usually moved every six months. Unusual movements or
developments in their neighborhood—suspicious-looking men
loitering near the house, mysterious phone calls, a sudden increase in the number of *balut* (boiled duck egg) vendors—would
send them packing. When another house was raided or one of

their comrades was arrested, it was also standard procedure for
them to abandon house. They never took chances. Like guerrillas in the jungle, they were always on the move.

"I was really surprised when Edjop was captured in 1979,"
recalls Tani. "When we were still together, Edjop was very conscious of security precautions. Once, he noticed a new vendor in
our neighborhood. He immediately decided to move to another
house. Sometimes I became quite irritated with these decisions
of his. *Konting bago lang, nag-aalsa-balutan na kami agad.*"

However, Alicia, then a committed though sometimes hysterical student cadre, was critical of what she considered Edjop's
laxness in security during their meetings in public places: "He
did not try to change the way he looked, as if his face had not
been splashed in the papers just a few years before." And once,
she was shocked to see him carrying stencils of *Ang Bayan,* the
CPP's official organ, which he did not bother to put in a bag or
a wrapper.

Cadres who lived together agreed on signals which described
the status of their UG house to comrades coming home. The
signal could be a window that was always kept open; a closed
window would be a warning that the house was no longer safe.
Other "danger signals," as they were called, could be a light bulb
that had been switched on; curtains in a specific window that
had been drawn closed; or a specific flower pot that had been
taken down from the fence.

The signals didn't always work, mainly because the cadres
themselves were not always alert to them. One evening Edjop
came home to find their UG house a mess: Papers, mostly party
documents, and clothes were scattered all over the living room;
cabinets and drawers were open. A big red flag with hammer
and sickle, used for party conferences in the countryside, or in
the swearing-in of new party members, had been unfurled on
the kitchen floor. *"Nabulatlat talaga ang bituka namin,"* says Eric.
"Our insides were exposed."

Edjop noticed that some of their appliances were gone. The
rest—an electric fan, a typewriter, and their refrigerator—had

been moved and were lined up in a row leading to the doorway. Edjop immediately thought the house had been raided. "He later told us how he had expected to be tapped on the shoulder and pounced on by the military," relates Jackie.

He soon realized it was a simple break-in. Still, there was the danger that the burglars would tip off the police about the house. Edjop took all the sensitive materials he could get his hands on. Before leaving, he switched on the light bulb that was meant as the danger signal to warn the others.

But most of his comrades either forgot about the signal or ignored it. "Despite the warning, each of us still went inside the house to get our belongings," recalls Tani. "We waited to see if we had been tipped off and if the house would be raided. Other comrades maintained surveillance on the house for the next few days. After a week, we decided to risk returning to get our things. We encountered no problems. But we had to move to another neighborhood."

27
Leading Cadre

Whenever possible, Edjop wanted all the members of the collective to live together in the UG house.

"He wanted a tight, harmonious collective life," says Tani. "This was important in our work. We had to have regular discussions and to share ideas and experiences. We had to be together to achieve a high level of political, ideological, and interpersonal unity. This couldn't be done if we just met sporadically, or if comrades treated their work for the revolution like a sideline or a hobby. *Hindi puwedeng pasawsaw-sawsaw.*

"As for those who couldn't or wouldn't live with the collective, Edjop required that they report to the UG house regularly and have a certain amount of discipline. We set regular meetings, with definite agenda. Edjop didn't like our work to simply go around in circles. He wanted it to advance in a concrete direction."

Jackie describes Edjop as an "organization man": "His training at the Ateneo—if you remember, he took up business management—and his experience as NUSP president made him a good administrator. He was a big help in trying to weld together a big and growing organization composed of people with different backgrounds and personalities. He was meticulous, and he paid attention to details."

He had a different style which his comrades, even veteran cadres, took notice of.

"Comrades never really developed the habit of taking down notes during meetings," relates Domingo, who was then head of the Party's Manila-Rizal Executive Committee (*Komiteng Tagapagpaganap ng Maynila-Rizal,* or KT-MR). "Edjop took pages of notes at meetings, writing down almost every item that was discussed. He was very keen on getting all the necessary data about a particular issue. His reports were always detailed and his presentation systematic, but clear and concise.

"Lenin mentioned two elements of an effective work style in waging revolution: 'Russian revolutionary sweep and American efficiency.' Edjop introduced efficiency to underground work. He was not limited to policies and principles, but also focused on concrete planning and methods of work, on how to get the job done."

Joma Sison saw the same potentials in Edjop, which is why the party chairman picked him to head the NDF group.

"Edjop had the ability to scan things and situations comprehensively and to focus on crucial details," says Joma. "Whenever he was assigned a detailed work, he never failed to do it excellently. He was bright, a very committed revolutionary."

An ordinary working day for Edjop meant a series of meetings in their UG house or in different parts of the city. He studied and wrote documents and pored over books on various concerns of the revolution. Time and again, he went on out-of-town trips, to attend conferences which were usually held in the countryside.

"Edjop set the pace of our work," says Tani. "He became decisive in getting concrete results from our group. At times, he was very demanding and pushy. But he did not directly pressure anyone, and he wasn't dictatorial. Still, the pace he set was enough to make you do the work better and faster."

Alicia came to associate Edjop with "work": "Every time we met, it was surely for some assignment or task he was going to give me."

Edjop was Adel Musidora's political officer. They met once a week, when they discussed the progress of work in the cultural department of the NDF Preparatory Commission, which Adel handled.

"Lampas-ulo ang trabaho niya noon," Adel recalls. "He was into everything. I would even consider as his major weakness that he assumed so many responsibilities which may have been beyond his own capabilities. Furthermore, he also had the tendency to assign tasks beyond a comrade's capacity.

"But the funny thing is, I never felt pressured. I took the work he assigned to me more as a challenge. Edjop thought I could do it, so I did it. To be frank about it, our working relationship was some sort of inspiration for me. I felt privileged to be working with him, despite the fact that I once treated him as an enemy of the revolution.

"Besides, Edjop also had a way of making a heavy load seem light. I knew he was saddled with so many things to do. But I never saw him get depressed. Each time he arrived in the house where we were supposed to meet, Edjop had a bright smile flashing from his chubby face."

His comrades remember him in many other ways.

"You couldn't help but develop a fondness for him," recalls Dong, a Central Committee member. "He was friendly, generous, polite, trustworthy, like a regular Boy Scout."

"Whenever we met for meetings, Edjop shook my hands CS-style, that is, with a lot of emotion and as if he was greeting a long-lost friend," recalls Ariel, a Manila-based cadre. "I sometimes felt uneasy whenever he did that. You shook hands that way in guerrilla camps, but not in the city."

Says Mauro: "When you put two people in the same house for an extended period of time, they both tend to get on each other's nerves. But Edjop and I were together for three years, and we developed a healthy friendship. We became very close."

"I sometimes attended meetings in their UG house," recalls Carlos, an NDF Prepcom member, "and one of the things that struck me was Edjop's attitude toward his son. Nonoy was then about three or four years old, and he naturally demanded attention from his father—asking questions, insisting that Edjop play with him—even while the meeting was going on. Edjop patiently answered every question and tried to give as much attention to the boy as he could, while still participating in the meeting. I mention this because I for one find it difficult to do two things at the same time. I am less patient."

"He was very puritanical," says Tani. "He rarely went to the movies, rarely watched television. All he did in the house was read and write. He didn't even play chess. I don't remember any of his pastimes, if he had any. Sometimes he told jokes. But they were so corny I don't remember any of them. They were the usual corny jokes of straight guys, the ones you hear over the radio. But Edjop was funny in his own way. His being so straight was already a source of amusement for most of us in the UG house."

"Yes, I heard him tell jokes," says Adel Musidora. "But they were usually old worn-out jokes. Still, he had fun telling them. He laughed at his own jokes, and out of respect for him I laughed along."

In meetings in the countryside, Edjop enjoyed playing basketball. Joma Sison relates with amusement how they played right in the middle of a barrio plaza: "He was very quick and showed a lot of spirit. *Parang propeller ng helicopter ang kamay niya*. He moved his hands like a helicopter propeller. He was not much of a shooter, but he was an excellent guard."

"Though he was short," recalls Gerry Bulatao, "he got most of the rebounds. He outjumped many of us."

In his late twenties, Edjop was five feet two inches tall. His height was often the subject of jokes and ridicule, but Edjop, says Mauro, was "always good-natured—he could laugh at himself."

Says Gerry Bulatao: "He used to brag that he was one inch taller than Deng Xiaoping, the leader of a billion people."

There were some who found the discipline Edjop imposed too serious, and the determination he expected of them too grim.

"With comrades who had a lot of angst, who had sensitive, or what is sometimes called artistic, temperaments, Edjop was not effective as a friend or a counsellor," says Tani. "They were often submerged in self-doubt, could not make up their minds about things, and bore many personal frustrations. Edjop was their exact opposite. He was definite about any decision he made. He knew what he wanted and worked for its fulfillment. *Hindi siya pabaling-baling*. He was never wishy-washy.

"Edjop was willing to listen and know about their problems. But Edjop could never really understand these types of people, because he was so different from them. He never went through the same anxieties, and he couldn't possibly comprehend such emotions.

"There was one comrade Edjop had to deal with. The fellow's heart was not totally into what we were doing. *Hindi buo ang loob sa trabaho.* Edjop tried to reach out to him, but I don't think he really knew how. The fellow simply left and went back to legal life."

Edjop rarely got into serious personal conflicts with comrades. "When he did, he never took a hostile or arrogant posture," says Tani.

One rift he got into was with an 18-year-old cadre named Selmo, who was in charge of the communications and other technical needs of the Party's Manila-Rizal Executive Committee, which Edjop headed in 1979. Selmo was of working-class origin and had once worked as a carpenter. He joined the movement at age 15 and became one of the most efficient and trusted com-tech (communications-technical) cadres of the movement in Manila.

He first worked under Domingo, then head of Manila-Rizal Executive Committee. Their UG collective, as he recalls, was like a *barkada,* a gang: "We were busy with many things. But we had time for jokes and laughter. Domingo sometimes even sparred playfully with me. We were very informal in relating to each other."

In 1979 Domingo was relieved, and Edjop took over as acting head of the Party organization in Manila. Selmo was retained as com-tech man. But he found a different atmosphere, under a different kind of leader.

"Edjop was so serious about everything," Selmo recalls. "*Nanibago talaga ako sa istilo niya.* He didn't seem like a comrade I could joke and laugh with. He was so different from Domingo and the other comrades I had lived with. He was formal and very serious. I didn't feel comfortable with him, and I kept my distance.

"He gave me my assignments, telling me the people I was supposed to contact and give letters or documents to. In giving me instructions, he enumerated everything I should do, covering all aspects of a particular task—where and when I should go, what route I should take to save time and money, what mode of transportation I should use. I often used a motorcycle, and once he asked: 'Won't you save money by commuting, instead of using the motorcycle?' He then computed how much gasoline I would use, comparing it with the cost of riding the jeepney or the bus. But since I could move faster on motorcycle, he let me continue using the bike.

"*Talagang ikinakahon niya ang lahat ng bagay.* He covered every angle of any task, making sure we were saving money and time. This was okay. But he took away initiative from a comrade, since he practically decided everything. *Nawawalan ako ng diskarte sa gawain.*"

To Selmo, Edjop was not so much a comrade as a stern administrator, an employer.

"I knew that the things he assigned were all for the struggle. They weren't for his own interests. But somehow I felt like an employee with Edjop as my boss. When I was able to carry out an assignment, he would give me a pat on the back and say, 'Good.' But when I failed, he frowned and muttered, *'Pambihira naman.'* He never yelled or lost his temper. But he made me feel guilty whenever I failed, as if he was keeping score on my achievements.

"But on the whole he was impressive as a cadre. He just took the revolution too seriously. If the rest of us had 70 percent determination, he had 99 percent. One thing I admired about him was his ability to consider the needs, not only of his unit, but of the entire organization. He was willing to share whatever resources we had with other comrades in other collectives, and even in other regions. The other units I was in didn't do this. They held on to resources even if they had more than what they needed. Edjop was more responsible. *Mas mataas ang kamulatan niya.* He could see the overall needs of the movement.

"For example, we had three motorcycles in our possession. We needed only one. Edjop decided that we should give up the other two. One was sent to Pampanga, and he asked me to make arrangements for the other motorcycle to be transported to Mindanao."

It took months for Selmo to carry out this particular task. His "boss," he says, was dissatisfied. Every time Edjop asked if the motorcycle had already been sent to comrades in Mindanao, Selmo explained that the needed papers were not yet ready. It was not his fault, he said, but those of the people responsible for preparing the documents. But Edjop frowned at him and said, "It's taking too long."

One evening, as he was heading back to the UG house after failing once again to finalize the business of the motorcycle, Selmo thought, "If he frowns at me this time, I'll surely answer him back. If he doesn't accept my criticism, I'll challenge him to a fistfight. *Magsuntukan na lang kami.*"

As expected, Edjop made a wry expression after Selmo reported that the task had not been completed.

"At that point I had had it up to the neck with him. *Punong-puno na talaga ako.* I was trying so hard, but he didn't seem to see this. I didn't wait for him to finish what he was saying. I suddenly turned my back on him and went to the room. I was lying in bed when Edjop came in. I think he already knew that I was angry.

"In a low, gentle voice he asked, 'What's wrong, Ka Selmo? What have I done to offend you? *May puna ka ba sa akin?* Do you have any criticism to share?' I didn't answer him. I felt so mad. He realized I wouldn't talk with him, and so he left. I then started to cry. Maybe he heard me whimpering from outside the room.

"Later, when I had already calmed down, another comrade, Ka Sarsi, talked to me. I agreed to a CSC (criticism-self-criticism) session with Edjop. But I was still mad at him. I was still ready to challenge him to a fight, if he didn't admit his mistakes. My behavior was no longer that of a kasama. It was no longer formal. I was very young then, and I may have overreacted.

"As we were about to talk, I grabbed a bench, put it down hard in front of Edjop, and sat down like I was about to punch him. Then I started talking about everything I hated about him, his style, his attitude—everything. I got all of it out of my chest.

" 'I thought Edjop would try to defend his actions. But he just sat in front me, listening, seriously considering every point I raised. It was then that I realized that I had been mistaken. He knew how to listen to and accept criticisms from other comrades. *Marunong pala siyang tumanggap ng puna.* He apologized for his behavior."

After the CSC session, Edjop went to a room where Joy was sleeping. "He woke me up," says Joy. "He said he wanted to talk. He wanted to share with me what had just happened. He was bothered by it, and it showed. He was in a very quiet, reflective mood. Until that time, he really wasn't aware of his negative attitude, of his tendency to treat Selmo and other comrades like employees. But he was thankful for being made to realize it."

"There were changes in Edjop's style and attitude after that," Selmo continues. "He let me decide how I should carry out my tasks. He became more friendly and cordial. I also made a self-criticism, and apologized for assuming that he wouldn't listen to what I had to say."

Selmo would later request to be deployed to the countryside. Edjop helped make the arrangements, and gave Selmo some parting words of advice: "Never keep your ill-feelings all bottled up inside you. Always be open with comrades about your criticisms, about what you feel. This is even more important to remember in the countryside, where you may find yourself in life-and-death situations."

"I never forgot what he said," says Selmo.

In November 1977, Joma Sison was captured in a military raid in La Union. The arrest had an immediate effect on Edjop's security. Sison was betrayed by a courier who was actually a military agent, and Edjop at one time was in touch with the same liaison man.

A day after Joma's arrest, Edjop and his comrades held a meeting in their UG house in Marikina to discuss precautionary measures. But danger was closer than they thought. While they were meeting, Lina, Nonoy's yaya, was taking the boy out for a walk. A man suddenly approached her and asked, "Excuse me, miss. Do you know where this man lives?" The man showed Lina a photograph. It was Edjop's.

Lina had never been involved in any underground activities. But she was loyal to Edjop; she respected and admired him. "I don't think I've seen that man before," she answered nervously. "Why don't you try the other end of the street?"

When the man left, Lina immediately reported what had happened. "We immediately packed and prepared to move out," recalls Eric. "Since Edjop had already been identified, we sent him ahead. Later, we learned that, even then, there were already agents all over our neighborhood."

In December, Edjop, Mauro, and Tani were called to a meeting in the countryside to discuss the implications of the CPP chairman's arrest. The trip was a welcome change for the three, for it gave them a chance to get out of the city and visit the *sona* to meet comrades and organized peasants. They traveled to a barrio in Pampanga where they met Cesar, a member of the Executive Committee of the Central Committee (*Komiteng Taga-pagpaganap ng Komite Sentral,* or KT-KS).

"When entering a barrio, it was common protocol for comrades to mix and chat with the peasants," says Mauro. "But for Edjop, it was more than an act of courtesy. He engaged peasants in discussions that lasted for hours."

"He asked about all sorts of things and listened to the people explain," says Tani. "He inquired about their problems in the barrio, how much they earned, how much they expected to harvest the next season and a hundred other things. I was really amazed by this. Here was a man who came from so different a background. Yet there he was making small talk with ordinary peasants. Other comrades would probably not have had the patience for that."

As the meeting proceeded one afternoon, sentries suddenly warned that enemy troops had entered the barrio.

"It was around three o'clock in the afternoon when we heard the news," relates Tani. "Cesar suddenly grabbed his M-16 and rushed out of the house. We followed him to a small space under the house, where we waited for the soldiers to come."

The soldiers were not aware of the group's presence in the barrio. But the cadres thought they were, and prepared for battle. Cesar handed a grenade to Mauro, a 9-mm handgun to Edjop.

"I remember being more afraid about Mauro dropping the grenade than about a gunbattle breaking out," Tani quips. "But I also thought that was the end for all of us. In those days, nobody survived an encirclement."

"It was a long waiting game," Mauro relates. "We were all afraid that the battle would begin any time."

The people in the barrio went on as if everything was normal. "If just one of them had talked," says Mauro, "we would have been finished. But we had their support."

The soldiers left before it got dark. Cesar led the others to another barrio where they continued their conference.

Edjop later confided to Mauro, "I can't imagine how we would have used those weapons."

"The only time we had actually fired guns was when we were in Tarlac," says Mauro. "But we hit rocks, not people. One thing about Edjop, he was not the type who easily got excited. He was a very balanced person. Of course, he was afraid at the time. But he took it all in stride."

In 1977 Edjop attended the 6th Plenum of the CPP Central Committee (KS), held in a guerrilla camp in Nueva Ecija. Among those who welcomed him to the camp was Tony Zumel.

"Our meeting was very warm," Zumel recalls. "Whatever differences we had had in the past had been forgotten. We greeted each other as comrades." Zumel remembers that Edjop walked around the camp with a .38 Beretta pistol tucked in a toy cowboy holster. "Kasama, that's some holster you've got there," comrades teased him. "I borrowed it from my little boy," Edjop answered.

The year before Joma's capture, the movement had already lost other key leaders. Satur Ocampo was arrested in January 1976. In August, Bernabe Buscayno, alias Dante, was captured in Nueva Ecija. In the same year, Victor Corpus, tired and frustrated with the defeats suffered by the NPA, surrendered to the military.

The burden of responsibility in the movement fell on the shoulders of second-liners. Edjop was among them. Earlier that year he had been raised from candidate member to full member of the party. (Communist Party chairman Joma Sison was reportedly surprised and disappointed that a cadre of Edjop's caliber had not been promoted sooner.) In the plenum in Nueva Ecija, Edjop was elected alternate member of the Central Committee.

"Edjop inherited a mountain of problems," relates Mauro. "But he saw it all as a challenge and was pushed to do more. During the years we were together, I never saw his morale ebb, ever."

28
Controversy

By 1977 Edjop was a ranking leader of the revolutionary movement. His comrades describe his ascent in the hierarchy as "meteoric," but are quick to add that it was "well-deserved."

As Edjop rose higher in rank, the nature and quality of his responsibilities changed. As a labor organizer for PAFLU, Edjop found fulfillment in being directly involved with workers and the urban poor. *"Nakalubog sa masa,"* immersed in the life of the people, as cadres would say. Now he was with the HO, the "higher organ," concerned with analyzing developments, setting policies, coordinating and administering committees and individuals under him—but with no direct and active link with the organized masses. He dealt with committees, cadres, and personalities, and spent most of his time in underground houses, doing paper work and participating in countless discussions.

Manny, an underground activist, explains the effect that such a change can have on a cadre. He was a barrio organizer in Central Luzon before being assigned to another task in Manila, where he stayed most of the time in a UG house.

"The adjustment can be difficult for any comrade," he explains. "When working directly in people's organizations, you always feel the pulse of the revolution, you see concretely the fruits of the struggle and how these are helping the masa. But in staff work, where you are often cooped up in a UG house and deal mostly with comrades, you somehow feel out of it.

"It's actually a dilemma. There is a need for people to perform administrative and staff work. But comrades performing such work must exert greater effort or be given more opportunities to integrate with the masses, so they don't feel so distant from the people they are supposed to be fighting for."

As head of the NDF Preparatory Commission, Edjop was also an ex officio member of the Manila-Rizal Regional Party Executive Committee and head of the MR United Front Committee.

213

"The Manila-Rizal committee was the first collective Edjop joined where discussions were often intense," recalls Mina, then a member of the committee. "I don't think he went through similar debates in the labor movement. The problems he encountered as a trade union cadre were more concrete and less ideological. But it was natural that, as a cadre assumed greater responsibilities as a member of a higher decision-making organ, the discussions became sharper and more ideological. *Mas nasasala, mas kumikinis at mas pumupuro ang usapan.* Edjop had to feel his way through these ideological tussles. He had to adjust."

In the mid-seventies, the Manila-Rizal (MR) committee was involved in an upsurge of protests in Manila, sparked by the La Tondeña strike. The national leadership, however, was apprehensive that comrades in Manila were giving too much emphasis to the city, at the expense of the struggle in the countryside. Armed struggle, the Central Committee's Executive Committee, or KT-KS, asserted, was still the "primary form of struggle." The KT-KS questioned many of the MR committee's policies and actions, including a proposal in 1975 to call for national elections, which the KT-KS branded as "reformist."

In 1976, the MR committee launched an urban mass campaign called "Unos," which hoped to achieve the level of protest reached during the First Quarter Storm.

"We did not believe that the movement in the cities should merely play a supportive role to the armed struggle in the countryside," says Ariel, a former member of the Manila-Rizal Regional Party Committee. "We felt that the urban mass movement must have its own dynamism, and must be able to carry the revolution to the very centers where the enemy is strongest."

Prominent in these debates was Domingo, a full-time cadre since the late sixties, and a top party ideologue and theoretician. According to some cadres, he had read and mastered all the works of Lenin, and could quote most of the significant passages verbatim. One story goes that, when one cadre asked him about

one of Lenin's articles, Domingo began his explanation by saying, "Ah, yes, I believe Lenin wrote that right after losing a game
of chess."

But Domingo had a crude debating style that turned off many
a comrade. One cadre compares him to Sonny Jaworski, the
popular Filipino basketball player known to be "brilliant, but
rough."

"He uses a full deck of dirty tricks in debates," says Manny.
"He will taunt you, intimidate you, and say things that can throw
you off, throw the whole discussion off. If you agree with him,
you will be mesmerized by his argumentation, and not notice
the coarseness of his style. But if you are on the other side of
the debate, you really get pissed off."

"He was often irreverent, and he showed no respect for other
people's views," says Obet, also a former member of the Manila-
Rizal Party Regional Committee. "Ka Domingo said things you
don't say to a comrade. In fact, you don't say them to anybody.
It's all a question of good manners and right conduct."

To one comrade who had presented his own analysis of a
situation, Domingo sneered: "*Saang lupalop mo nakuha ang teory-
ang iyan?* Where in the world did you get that theory?" To a
comrade of upper-class origins, he snapped in the middle of an
argument, "*E taga-Arrneow ka kasi, e!* We all know you went to the
Ateneo."

In fact, most debates in the MR committee were characterized
by impassioned, polemical speeches, delivered in stinging Pilipino, and accentuated with English quotations from the works
of Marx, Lenin, and Mao. "*Durugan talaga,*" Domingo describes
it. "Each would try to smash the other's ideas. You don't think
about friends anymore."

Edjop stayed clear of most of these ideological jousts, as Domingo recalls: "I don't remember Edjop being that active in
political discussions. He was more concerned with getting things
done. His approach to discussions and debates was more practical than theoretical. He supplied the practical data to give a

more concrete view of the problem and help the discussion move along. He would ask, 'What is the basis of your position?' He argued based on the facts he had, not so much on theory.

"Edjop also did not join in the yelling and shouting. His Ateneo breeding always showed. He was always refined in arguing his position. Never did I hear him quote from Marx, Lenin, or Mao. That was not his style."

Despite their contrasting styles and personalities, Edjop and Domingo were "allies" in many debates on particular issues. Both pushed for the creation of an underground organization of workers who believed in the national democratic revolution, but who may not be ready to enter the Communist Party. When other party cadres asserted that the party was the revolutionary organization of the workers, Domingo snapped: "What kind of a party is this that is so jealous and insecure of its vanguard role? I don't think I like this kind of party!"

Both Edjop and Domingo were overruled at the time, though Edjop would later carry out this plan in Mindanao, where he helped form an underground national democratic mass organization of workers; and today one such assemblage, the Revolutionary Committee of Trade Unions (RCTU), is a member-organization of the NDF.

Mina remembers a particular meeting in July 1976 which illustrates another aspect of Edjop's character:

"Ka Domingo and I were arguing on the direction of the workers' movement after the upsurge in 1976. As usual, the discussion was very heated. There was shouting and a lot of intense argumentation on both sides.

"Edjop was not involved in the debate, but he tried his best to mediate, to reconcile the positions of the two contending sides. He kept butting in, saying, 'I don't think there are major differences in the points you are raising. There is nothing to argue about. *Hindi kayo dapat magtalo.*' But, in fact, there were differences in our positions. Only, Edjop could not see it. At one point I became so irritated with him that I yelled, 'Why don't you just keep out of this! We have different positions, and they simply can't be reconciled!'

"Edjop became silent. Later, I apologized for snapping at him, explaining, 'It is wrong for us to try to agree when there are clearly differences in our perceptions. But to argue doesn't mean that we are fighting each other. If we don't thresh things out thoroughly, nothing will be clear and there will still be no unity.'

"Looking back, I think Edjop was always uneasy to see people who are supposed to be comrades quarreling or giving the appearance of quarreling. He was a very cool person, and he didn't like heated and intense debates, especially among kasamas."

People like Domingo had been studying the works of Marx and Lenin (what is referred to, in the movement, as the "classics") since they were student activists. This gave them a clear edge in theoretical discussions. On the other hand, Edjop spent his formative years as an activist with the reformist bloc. "Most of the other leading cadres were UP intellectuals who had begun reading and debating Marxist ideas since they were in college," says Alicia. "But there wasn't much intellectual discussion on revolutionary theory at the Ateneo."

With the work load he bore in his early years in the underground, Edjop didn't have much time for a deep and comprehensive study of Marxism. He was not a top party theoretician, as his comrades readily admit.

"Edjop was not really brilliant when it came to expounding on and formulating new ideas on revolutionary theory," says Tani. "One couldn't expect any extraordinary creativity from him in that respect. At that time, he was more of a doer, a man of action, than a thinker. He was best at understanding and then realizing concepts and programs. He didn't engage much in polemics and intellectual exercises. *Hindi siya mahilig sa paglalaro ng mga magagandang ideya.*"

"This didn't mean that Edjop was incompetent as a leading cadre," adds Raul, a member of the Manila-Rizal committee. "He may not have been as theoretically and ideologically sharp as the other leaders. But I always looked up to him when it came to policy making. He was superior to a great many cadres. He was definitely of HO caliber."

One cadre cites characters from Tolkien's *Lord of the Rings* to describe Edjop:

"If Joma Sison was Gandalf the wizard, and Bernabe Buscayno was Aragorn the warrior, Edjop would be Frodo Baggins the hobbit. I'm not just referring to Edjop's physical attributes. A hobbit was a humble, simple creature who was best at keeping a house in order. That's exactly what Edjop was then, a cadre who improved on how the organization was being run and thus helped get things done better and faster."

Edjop's first major test as a leading cadre involved a major debate within the revolutionary movement. Not all cadres are willing to discuss the underground's role in the Interim National Assembly elections in 1978—and the crises that plagued the movement afterwards. The decisions made and the questions raised during this period are still "under study," and some would rather not discuss it, except perhaps in formal party fora. It is a highly complex debate which would take an entire book to discuss clearly and thoroughly. But there are some who are willing to talk, if only to shed some light on Edjop's role in the debate, and on how it affected him as a revolutionary and as a person.

In late 1977, Marcos, under pressure from the administration of U.S. President Jimmy Carter, announced the holding of general elections for an interim national assembly. The polls, set for April 7, 1978, were supposed to be part of a process of "normalization" that would pave the way for the lifting of martial law.

Traditional opposition parties accepted the challenge. Benigno Aquino, then the country's most prominent political detainee, announced that he was going to run as candidate from prison.

The MR committee, including Edjop and members of the NDF Preparatory Commission, voted to participate in the elections. According to Domingo, their position received the tentative support of some members of the national leadership, though he expected the KT-KS to have reservations about their decision.

"We did not have too many illusions about winning in the election," says Domingo. "We were more concerned about maximizing the opportunity to propagate the national democratic line and expand to other areas."

Traditional opposition leaders, aware of the left's organizational strength, agreed to a tactical alliance with the national democrats. Cadres were pulled out from their regular units to help in the campaign. Edjop himself got in touch with allies from traditional parties to help form a slate and set up an election machinery. Not a few politicians were surprised and glad to deal with the former NUSP president.

"There was one personality who was so disgusted with the left that he wouldn't have anything to do with us," recalls Ariel. "*Talagang diring-diri siya sa amin.* He himself said that he always thought Communists were devious creatures who ate people up. But he was willing to talk and deal with Edjop, whom he still considered to be of the upper class."

The natdems helped set up the *Lakas ng Bayan* (People's Power or LABAN) party. Included in the slate was Alex Boncayao, a working-class leader, respected in many urban poor communities in Manila. He was also a Communist cadre.

Rallies were held almost daily in different parts of Manila. Candidates and opposition leaders lambasted the Marcos dictatorship, and called for the people's support for the LABAN slate. Others, like Boncayao, attacked U.S. support for Marcos and called for " an overhaul of the social system"—another way of saying "revolution."

The campaign had already started when the KT-KS came out with its position to boycott the elections. Stated in so many words, the national leadership believed that the elections would delay, rather than advance, the revolution; it would only draw more people to the "reformist" path.

The MR committee believed otherwise. To Domingo and other cadres, the election campaign was an excellent opportunity to propagate the national democratic line.

Edjop, Domingo, and Mauro, the deputy secretary of the NDF

Preparatory Commission, met with KT-KS members in Nueva
Ecija. The national leadership affirmed the boycott position. As
party members, the three cadres from Manila were duty-bound
to abide by it. Domingo was instructed to return immediately to
the city and implement the policy. Edjop and Mauro stayed behind in Nueva Ecija.

What happened next is unclear and remains a controversial
issue in the history of the movement.

According to Domingo, the new policy was handed down only
a few days before Election Day. When he convened the Manila-
Rizal committee and announced their withdrawal from the campaign, the other cadres were "shocked and resisted the
instructions."

But the KT-KS claims that Domingo deliberately delayed the
announcement and that he suppressed KT-KS memos which explained the boycott policy.

Still, says Domingo, the MR committee informed cadres in the
lower units, as well as allies, about the shift in tactics.

"Minura kami ng mga alyado," says Raul. "Our allies cursed us."
According to Jackie, the move reinforced the fears of "bourgeois
allies" that they "can't trust these Communists who are only out
to use them."

Among cadres and activists, the reactions were just as intense.
Party members threatened to resign, and sympathizers threatened to withdraw their support.

The MR committee reconvened to discuss the situation. It was
decided that to push for a boycott of the elections meant a political and organizational disaster for the movement in Manila. The
committee voted unanimously not to implement the KT-KS
policy.

"We knew we were defying the official Party position," says
Remo. "But we did so for very practical reasons. If we pushed
for boycott, there would be chaos and confusion in our ranks,
not to mention among our allies."

A committee member was sent to Nueva Ecija to explain the
decision to the KT-KS and try to get the leading body's support.

But a heavy military presence in the area prevented the cadre from reaching the main camp.

Meanwhile, cadres in Manila went on with the campaign. On April 6, 1978, a noise barrage was successfully launched in the city. Amid massive cheating and terrorism, not one of the LABAN candidates made it. To pre-empt post-election protests, Marcos ordered a crackdown against the opposition. Activists and leaders, including former Senator Lorenzo Tañada and human rights lawyer Joker Arroyo, were arrested. Cadres who had surfaced during the campaign went back underground.

Nevertheless, from the point of view of most cadres in Manila, the electoral campaign was successful. "We were able to organize and propagate the ND line in factories, communities, schools, and places which we could not penetrate in the past," says Domingo. "New members were recruited and new organizations and underground collectives formed."

The KT-KS, however, did not take the infraction of official policy lightly. Mauro returned from Nueva Ecija and informed Domingo that he had been relieved of his position. Edjop was the new secretary of the Manila-Rizal committee.

Domingo was indignant: "I couldn't understand how Edjop and Mauro could accept such a decision, how they could simply abandon me and the MR committee, when all along we were together in pushing a common position for the elections. They should have understood the problems we would have faced if we had pushed for the boycott position in the middle of the campaign."

Later, Edjop himself returned and met with Domingo. "I was furious at him," recalls Domingo. "I asked, 'How could this happen? What did you do?' But he could not give me a straight answer. All he said was, 'That's the decision. We must implement it.'

"I questioned his right to succeed me as KT-MR secretary. *'Bakit ikaw?* Why you? Do you think comrades in MR will simply accept this decision? Do you think they will accept you?' I said some very nasty things against him. I practically accused him of having schemed to get my post. I didn't really mean that. Edjop was not that kind of comrade—or that kind of person. But I was angry and felt betrayed. I had had a lot of differences with the KT-KS, and now they were hitting back at me. I told Ed, 'People will answer for this kind of maneuvering. Heads will roll.' "

This statement later became part of the controversy.

"Edjop and other cadres took what I said literally. *Na pupugutan ko sila ng ulo*. They thought I planned to use force to vindicate myself. All I meant was I would file a case against the leadership and struggle it out in formal party fora."

Domingo resigned. The majority of the MR committee members rallied behind him. Barely ten years after it was re-established, the CPP was facing its most serious internal crisis.

Edjop was caught in the crossfire. He had assumed the leadership of the MR organization, but found few comrades willing to cooperate. "We hated him," says Remo. "We condemned the leadership's underhanded approach to our differences, and we saw Edjop as an agent of this scheme."

Jackie belonged to the NDF Preparatory Commission, but she was more sympathetic with the MR group. "In our meetings after the elections, I listened to Edjop put much of the blame on Domingo and other comrades from the MR committee. But he had been part of the decision to participate, as much as the others. I found this unfair to the other comrades. To me, Edjop seemed to be denying his role in the MR decision, as if he was washing his hands of the entire mess."

Others questioned Edjop's own abilities as a leading cadre.

"I always looked up to comrades in the HO as people with exceptional achievement and experience in the revolution," says Ariel. "But, at that time, I didn't see Edjop as such a person. I began to question his qualifications to be part of the HO. Was he that theoretically equipped? Had he really undergone comprehensive revolutionary work? Up to now I still don't understand why he shifted position. It's one of the strong negative impressions of Edjop that has remained in my mind."

"I don't remember hearing him raise any question against the policy," recalls Raul. "My impression was that Edjop was for participation all along."

Jackie offers this explanation: "When it came to taking sides in ideological debates, Edjop, I think, was handicapped by his shortcomings in theoretical studies. He didn't know how to defend his position from the best ideological standpoint. He was not as confident as Domingo or other comrades. Of course, Domingo's intimidating style aggravated this. Edjop may have actually been for boycott all along. But he didn't know how to argue it out with comrades like Domingo, who really dominated the discussions. But then he found comrades with like views in the national leadership who could better confront Domingo and the MR cadres on a stronger ideological foundation. That may have been the reason for the position he took later on."

Mina of the Central Committee disputes this view. "I cannot accept the idea that Edjop carried any position without actually believing in it. He was a strong person, though not as overconfident or overbearing as other comrades. I still believe that he was for participation in the beginning, but was later convinced about the boycott position."

In the heat of the conflict, cadres resorted to labels and name-calling. The KT-KS came out with a 200-page critique of the MR position. In it, the national leadership branded the KT-MR as "reformists, worse than the Lavaites," referring to members of the Partido Komunista ng Pilipinas, who had surrendered to Marcos after the declaration of martial law (PKP leaders prefer to say they "entered into a political agreement").

In the national democratic movement, to be called a "Lavaite" is as insulting as it is for a Cory supporter to be branded a "Marcos loyalist." Not surprisingly, the MR group answered back, calling members of the KT-KS "imbeciles" and "ultra-leftists."

Edjop got his share of the brickbats. As a student leader, he had been tagged a "clerico-fascist" and "bourgeois reactionary" by radical students. Now his radical comrades had a different set of names for him. He was branded a *balimbing,* an unprincipled cadre who arbitrarily shifted position on an important issue. Some described him as *sipsip sa HO* or *tuta ng liderato,* or called him a *transistor,* a mouthpiece of the national leadership. Others accused him of being a *karerista,* of ingratiating himself with the KT-KS to attain a higher position in the party. Jackie would rather not recount the other names Edjop was called. "They were things said in moments of anger, and are best forgotten."

The insults came mainly from disgruntled members of the MR group led by Domingo. Most other cadres, like Mauro, found the verbal attacks against Edjop "childish, naughty, and unprincipled."

Members of the MR group now admit that there were excesses on their part, that most of their criticisms against Edjop were unfounded and unfair.

"I take back the nasty things I said against him," says Domingo. "Edjop got caught in the middle of a bitter conflict within the movement. *Naipit siya talaga.*"

But as it was during the First Quarter Storm, Edjop did not react with vindictiveness. Never, his comrades attest, did he answer back in anger.

"He was quiet and reflective," recalls Jackie, "He was never outspoken and did not have flare-ups like Domingo and the rest. I never heard one bitter statement from him during this period. He was still careful about what he said and how he said it. He never resorted to backbiting."

"He was a very diplomatic person, and I guess we mistook this for opportunism and dishonesty," says Remo. "But he never engaged in tit-for-tat exchanges."

"In the middle of all the quarrels, he had the time to worry about the safety and welfare of other comrades," recalls Jackie. "There were a lot of arrests and disappearances during that time. I'll never forget how Edjop cared enough to help make arrangements for my safety."

29
A Struggle Within

A major party conference was set to settle the conflict between the KT-KS, the Central Committee's Executive Committee, and the KT-MR, the Manila-Rizal Executive Committee. Both bodies girded for an intense ideological battle. Domingo and his group held rigorous theoretical study sessions. Meanwhile, Edjop was tasked by the KT-KS to investigate the effects of the election campaign on the underground organization in Metro Manila.

In January 1979 cadres from Manila set out for Nueva Ecija in several batches. Edjop traveled with Remo and Raul, both of the MR regional committee. They rented a private jeepney and drove to a barrio at the foot of the Sierra Madre mountains, where peasants and NPA guerrillas welcomed them. They spent the night in a farmer's house and the following day began the two-day walk to the camp.

"There were military patrols, and we had to be alert," says Raul. "We were all conscious of the danger we were facing. Everybody cooperated."

It was during their trek to the camp that Remo had a change of attitude toward Edjop. "It was a very long walk, and not once did I hear Edjop complain," he recalls. "He was very patient, and even took the time to ask how I was doing. I wondered how a person with his background could take it. I was really impressed."

They spent the first few days in camp setting up tents and bringing in supplies. The cadres were divided into teams, and they took turns carrying sacks of rice, vegetables, and other goods from the barrio to the camp. They bought a cow in the barrio and had it slaughtered. Each cadre had to carry ten kilos of raw beef up to the camp. It was exhausting work, as it took a whole day to go up and down the mountain.

There was always the danger of enemy attack, and all cadres were issued firearms while in camp. Once, the camp went on

225

the alert when a carbine went off; a cadre had accidentally dropped it. Another time, an NPA squad left the camp to rejoin their mother unit in another part of the guerrilla front. A few minutes later, shots were heard from afar. Again, the whole camp went on the alert. They were relieved to see the guerrillas who had just left camp coming back with the carcass of a wild boar. Cadres and guerrillas had a feast.

Despite these false alarms, the atmosphere in the camp was relaxed, even jovial. Cadres from both the national and MR bodies set aside differences for a while to enjoy life in the sona. "We were there for almost two months, and, of course, you get tired talking about politics all the time," says Raul. "Sometimes we just talked about our children, nature, the forest, and things like that."

There were the usual jokes and wisecracks from the MR group. Once, a cadre from MR kidded about an NPA advance point called the *ublag,* where guerrillas had to sleep with no mats or mosquito nets. This cadre quipped: "Those who don't behave will be made to spend the night in the ublag."

Edjop didn't like the joke. "Comrades, we should not make fun of the ublag and comrades assigned there," he said in a serious tone. "We should even be thankful that they are making that sacrifice for our protection."

"I think the man left his sense of humor in Manila," somebody whispered to another cadre. "Talk about a killjoy."

But there were times when Edjop himself joined in the fun. At age 30 he had begun to lose his hair and had a bald spot in the center of his head. *"Nakakalbo ka na, kasama.* You're getting bald," cadres teased him. *"Di bale. May buhok naman sa dibdib.* At least I have hair on my chest," Edjop answered, playfully showing off the patch of hair on his chest, to the laughter of his comrades.

After a few days, the conference began. The cadres agreed on a ten-point agenda, covering the major aspects of the debate. At 22, Ariel was one of the youngest participants in the conference. It was the first major party gathering he had attended. "I was both excited and apprehensive," he recalls. "It was my first experience in higher levels of struggle. But I was part of a group which had dared quarrel with the national leaders of the movement. I didn't know if I was competent enough to join in such a struggle. I didn't know what to expect."

He learned soon enough. The conference was a cross between a highbrow intellectual discussion and a rowdy high school shouting match. "I was shocked," says Ariel.

As in the past, the exchanges from both sides were heated and intense. They traded arguments and theories, with the usual quotations from Marx and Lenin. "But this time, there was a lot of nitpicking and hair-splitting on the points raised," says Ariel. "Every sentence, every word was debated on. There was a lot of yelling and shouting. Not much respect was shown for the points raised by other comrades."

Domingo would often ask one question after another until he had cornered his opponent on a particular point. But this tactic was eventually exposed to the other side. When Domingo tried to pull the same trick again, a cadre warned, "Watch out, he's leading you. It's a trap!"

Cesar of the KT-KS always used a historical approach, and often went on long discourses to prove a point. Domingo was often irritated with the length of Cesar's speeches, and once he snapped: "Will you keep it short and give the others a chance!"

Most of the national leaders remained cool in the discussions, but others lost their temper. In the middle of an exchange, Pol, a Central Committee member, stood up and with expansive gestures lambasted Domingo's debating style: "You are a disgrace!"

Edjop was not that involved in the debate, though he made notes on the points raised by both sides. He reported on his investigations into the state of the movement in Manila. He focused mainly on the weaknesses of the movement in Manila under Domingo's leadership—the lack of consolidation in specific districts, the decline in membership, the units that had collapsed. For this, Edjop earned another label. "Some comrades called him *bala ng national*, the national leadership's hatchet-man," says Raul.

"We didn't question the accuracy of the facts he presented," says Domingo. "But he had not been that objective. A lot of the gains and strengths in the past years were not mentioned in his report. I don't think Edjop intended any malice. I would say that it was more the people from the national organ who planned it that way. But I was disappointed that Edjop didn't even try to talk to us about it, that he didn't even try to get our side of things. Instead, he let the KT-KS use the information he had presented as ammunition against us."

It is one point that even Mina of the Central Committee, who has always defended Edjop's posture in the struggle, concedes: "I may agree with some who say that Edjop was not very objective in presenting the situation of the organization in Manila under Domingo. In wanting to strengthen his own position in the debate, he may have omitted very important aspects in his report. But Edjop did not enjoy his role as the supplier of information against the Manila-Rizal group. *Naipit talaga siya sa ganoong proseso.*"

After five weeks, the cadres were still discussing Item Number One on the agenda. "The conference was dragging on without anything being resolved," says Raul. "We were getting nowhere."

Cesar announced that the discussion had to be adjourned. But there were still organizational matters to be tackled. The KT-KS passed sanctions on those who had violated official policy in the elections. Domingo and other members of the MR committee were also accused of "factionalism"—a charge Domingo denies up to now.

Edjop and Domingo never saw each other again after the meeting in Nueva Ecija.

"I wanted to forget everything that had happened after that," Domingo recalls. "I just wanted to concentrate on my new assignment in the countryside. I worked in an area that was heavily militarized. There was a military detachment in literally every barrio. We had no mass base to speak of. We had to organize, moving from one barrio to another, with the military on our tails. Two or three months later, my wife died in an encounter.

Nobody wrote to me to express their sympathies, not even comrades I worked with in Manila. I became even more bitter. I didn't try to write to anyone, not even friends. So I simply tried to erase everything from the mind. *Kung baga sa tape, binura ko dahil sa sama ng loob.* Even the things that had happened between me and Ed.

"Several years later, Ed sent word that he would like us to meet, so we could patch things up between us. I wanted that, but the opportunity never came. I was in a guerrilla camp when I heard about his death. *Sayang talaga.* He died without us ever having the chance to talk. *Hindi man lang kami nakapaglinawan.*"

In late February 1979 the Manila cadres who had attended the Nueva Ecija conference returned to the city bitterly disappointed. Domingo was transferred to another region. Edjop remained secretary of the Manila-Rizal committee. But the struggle was a big emotional drain on him. "He admitted to me that the 1979 debate was one of the worst crises of his life," says Mia, a cadre who later became close to Edjop. "During the struggle, he felt like he was being torn to pieces."

This was true for the revolutionary movement as well. Though many cadres believe that the charges of factionalism against Domingo and his group were unfounded, the debate uncovered rifts in the movement. It had never been as sharply divided on an issue before. The 1979 conference in Nueva Ecija is still a major unresolved debate in the history of the national democratic movement.

"After the 1979 struggle, everything that the KT-MR under Ka Domingo did and all that happened in Manila was considered a mistake," recalls Jackie. "There is a need to correct this view. While we must learn from the mistakes, we must also recognize the gains during this period, and the lessons learned, not only on how to launch an anti-fascist struggle, but also on how we handle internal differences. Instead, the movement developed blinders which caused problems and mistakes in later years, especially in 1986, right before the Marcos dictatorship was overthrown.

"The movement has a lot to learn from what happened in 1979. But I think some comrades would rather erase it from memory. This is a mistake. We shouldn't follow the examples of the Chinese during the Cultural Revolution, when they rewrote parts of their history to suit their needs, or scratched out from photographs the faces of the people they didn't like.

"What happened also had an effect on how I viewed Ed. I became more realistic about him and about other leading cadres in general. Ed was not a saint. He was a human being who had weaknesses. Despite everything, I admire and recognize him as one of the best, most committed and kindest revolutionaries I ever knew. But we must not put anyone on a pedestal. We should never romanticize our martyrs."

Most cadres admit that the debate was a reflection of "major ideological weaknesses" of the revolutionary movement. "The movement then still had far to go in developing cadres who were ideologically sharp," says Raul. "The debate was something new for all of us. We were all very young then, mostly in our early and late twenties. Although a lot of us had been full-time cadres since 1972, we still had a lot to learn about fighting a revolution."

According to Mina, the 1979 debate "sparked greater interest in many comrades for ideological studies, for deeper understanding of revolutionary theory. Edjop was among those who began to read and appreciate the classics and the practical experiences of other revolutionary movements."

Edjop, now known as Ka Rodel, inherited a load of problems as head of the MR organization.

"A lot of comrades remained bitter about what had happened," relates Mina. "A lot of them lay low, others resigned. The organization was practically in a shambles."

Edjop and other KT-MR members met with leading cadres of different sectors and districts. They tried to explain the decisions reached in Nueva Ecija. They held ED, or educational, sessions, and helped draft programs and consolidate units affected by the internal struggle.

"The main objective was to reunite the organization in Manila," says Remo. "It was a difficult task for Edjop, given the antagonistic attitude some comrades still had towards him. But one thing about Edjop, he had the courage to face up to the organization. He was persistent.

"He also had a style of dealing with comrades, different from the style of Domingo, who was often overbearing and too much a *komandista*. Edjop was also firm, but more understanding and caring about comrades. He tried to understand their problems, whether political or personal. He was more democratic. He did not simply impose a policy, but always discussed it with comrades. This style became contagious in the organization. *Lumaganap ito sa ibang mga yunit.* Other comrades began to follow his example.

"Edjop was not as brilliant and creative as Domingo had been. But I think, given more time in MR, he would have really developed. There were many things he would have accomplished for the movement in Manila."

But Edjop was never to have that opportunity. He served only four months as KT-MR head, from March, when he returned from Nueva Ecija, to that night in June 1979 when the enemy finally caught up with him.

30
The Face of the Enemy

Bernabe Buscayno, alias Dante, was kept in isolation in a cramped cell of the Constabulary Security Unit (CSU) headquarters in Camp Crame. The room had a small window with iron bars, and through it Dante could see the quadrangle where prisoners were allowed to stretch and get some sunlight. But the window was too high for Dante to reach. Whenever he wanted to peer out, he had to stand on top of two chairs placed one on top of the other.

Early in the morning of June 14, 1979, Dante heard people passing through the quadrangle. He went up to see who they were.

"They were blindfolded and handcuffed, while being led by soldiers. I noticed how they walked sluggishly and with heavy shoulders. There were bruise marks on their faces. They had obviously been beaten."

From the few visitors allowed to visit him once a week, Dante later learned that the new prisoners were kasamas, and that among them was Edjop.

"I wanted to see him and talk to him again, but I didn't know how. One morning I heard voices in the quadrangle. I immediately peered out. I saw Edjop and other comrades getting some sunlight while being watched by guards. Edjop saw me looking out of my cell window. He smiled, raised a clenched fist, and said, 'Mabuhay!' (To Life!) I replied, 'Mabuhay!' The guards took them away. That was the last time I saw Edjop."

Edjop had been arrested with six people: Winfred Villamil, Romeo Candazo, Mario Galang, Caridad Magpantay, Oscar Armea and a certain Marie.

In an "open letter to the Filipino people," Edjop would later give a detailed account of their arrest and prison ordeal:

"We were arrested at three a.m. of June 14th at Periwinkle Street, Talon Village, Las Piñas, Metro Manila. My wife and I rented the house in the last week of March. My wife was not arrested with us because she had just given birth to our second child [Scarlet Victoria or Joyette] at the time of our arrest. . . .

"The arresting officers were from the 5th CSU, now disguised under the name RSU-4 (Regional Security Unit-4), headed by Captain Robert Delfin and Master Sergeant Ricardo and supplemented by a force from NISA [National Intelligence Security Agency] headed by Captain Braganza. . . .

"It was Captain Delfin and Lieutenant Datuin who painstakingly surveyed all the subdivisions in the Alabang-Zapote-Las Piñas area after receiving reports from NISA and MSU sources that I stayed in that general area. They looked for houses or apartments for rent until they stumbled on a house for rent in Angela Village which we had occupied until the last week of March. From neighbors in Angela Village, they were able to get my description, and that of my wife, my child and his yaya. It was not difficult to trace our house in Talon Village after that, with the help of the barangay official, a former PAF [Philippine Air Force] colonel.

"[They] surveilled the house starting the 2nd or 3rd of June. They took photographs of my four-year-old son and his mama, and everyone entering the home since that time, including friendly neighbors. They only confirmed my presence in said house on the 13th of June, 7 a.m., when I closed the gates after a friend went out. . . .

"A group of 20 to 25 officers and men armed with M-16 Armalite rifles surrounded our house and banged on the door. After five minutes, the raiding team headed by Captain Delfin broke the door lock and forced their way in. They ordered everybody to lie face down on the floor. . . .

"The arresting unit manhandled everybody, including my four-year-old son, who cried out loud while the arresting unit shoved and kicked us.

"The arresting unit ransacked the whole house, cabinets, suitcases, mattresses. Cash amounting to P6,000 of our five-year savings was confiscated from my wife's purse. Wallets, handbags, and pocket money amounting to P700 were likewise confiscated. The wristwatches of some, including Winfred Villamil's, were likewise confiscated. An aide of Captain Braganza took my wallet which contained P200 and family pictures. I saw Captain Delfin himself take my wife's purse with P6,000 in it. None of these cash amounts were listed officially in the CSU list of confiscated items. . . .

"After our arrest, we were thrown into four cars and one van. One of our neighbors, a retired Air Force colonel and now a barangay official who owned the corner store in our neighborhood, helped the raiding team.

"Captain Braganza, with four assistants whom I can identify only by face, served as my guards. My son was allowed to ride in the same car with me. On the way [to Camp Crame], I tried to explain to my son who was arresting us and why we were arrested. . . .

"We were led straight to the 5th CSU office, adjacent to the gymnasium behind the grandstand. Upon arrival, I saw some students being interrogated while blindfolded. After a few seconds, I was blindfolded and my son forcibly taken away from me. While my son was crying, *"Papatayin nila ang tatay ko!"* [They are going to kill my father!], I was whisked off to the anteroom of the Commanding Officer's office for interrogation. Since June 1st, Colonel Ishmael Rodrigo (a veteran of the Vietnam war as project head of Frisco San Juan's Eastern Construction Company and later on attached to the Green Berets Intelligence Team with the rank of colonel) had replaced Colonel Miguel Aure, the infamous chief of the 5th CSU. (I suspect that he has been transferred or promoted elsewhere, since he still regularly visits Colonel Rodrigo's secretary, Edna Olazo.)

"Inside the room, I was bombarded with questions by some five men trying to extract information which would lead to the arrest of others. When I refused to cooperate with them, I received two fist blows in the chest. Another interrogator pressed his ballpen to my left thigh, my left arm and my chest.

"Interrogation like this was to go on for many days until I got out of CSU. In my first three days of detention, I had a total of only around 10 hours of rest and sleep. The rest of the time was spent on continued interrogation. . . .

"I proudly asserted I have been a national democratic activist, advocating the National Democratic Front's 10-point program and working under the direction and coordination of the NDF Preparatory Committee.

"I was detained at a time when the vigorous protests of the political prisoners and the broad national democratic movement outside prison had begun to bear fruit. Colonel Rodrigo and his staff tried very hard to pretend that the old 5th CSU with its infamous version of torture and maltreatment had been relatively soft on me. . . .

"[Colonel Rodrigo] was very excited over my arrest. He desperately wanted to erase the 5th CSU stigma exposed by hundreds of political detainees earlier. He wanted to extract tactical and strategic information through the psywar method. To him, hunting down suspected subversives and extracting information from them were some sort of sport. Like in *The Deer Hunter* starring Robert de Niro, he wanted to get suspected subversives with 'one shot.'

"His patience started running out after the third day. He told me, 'We want to use persuasion, but, of course, if this fails, we use the iron fist. . . . The right hand does not know what the left hand is doing. . . . The end justifies the means. . . . Our end is to make suspected subversives admit their crime and pinpoint their associates. . . . You see, good Communists are dead Communists. . . . You [should] never trust Muslims also. Only dead Muslims are good Muslims.'

"That same evening [June 16], torture sessions were intensified. Captain Robert Delfin, Master Sergeant Ricardo, Sergeant Rocky and several others participated in such sessions.

"The next day, when I protested against the torture. Colonel Rodrigo asserted that he was not aware of such torture. Besides, he was not around, if it did occur. He added, 'You see, it could have been worse. There are techniques perfected by our counterparts in the U.S. and Europe. It is worse in Russia and China . . .

"They had begun to use the old CSU method of beating up, stripping, strangulation and electric shock. The first target of this vicious attack were those whom the military thought had no influential relatives: Oscar Armea, a worker from Consolidated Can who hails from a poor peasant family in Lagunoy, Camarines Sur; Doris Manero, a household helper from a poor peasant family in the Visayas.

"Oscar was beaten up even in his first few hours of detention. After a few days, this was repeated. He was strangled twice. He was stripped naked. His pubic hair was burned and electric shock was administered on his genitals. Captain Robert Delfin, Major Saldajeno, a lawyer representing JAGO [Judge Advocate General's Office], C2 [intelligence] Office, and Master Sergeant Ricardo, who hails from Marikina, Rizal, led the torturers.

"Doris, on the other hand, was stripped naked and subjected to indignities. Captain Robert Delfin and Master Sergeant Ricardo led the torture of Doris Manero.

"Wilfredo Villamil was likewise tortured. He was beaten up, strangled by Captain Braganza, ordered to take off his shirt and to press his sweating back against the air-conditioner. Captain Delfin and Master Sergeant Ricardo led the torture and maltreatment of Villamil. . . .

"Except for one day with fellow detainees [the same day Edjop and Dante saw each other again], I was placed in solitary confinement at OIB [Office of the Interrogation Board] headed by Major Totoy Poblete. For six hours, I was placed in a bartolina-like cubicle with no ventilation. This was after I joined the protest of other detainees in the evening of the 16th. I was blindfolded, tied and handcuffed to a chain. Every 15 minutes, agent Rocky, after drinking liquor, would enter the cubicle and interrogate and threaten me with the water cure.

"The methods of questioning and interrogation were carefully calculated to put maximum mental torture on the detainees.

Most of the interrogations were conducted in the middle of the night.

"The interrogators would first prepare themselves by drinking a case of beer and several bottles of hard liquor. At about 10:30 p.m., they would start pulling detainees from their beds one by one for interrogation. The detainees would only be returned to their cells usually before sunrise.

"I myself underwent the so-called marathon interrogation. Colonel Ishmael Rodrigo himself interrogated me from 10 a.m. to five in the morning of the next day (20th of June). He only stopped when he himself could no longer keep his eyes open.

"Captain Braganza of NISA used another tactical interrogation trick. After asking questions which I refused to answer, he would dangle pictures of my wife and four-year-old son, implying, of course, that harm would come to them if I did not cooperate."

In a taped message to his son, Edjop would later talk of how he coped with torture:

"Alam mo, Nonoy, noong pinahirapan ako ng kaaway sa loob, sinuntok nila ako at ikinulong sa kuwartong madilim, 'tapos itinali, kinakanta ko lang ang mga awit natin para hindi nila ako matakot at hindi naman ako natakot sa kanila. Kaya nakakatulong din kung alam natin ang mga kanta ng masa. Nakakabigay sa atin ng tapang at lakas ng loob."

[You know what, Nonoy, while I was in prison and the enemy was giving me a hard time—they punched me and kept me in a dark room, then tied me up—I was singing our songs so the enemy couldn't scare me, and in fact they weren't able to scare me. So it really helps if we know the songs of the masses. They can give us courage and strength.]

Early in the morning the day after the arrest, Nonoy and his maid Pits were released. They were the ones who informed the Jopson family about what had happened. (The military would later apparently regret having let Pits go. They visited the Jopson residence several times to try and get her back. But the Jopsons had whisked her out of the house and into a safer place.)

On June 16, Hernan Jopson went to Camp Crame. But the military refused to let him see his son, according to the elder Jopson. Major Saldajeno said Ed was still under investigation: "Your son is facing a serious charge. But if he cooperates, we will make it easier on him."

Mr. Jopson returned the next day, with bags of clothes, medicine and food. Again, the military refused to let him see Edjop. He recognized Colonel Rodrigo, who was once a regular customer at their supermarket. "Your son is our big catch," the colonel said. "We've been after him since he left law school. Your son is very intelligent, he has charisma. He could lead the intellectuals."

Mr. Jopson again asked permission to see Ed, but was refused for the same reason Major Saldajeno had given: "Colonel Rodrigo said Ed was under interrogation." Mr. Jopson was about to leave when the colonel changed his mind. The elder Jopson was told to wait in an office. Soldiers then brought in Edjop, blindfolded and handcuffed. The blindfold and the handcuffs were removed, but Colonel Rodrigo and Major Saldajeno stayed in the room while father and son talked.

"I wish we could have met under better circumstances, Daddy," Ed said.

"Are they hurting you?" the father asked.

"Patapik-tapik," Ed answered. "A little bit. Do you have some money, Dad?"

"What do you need it for?"

"Panigarilyo. For cigarettes."

The father pulled out his wallet and gave his son five hundred pesos. Mr. Jopson recalls that either Saldajeno or Rodrigo suddenly told Edjop: "Go ahead and take it. That's your father's money."

"What did you mean by that?" the elder Jopson asked.

"They took thousands of pesos from me," Ed explained. And the two officers shot back, "But it's the Party's money anyway, right?"

Edjop and his father saw each other again two days later. When they embraced, Ed whispered, *"Daddy, pinapahirapan nila ako*. They are giving me a hard time. He won't let me sleep. Please ask Colonel Rodrigo to let me sleep."

Before Mr. Jopson left, Ed asked for some more cigarette money. "You mean," Mr. Jopson asked in surprise, "you spent 500 pesos on cigarettes in just a few days?"

"But I thought he had some plan," Mr. Jopson would later recall. "I gave him a thousand pesos."

Before leaving, Mr. Jopson confronted Colonel Rodrigo about what they were doing to his son. The colonel denied the allegations and said: "Time is running out. Your son has to cooperate."

During one visit, Edjop warned his father, "Daddy, if anybody from the military asks for money in exchange for my release, don't believe them."

"He said these people were professional killers," Mr. Jopson explains. "They let you go, then shoot you before you get far."

Edjop was considering all the possibilities in trying to get out. He got a chance to talk to a fellow prisoner with the codename Carlo one morning as they were brushing their teeth in one of the bathrooms of the RSU headquarters. After the usual exchange of amenities and information, Edjop looked to see if anybody was around, then whispered, "Listen, what would you say if I told you I could escape?"

Carlo asked how.

"The price on my head is P30,000. I've been talking to one of the officers. I offered to give him P60,000 if they let me go. He agreed." Edjop paused. "What do you think? Is it a principled thing for me to do?"

"It depends on what you plan to do."

"I'm worried that if I escape, the military might give you and the others a rougher time. *Baka kayo ang mapahamak.*"

"Don't worry about us," said Carlo. "Do what you think is best. We'll make it."

"I knew Edjop had a good chance of escaping since he was being held in a regular office, while the rest of us were in cells," Carlo recalls. "But I didn't know his plan."

Another time, Edjop talked to Tessie, another fellow detainee, in one of the interrogation rooms when their guards left them alone for a brief moment. "They want me to cooperate," Edjop whispered. "They want me to be their *ahente*. I'm thinking of playing along to get out of here."

"You decide," Tessie told him. *"Ikaw na ang dumiskarte."*

"It was standard procedure for the military to ask detainees to become informers," says Tessie. "A comrade can ride on that, so long as he or she does not betray any tactical information that could hurt other kasamas or the movement. Edjop knew this. I trusted him."

On June 24, ten days after the arrest, Tessie and the other detainees learned that Edjop was gone.

"The military said that he had escaped," Tessie relates. "But we weren't that sure. He could have been salvaged or taken to some safehouse. *Kinabahan kami.*"

That night, Mr. Jopson got a call from Colonel Rodrigo. As Mr. Jopson tells it, the colonel reported: *"Naku, Mr. Jopson, naisahan kami ng anak mo.* Your son escaped. He put one over on us."

The elder Jopson found the story hard to believe. "How can he escape when you have him cuffed and blindfolded in a room?"

Rodrigo asked Mr. Jopson to come to headquarters, and the worried father went immediately. He was shown the room where Ed had been detained, and he saw the handcuffs, still locked, and the pair of pants he had given Ed. "How could my son have escaped when the handcuffs are still locked?" the elder Jopson asked.

"That's what we are also wondering about," Rodrigo said. *"Naisahan niya kami."*

Mr. Jopson was then led to the bathroom beside the room. There was a pair of rubber slippers by the toilet bowl. Rodrigo told him that they belonged to Ed.

"I still don't believe he escaped," said the elder Jopson. "Maybe you made him go through too much torture. The last time we talked, my son said that you didn't let him sleep while you were subjecting him to continuous interrogation. Maybe you ended up killing him! And now, you are telling me that my son escaped?"

But Colonel Rodrigo, according to Hernan Jopson, stood by his story. He said the guard had fallen asleep, and that the officer in charge of Ed had been at a party the night Ed disappeared. Rodrigo said, "If he contacts you, tell your son to surrender to me. If another unit captures him, he will be killed. We have spread the word that we let him go. His comrades will think that he has turned informer, and will also kill him if they find him. So he must surrender to me."

The next day Beng, one of Edjop's younger sisters, received a mysterious call from someone pretending to be one of the Jopson Supermarket's regular Chinese suppliers. After hanging up, she excitedly rushed to her parents and said, "Ed is alive! It was his voice!"

Unknown to the Jopsons then, Edjop was still in military hands. Beside him as he made the call to his parents' house were intelligence operatives of the C2, led by Captain Rodolfo Aguinaldo.

31
Counterfeit Traitor

Edjop would later tell his comrades he had made a deal with Aguinaldo—he agreed to be a spy. But his task was more than simply to relay secret information to Aguinaldo's unit. He was supposed to push for changes in the movement's overall strategic line, which, Aguinaldo hoped, would lead to mistakes and, eventually, the defeat of the underground organization.

Mauro, Edjop's former deputy in the NDF Prepcom, explains: "By the late seventies, the military had succeeded in capturing major leaders of the movement. But the arrests did not stop the movement from growing bigger and stronger every year. The AFP probably realized that it would take more than the nabbing of top-ranking cadres to break the momentum of the revolutionary movement. The movement itself must be forced to commit major strategic blunders that would lead to its downfall."

Edjop, Aguinaldo thought, was the man for such a task. A former moderate, he was considered a dove among the hawks or hardliners of the movement. Among the documents captured in the Las Piñas raid were Edjop's notes on the debate in Nueva Ecija, and Aguinaldo had figured that Edjop was among those who opposed official Party policy.

Aguinaldo courted his prisoner, playing on what he believed to be Edjop's growing disillusionment with the movement. He also gave Edjop gifts and once bought him a jacket.

Edjop draws a picture of Aguinaldo in his "open letter to the Filipino people":

"His [Aguinaldo's] views are typical of an intelligence officer: 'Each man for himself.' He doesn't trust even his fellow officers. He loves to conspire and sow intrigue. He enjoys manipulating people and making people fight each other. He despises the national democratic principle of serving the people. He said that if one places a finger in a bowl of water, one creates some ripples; but once that finger is removed, the water soon settles down. By this, he implied that 'dying for the people may create some ripples, but soon these ripples will disappear and the water will settle down.'

"Since he doesn't trust his fellow officers, he hardly gives written reports; he changes his project colleagues often; he refuses to teach his fellows the tricks of the 'trade,' or share with them his knowledge of the [underground] movement. If he does, he says, he may soon become dispensable and subsequently be replaced. . . .

"Aguinaldo loves intrigues. He enjoys courting and seducing wives and sisters of political detainees. He relishes the ensuing misunderstanding between husband and wife and among siblings. In interrogation sessions, he loves to pry into the marital problems of detainees and activists, or the love [problems] of single female activists and detainees—all for the purpose of sowing intrigue in the movement.

"Aguinaldo usually offers an early release from detention to the wives of detainees, whom he uses as some sort of 'hostages.' If and when an ex-detainee decides to rejoin the movement, Aguinaldo would threaten to harm the wife and relatives of the ex-detainee."

Aguinaldo, other detainees say, is also familiar with Marxist-Leninist ideas. According to one prisoner, he tried to start political discussions with detainees whom he suspected were with Domingo's group in the 1979 debate.

"You know, your group took the correct line," Aguinaldo reportedly said. "Look at what happened in the Russian Revolution. Lenin and the Bolsheviks participated in the Duma and this led to their victory. *Kaya tama kayo.* You were correct. If I were you, I would regroup with the former members of the Manila-Rizal committee and dislodge Bilog. *Utak militar iyon.* He's a militarist." Bilog is supposed to be the alias of Rodolfo Salas, who was suspected of having replaced Joma Sison as CPP chairman.

Early in the morning of June 24, Aguinaldo's men had sneaked into the CSU headquarters. The guard must have been asleep, as Colonel Rodrigo said, or he could have been secretly involved in the operation. The men got Edjop out and led him to a car parked right outside the building. Aguinaldo himself was waiting in the car. Edjop was then taken to a military safehouse in San Francisco del Monte in Quezon City.

In the safehouse, Aguinaldo started training Edjop to be an informer. According to a cadre, he even gave Edjop the names of some of the military agents in the movement.

But Edjop had his own plan. The safehouse where he was kept was only a few blocks from his parents' house, and it was located in a neighborhood he was familiar with.

On June 30, Aguinaldo instructed Edjop to contact Joy. (According to a cadre, Aguinaldo planned to make Joy a hostage, in case Edjop reneged on their deal.) Aguinaldo sent two of his men to accompany the detainee.

Along the way, Edjop said he had to make a phone call to check if his wife was home. They stopped at a sarisari store with a telephone. Edjop went in to make the call, while his guards waited for him in the car on the other side of the road. A few minutes passed. When the guards checked on him, Edjop was gone.

The guards frantically drove around the area, looking for their detainee. But Edjop, who as a boy had played with the kids of that neighborhood, had succeeded in outmaneuvering them. He had found his way to the house of a labor leader whom he knew at PAFLU.

To delay any reaction from Aguinaldo, he called up the safehouse and reported, "I got separated from my guards. They seem to have gotten lost."

"Never mind," an unsuspecting operative replied. "Come on back."

Edjop sent word to his comrades about his escape. Arrangements were made for him to be taken out of Manila. The military had launched a city-wide manhunt for him, and his comrades had to move fast. Sometime in early July, Mauro and Edjop secretly left Manila and headed north toward Bataan province.

Asked if he ever suspected Edjop of having turned traitor, Mauro is quick to reply: "I never would have doubted him. Never."

Edjop later explained to Mr. Jopson that he had used the money he got from his father to bribe and gain the confidence of military personnel in the camp. He had used his prison experience to "learn from the enemy."

After his escape, Edjop came out with a stunning exposé on the military intelligence community and their operations. Aside from relating his prison ordeal and that of other detainees, his letter described the structure of the AFP intelligence organization and the kind of people who ran it.

"In my short detention," he wrote, "I was able to interview around 40 intelligence personnel and agents attached to the C2. Many of the janitors and C2C and C1C personnel come from humble backgrounds and were forced to enter the military service because it was the only source of livelihood open to them. Most of them have many legitimate gripes: low pay, misappropriation of funds intended for them, and brutal and inhuman treatment by many commissioned officers.

"On the other hand, many of the officers I met come from dubious backgrounds and engage in nefarious activities.

"One agent confessed that he was a killer for hire. For a five- to six-figure fee, he and his associates were willing to liquidate anybody. Another disclosed to me that they engaged in protection rackets. Another confessed that he was a former carabao rustler, and was recruited into the intelligence service from a provincial jail. Another agent was a mental patient in Ward 24 when he was recruited for the intelligence service by a *kababayan* [townmate]. Several agents offered to set me free or help me escape for a five- to six-figure fee. Their womanizing, gambling and drinking are flaunted right in the detention center. Another agent admitted that he engages in holdups and robberies. Most confessed that salvaging detainees is part of their tradecraft. Covering up these incidents goes along with the ethics of the trade."

Edjop drew profiles of top intelligence officers and notorious torturers in the military, complete with details on almost every aspect of their backgrounds, appearances and personalities.

"[Colonel Rodrigo], around 54 years old, was born and raised in San Juan, Rizal, although his parents allegedly come from Batac, Ilocos Norte, or 'Bethlehem,' as the military calls it. In his childhood, Colonel Rodrigo had Americans for neighbors. According to him, they helped him develop his facility for the American language and slang. . . .

"[He] is 5 feet 6 inches, has dark complexion, with eyes and nose similar to those of Pacifico Marcos. . . . He likes to carry and use bugging devices. Once he bugged his own agents to find out whether they were plotting against him. His wife, according to agents, is a plump, strong-willed woman who is an accountant by profession. She constantly checks on his womanizing. . . .

"During his stint in Vietnam, he met William Colby, head of the CIA [Central Intelligence Agency]. He took some time off to further his knowledge of U.S. intelligence 'tradecraft.' He took up courses in intelligence in the U.S. . . .

"Aguinaldo, 'Aggie' or 'Rudy,' hails from Laoag, Ilocos Norte. He related how he forged signatures, including that of his teachers and the school principal, as early as his high school days. Up to the present, he is proud of his golden-arm proficiency. He easily forges the signature of his colleagues, including Major Garcia's [Garcia was Aguinaldo's commanding officer at the time]. . . .

"[Aguinaldo] is about 5 feet 6 inches. His eyes, high cheekbones, and his face and muscular build make him look like basketball star Lim Em Beng. . . . He carries a 9-mm Belgian-made Browning pistol. He carries this pistol tucked in his waist, just to the right of his navel. When riding in his car, a Toyota 77–78 Corolla (brown or maroon), he places his gun under the bucket seat to his right. . . .

"He related with put-on sentimentality how the death of his driver [during an encounter with the NPA] pushed him to fight the movement all-out. . . .

"From then on, he narrated, he studied the movement seriously. He hung around UP for a long time, getting to know the active students and trying to recruit some of them as his informants and agents....

"He became infamous because of his brutal torture and psywar methods. A storm of protest from detainees isolated him from the general public.

"According to him, he got his big break sometime in late October 1977 [when Jose Maria Sison was captured]. He said he obtained information on the car and motorcycle used by Sison. After a month and a half of survey work, and a few days of actual surveillance, he was able to capture Sison and company. Up to now, he keeps Sison's Volks Beetle parked just outside [his office], as some sort of trophy....

"[Colonel Miguel Aure] is now retired from AFP service. His former agents openly accuse him of enriching himself in office by dipping into intelligence funds.... To justify his hidden wealth, he and his wife reportedly opened an orchid business [and] reportedly supply the big orchid outlets in Metro Manila...."

On safehouses, Edjop wrote: "Safehouses usually have their windows always shut tight. They are usually covered with high walls. One would usually detect [safehouses] through the traffic of motorcycles and cars, going in and out of the house at irregular hours. Burly men usually 5 feet 4 inches, armed with pistols tucked in their waists or in clutchbags, usually drive these vehicles."

Edjop ended his letter with an appeal to other political prisoners "to continue exposing and opposing military atrocities including the big shots in military intelligence."

"I call on the national democratic activists and all freedom-loving people to study the enemy well, especially its military apparatus working for U.S. imperialism and the landlord-comprador ruling class....

"I am writing this letter a few hours before my scheduled departure for a distant province. I have decided to continue working for national freedom and democracy among the poor peasants and workers in that area."

32
Samal

In Barrio San Roque in the town of Samal, Bataan, it was common knowledge that a newcomer who volunteered to work in the ricefields was either a guerrilla or an aktibista. That was why nobody really believed Aling Osang when, one afternoon in 1979, she introduced a young man who had come to help her plant in the fields as "a nephew of mine from Manila."

But it was no big deal for the other peasants. As far as they were concerned, Gusting, as Aling Osang's "nephew" was called, was a kasama. And if Aling Osang said he was her nephew, then that was what they would say to anyone who asked about Aling Osang's guest.

Aling Osang often had guests whom she introduced as a "nephew" or a "niece" or, if the guest was a little older, a "cousin." Everybody knew they were kasamas.

Sometimes several visitors would stay in Aling Osang's house at one time. "*Ay*, look, there is another fiesta in Aling Osang's house," her neighbors would say.

"We worry about you, about all the kasamas you take in," some of her friends often told her.

"*Aba'y* I'm not doing anything wrong," she would reply.

"What if you get arrested?"

"*Bahala na*. Only the Lord knows what will happen to me. Besides, those people whom I let stay in my house are good people."

Gusting, the residents of San Roque could see, was definitely not of the NPA. His skin was too smooth and his complexion too fair for him to be a member of the hukbo (or the "H," as the local activists would say). "*Ay, kaputi niya, e,*" says Aling Osang. "He would come home from the fields red like a tomato." He was also too clumsy to be a guerrilla—he stumbled a lot when he walked on the levees.

Gusting was not much of a farmer either. "He planted the

seedlings too close to each other," says Aling Osang, bursting into laughter.

But he showed a lot of spirit in the work, perhaps too much for someone not used to working the whole day under the blazing sun. Aling Osang would tell him not to strain himself, and he would reply that he would soon get the hang of it: "I'm still learning, that's why I'm a little slow." Not surprisingly, Gusting came down with the flu one evening after working in the fields. "Ay!" Aling Osang exclaimed. "Didn't I tell you not to work anymore? *Ay, kay tigas ng ulo!* You're so hard-headed!"

One day Gusting's wife arrived. She was called Gina, and it was said she had just given birth in Manila. The military were looking for her husband, and they had been harassing her as well. Aling Osang understood, and took her in as another "pamangkin."

Aling Osang cooked for the young couple, but it was Gusting and Gina who set the table and washed the dishes. The couple never complained about the food. "They ate whatever we had on the table," says Aling Osang. Once she offered Gusting a spoon and a fork. Gusting turned down her offer and ate with his fingers.

Sometimes Gina would set out for Manila and come back with bags of groceries for the household. Aling Osang noticed the name on the bags: "Jopson's."

On some days, Gusting simply stayed home and read. "He had dozens of books of all kinds. He just pored over them the whole afternoon. I never thought of bothering him."

But other times he went out to chat with the villagers. He grew especially fond of talking with a group of teen-agers, aktibistas of the local chapter of the revolutionary youth organization. News of kasamas in the barrio always got these boys excited. Gusting was not of the "H" and had no stories of spectacular gunbattles with the kaaway to tell. But he was a good talker; the youngsters enjoyed his company. *"Nakakaengganyo,"* says Luis, who was 15 when he met Gusting. "He was very friendly and soft-spoken."

Gusting sometimes helped the kids with their schoolwork. But most of the time they just got together and had discussions on all sorts of issues—politics, life in the barrio, the rebolusyon. One particular conversation remains fresh in Luis's mind.

"Sometimes our parents worry about our involvement in the kilusan," the young activists told Gusting. " 'What will become of you?' they ask."

"Yes, I know what you mean," Gusting said. "I went through the same thing with my parents. They expected a lot from me. But I saw that I was needed and could be of greater service in the movement."

Gusting gave some words of advice: "You will have to make the same decision, and then try to explain that to your parents. Naturally, they will try to discourage you, because they are worried about what will happen to you. You will have to show them that you know what you are getting into, that you are strong enough for it. Eventually, they will recognize, and even respect, your decision.

"Always stand by what you see is right. Never let anything or anyone prevent you from taking a stand. If you realize that you have been wrong, never hesitate to change position. *Hawakan ninyo parati ang tama.* Always stand for what is right."

Sometimes, other kasamas fetched Gusting for a meeting at a nearby guerrilla camp. He mingled with the "Red fighters," chatting with them on various topics. He was willing to talk, even late into the night. "He did not have airs. *Hindi suplado,*" Delio, who served in the security force, says of Gusting. "He was easy to approach and talk to."

Gusting explained complex issues such as the economic crisis or the national situation—*"detalyado at malinaw,"* says Luis: detailed and clear—and gave advice on the handling of personal relationships within the kilusan.

Once a guerrilla asked permission to visit his wife and children in another barrio. *"Ayos lang,"* Gusting said. "I'll go with you. We can stay there for two days."

While walking on the levees one day, Gusting challenged Delio: "Whoever slips or falls, gets a pinch in the ears." Delio agreed to play the game. After a few minutes of walking, Gusting stumbled into the muddy water.

"Well, Ka Gusting?"

"A deal is a deal, kasama," Gusting gamely replied. Delio helped him up by pulling on his ears. Their laughter echoed across the ricefield.

Another afternoon, while Gusting was at a meeting with kasamas in Barrio San Juan, there was an explosion from one of the nearby houses. Guerrillas immediately took battle positions. Some got Gusting and the cadres out of the area.

After a few hours, when no sign of enemy presence was reported, Gusting and the other kasamas returned. They learned that a guerrilla, who had gone into a house to cook rice, accidentally unclipped a grenade as he was taking off his gear. He and another guerrilla were killed.

Gusting helped bury the comrades. Delio noticed how he didn't laugh or tell jokes several days after the incident.

In those days, there was a notorious military officer in Samal named Lieutenant Areston Corporal. Delio was one of his victims. He had beaten up Delio, burned his lips and face with cigarettes, and pushed his face repeatedly into a pile of carabao dung. The people started to whisper among themselves, "When Corporal dies, we will prepare lechon."

In July 1979, NPA partisans ambushed and killed Corporal. The lieutenant's men went amok. Several nights later, Aling Osang, Gusting, and Gina heard the staccato of automatic fire, long and uninterrupted. "That's not ours," Gusting said. "The kasamas don't fire that way." NPA guerrillas fired short bursts followed by single pops, to conserve on ammunition.

Aling Osang and the couple stayed on the alert the whole night. The next morning, they learned that seven youths walking down a barrio road had been sprayed dead by armed men in a white Fiera.

The kasamas decided it was no longer safe for Gusting to remain in Samal.

"We have to leave, Inang," Gusting told Aling Osang one day. "We'll go tonight. Thank you for everything."

"Yes, I understand, *anak*. God be with you."

Aling Osang never saw Gusting again. Sometimes she asked the kasamas where he had been sent. "Somewhere in the south," she was told. Three years later, a neighbor pointed out a picture on the front page of a newspaper. *"Si Gusting!"* she exclaimed upon seeing the face of Edgar Jopson, who had been killed in Mindanao.

It was only then that she knew who Gusting really was. "To think that he actually set my table and washed my dishes," says the old woman. Of all her "nephews" and "nieces," Aling Osang adds, "Gusting was closest to my heart." On one of her visits to Manila, she made it a point to pass by Jopson's Supermarket in Sampaloc.

Edjop, as Ka Gusting, had seen the fruits of the rebolusyon while he "rested" for two months in Samal, Bataan. This town of around 4,000 people, mostly peasants, was then already a major base of the revolutionary movement.

Samal had a long history of militance and revolution. In the 1930s, Filipino revolucionarios in Samal fought for independence against American colonial forces. In the Second World War, the town was the scene of fierce resistance from Filipino anti-Japanese guerrillas. In the fifties, Samal became one of the base areas of the Hukbong Mapagpalaya ng Bayan (HMB) or Huks, the military arm of the old Partido Komunista ng Pilipinas.

Through the years, different homegrown and external forces, presenting themselves as friends, tried to win the allegiance and support, the hearts and minds, of the people of Samal. But it was the people themselves who made distinctions, who defined the nature of the diverse movements, parties, and regiments that appeared in the barrio. They might not fully understand or accept the programs and ideologies of the contending forces; but from the way these groups behaved and treated them, they were able to tell who their friends and enemies were.

The NPA in Bataan was organized in Samal in October 1972. Like the Filipino resistance fighters during the American and Japanese occupation periods, the NPAs took on the role of kasamas, comrades—the "protectors of the people." On the other hand, the AFP, like the Americans and Japanese invaders, were perceived as the kaaway, the enemy. It was in Samal that the term "Hapon" was first used by the civilians—and later by the rebels—to refer to government soldiers.

By the time of Edjop's stay, cadres in Samal had reduced the rent that peasants paid to the landlords from 30 cavans of rice per season to 10. They had led the local residents in a successful campaign against the pollution caused by the Bataan Pulp and Paper Mills, and had begun to implement a "revolutionary agrarian reform" program. The town also had the strongest, most consolidated underground mass organizations in the province.

The kasamas couldn't have picked a safer place to hide a leading cadre. But by late 1979 Edjop was preparing to take on a new assignment. He was now one of the most wanted men in the country, with a P180,00 price on his head.

In August, guerrillas escorted him to Pampanga for a top-level party meeting. The meeting was held in a sugarcane field where a camp had been set up. There, Edjop met again with Ariel, Raul, and other former members of the Manila-Rizal Committee.

"We embraced and shook hands like long-lost brothers," recalls Ariel. "We had already forgotten all the bickerings and our personal differences. We stayed up the whole night, as Edjop shared his experiences in prison."

Edjop also met Nick, one of the top party leaders in Mindanao. By the late seventies, the movement in Mindanao, which had been under one island-wide party committee, had grown too big for only one body to lead. In the meeting, the national leadership decided to divide the Mindanao organization into four sub-regions. The Mindanao Commission was created to act as coordinator of the four new regional committees.

Nick explained that the Mindanao movement suffered from a dearth of cadres who could serve in the leading bodies and help in the reorganization. It was then, according to Nick, that Gusting expressed a desire to "engage in comprehensive revolutionary work" and volunteered for Mindanao.

The other kasamas in the national leadership appointed Gusting to the newly formed Mindanao Commission. Later, Nick asked other comrades about Gusting. From the stories he heard about Gusting's record as a student leader and a leading cadre of the Manila-Rizal region, Nick concluded, "Yes, he will be of great help to Mindanao."

33
Stranger on the Island

Edjop, now called Gimo, left for Mindanao in November 1979. Leon, who had also been appointed to the Mindanao Commission, came to Manila in order to accompany him on the trip to the island.

Gimo and Leon shared a private cabin during the overnight trip to Cebu. But on the ship from Cebu to Cagayan de Oro City, there were no passenger cabins, and the cadres had to travel economy class, bunched up with hundreds of other passengers—including military men. Both of them risked being spotted, especially Leon, then one of the most wanted men in Mindanao.

Leon had a .45-caliber pistol ready for their defense. Edjop had brought along an old dilapidated .22-caliber pistol; it didn't look like it could still fire. When he saw Edjop's gun, Leon smiled and said, "Ka Gimo, I think you better just put that away. It is bound to get us into more trouble."

The two men arrived safely in Cagayan de Oro, where they were met by other comrades. They stayed in the city for a few days before proceeding to Davao, where the Mindanao Commission was based.

Edjop was a stranger to Mindanao. He had visited the island only several times in the past, during sorties as NUSP president. As a member of the Mindanao Commission, he had a new language to learn, a new culture and a new history to study. There was also another armed revolutionary force, with a different aim in mind for Mindanao, for Edjop to understand and deal with.

In the early seventies, the revolutionary movement in Mindanao was a negligible force. The NPA then was a ragtag band, still in the process of learning the fine points of guerrilla warfare.

In 1974 more than 20 cadres from Manila had been sent to

255

Mindanao to boost the underground organization there. By the time Edjop was deployed on the island, most of those cadres, including the renowned poet and Edjop's friend, Emmanuel Lacaba, had been killed in encounters. Given the inexperience of the movement, and in the face of superior government forces, NPA units were time and again wiped out in one-sided encounters. Some barrios where cadres had gained a foothold in organizing work often had to be abandoned, due to intense military operations. By 1975, only four NPA squads were left on the entire island.

In 1979, the year Edjop arrived in Mindanao, the picture was drastically different. By then the NPA had established five guerrilla fronts on the island—the Zamboanga peninsula; Davao Oriental; Davao del Norte; the Davao del Sur-Davao City boundary; and the Misamis Oriental-Agusan boundary. The standard formation of the guerrilla army had grown, from squads, to undersized platoons; more underground mass organizations had been formed in barrios and towns in almost every province.

The party organization, for its part, was subdivided into four regions—South, East, West, and North Central—with one leading committee for each region. The Mindanao Commission was formed in September 1979, as the administrative arm of the CPP Central Committee on the island. After the eighth Central Committee plenum in 1980, the commission was given policy-making powers, making it the highest body of the movement in Mindanao.

Edjop's first assignment was to conduct a preliminary social investigation (PSI) of the conditions in Mindanao. For three months he traveled from province to province, gathering data on different aspects of the life on the island.

Leon would later recall how, on their voyage to Mindanao, Edjop had "asked a lot of detailed questions, a practice which, I later learned, was his way of getting a grasp of a new territory, and a new field of work."

Fresh with idealism and zeal, Edjop took to Mindanao like a young recruit to the rebolusyon. Fidel, also a member of the Mindanao Commission, describes him then as amusingly naive, "like an innocent boy with a lot of questions, eager to learn." At one meeting in a guerrilla camp, Fidel pointed out a tall tree to Edjop and had told him it was a "giant santol tree." It was actually just a lawaan, a common tree in Mindanao. But Edjop believed Fidel and started telling other people about the "giant" tree.

Leon and Fidel accompanied Edjop to plenums and conferences of different regional and front committees. Of the members of the Commission, Edjop was the least known to the other leading cadres on the island. But in the meetings he attended, he stood out as the little man with a deep full voice, who asked an infinite number of questions. He probed into minute details about a particular region, province, or town—its general political and economic profile; the state of the revolutionary movement there; the climate, terrain, and social customs of the people.

These may have been some of the questions he asked, on a particular province:

What crops do the peasants grow? How much do they earn in a season? How much rent do they pay to the landlord? What religious festivals do the people celebrate? How many children do the peasants usually have? What schools do they usually send them to?

Who are the big politicians? Who are the top military commanders? How many AFP troops are deployed in the territory? How many barrios are influenced by the revolutionary movement? What level of organization has been reached? How many tactical offensives were launched in the past year? How many rifles were captured from enemy troops?

How heavily forested are mountain areas? How many rivers, creeks, and rain forests can be found? Is there a possibility of setting up another guerrilla front?

At meetings, no sooner had cadres thought that all questions had been answered than Edjop popped another point to ponder. Some were annoyed by the seemingly endless stream of queries, complaining, "This comrade asks too many questions."

Edjop was based in an underground house in Davao, together

with Fidel and Leon. In their first months together, he worked day and night, poring over piles of books and documents, writing and editing his report. Time and again, even during meals or while doing household chores, he consulted Leon and Fidel. On a visit to their underground house, Buddy, an NPA cadre in Southern Mindanao, was awed to see the stacks of books and documents around Edjop's desk.

Edjop availed himself of various materials in writing the PSI. Aside from consultations with Mindanao cadres, he made use of government reports on the economic conditions on the island, including publications of institutions such as the National Census and Statistics Office and the National Economic Development Authority.

The result was one of Edjop's major contributions to the movement in Mindanao. The cadre who only a few months before had been a virtual stranger to Mindanao, had prepared the most comprehensive study on life on the island ever written for the revolutionary movement.

The PSI document is more than 200 pages long. The first part discusses Mindanao geography and topography. It describes the terrain in the different parts of the island, specifying the number of creeks, rivers, and mountain ranges, where tactical centers and guerrilla bases have been, or could be established. It talks about the peoples of Mindanao, their origins, customs, traditions, and histories, and the general flow of the population on the island.

The second part is on the Mindanao economy, and deals with the state of industry and agriculture on the island. It lists the big corporations in Mindanao, both local and foreign; the people who control them; the profits these establishments earn a year; and the wages and the general working conditions of their employees.

The third part describes the political setup on the island—the warlords and kingpins of different regions; the extent of their influence and power; their respective political records; their enemies and allies. The document also talks about the AFP organization on the island, the names and records of the regional and provincial commanders, the number and formations of troops deployed, the type of operations they undertake, and the origins of different paramilitary groups.

In fact, there is nothing spectacular about the Mindanao PSI. Cadres admit that it contains no new or earthshaking ideas on political analysis and strategy. But it was painstakingly researched, and systematic in its presentation of data. Some leading cadres thought it was so detailed that comrades tended to miss the essential points of the investigation. But to others, the PSI provided a broad overview of Mindanao, which helped define the orientation of various organs of the movement on the island. Though the document was a preliminary study, it is said to have contributed a great deal to the development of the Mindanao movement in the eighties.

The military once got hold of a copy of the Mindanao PSI during a raid on an underground house. A cadre arrested in the operation relates how the interrogating officer grilled him on who wrote the document. The officer had commented, "Whoever prepared this document is indeed brilliant."

Since the 1979 debate, Edjop had put much value on theoretical studies. In Mindanao, he is credited with having helped raise the level of theoretical and ideological preparedness of the underground organization on the island.

The CPP Central Committee had launched a theoretical education campaign in 1979 for cadres in different parts of the country. Party members and recruits throughout the archipelago were required to undergo a 10-day Basic Party Course (BKP) which covered topics from Marxist-Leninist theory to the history of revolutionary movements in the Philippines.

Edjop helped translate the newly-issued BKP manual into Visayan, and was one of the instructors in the very first BKP session held in Mindanao. Hundreds of books, mostly on Marxism-Leninism and on the history and experiences of other revolutionary movements in other countries, were reproduced and distributed among cadres. The technical staff of the Mindanao

Commission, which was directly under Edjop's supervision, was often busy translating and reproducing the countless articles, minutes, primers, and orientation papers that came out in this period. Edjop requested friends and allies who were going abroad to send books and other reading materials which could be of use in ED sessions.

"At major meetings," Fidel relates, "while Leon and I had with us just a small bag and a notebook each, Edjop brought along volumes of books and documents. Whenever we moved to another house, he always had cartons of materials. In the house he read, wrote, and engaged us in discussions."

In fact, Edjop was responsible for the sudden popularity of the writing of drafts and documents as part of the day-to-day work system in the underground. Fidel, who had been a leading Mindanao cadre since the early seventies, admits that the Mindanao PSI made cadres see the importance of paperwork in waging revolution: "The Mindanao organization then was growing. There was a need for a more systematic, and formal, way of communication. I realized that I had to force myself to write."

The Mindanao organization had a great deal of experience in revolutionary struggle which, once processed and put down on paper, could be of great use to the movement as a whole. Edjop was well aware of this, and he did not waste time trying to break his comrades' chronic aversion to the written word.

He "bullied" Leon into summing up the movement's military experiences in Mindanao. "I really found it difficult to write. I didn't think I could do it. Sometimes I was just lazy. But Edjop kept on pressing me to do it. When I felt like giving up, he was always there to tell me, '*Kaya mo iyan.* You can do it.' He never let up on me, until I actually sat down and did my work." In 1987, the NPA General Command came out with two volumes of guerrilla warfare manuals which were partly based on the writings of Leon.

Edjop religiously took down notes at meetings even if a scribe had been assigned for the task. In fact, even in informal or friendly chats with a comrade, a leading cadre or an ordinary peasant, he would continually scribble on yellow pad paper or in a small notebook he always carried with him.

He asked comrades with a new project or policy in mind to present drafts of their proposals. After every meeting, he prepared minutes, which he had reproduced and distributed among kasamas. Soon, different collectives, and even individual cadres, were coming out with documents of all sorts—primers on trade union work, regional situationers, youth and student orientation papers.

In this kind of work Edjop was by far the most prolific—and the most creative. In his consultations on the labor situation with a worker-cadre named Berting, he took down pages and pages of notes and, by their next meeting, had prepared a primer on trade union work. Manding, one of the leading Mindanao cadres of the time, talks about the significance of this document: "Workers could not appreciate the heavy language of classical Marxist literature, so they were often discouraged from taking up higher theoretical studies. The trade union orientation paper, which Edjop prepared, was comprehensive enough to cover all vital aspects of labor organizing, but simple enough for even an ordinary factory worker to comprehend. It was also very handy, published in booklet form, small enough for organizers and union members to bring along in their pockets—and to hide in case of security problems."

Edjop wrote most of the documents in colloquial Tagalog. Some cadres found his writing style crude and badly in need of editing. Mindanao cadre Lucas Fernandez, for instance, notes Edjop's frequent use of the word "siyempre" in stressing a point, as in "*Siyempre, kailangang patibayin ang pagkakaisa ng mga unyon, para sumulong ang kilusang paggawa.*"

But Edjop was less interested in being revered as a master stylist than in arming his comrades with a framework for getting the work done. He "revolutionized" the conduct of underground meetings in Mindanao. Lucas Fernandez, who came to Mindanao in the late seventies, describes the meetings before Edjop's arrival: "The gatherings were usually very informal.

Comrades, even those in the leading committees, lolled in their seats and cracked jokes. *Pakengkoy-kengkoy.* It was more like a *barkadahan,* a gang meeting, than an underground meeting. There were rarely any prepared documents and very few took down notes."

Edjop changed all that. He always had a prepared agenda when he arrived for a meeting. As he laid down the topics to be tackled, he was serious, though never grim, his voice steady and with authority. Before opening the discussion, he asked if his comrades had questions or comments. Each item was then exhaustively discussed, with Edjop posing question after question to his kasamas.

"Edjop was actually a facilitator," recalls Bruce, another Mindanao cadre. "He did not come to a meeting with a ready-made set of ideas and proposals. Sometimes, those of us at the meeting knew that Edjop already had his own ideas. But he did not pre-empt our views on the matter by presenting his own ideas at once. Nor was he patronizing in the way he asked questions. He was sincerely interested in a kasama's point of view.

"By the time we were finished with the meeting, each comrade in the collective had internalized almost every aspect of the matter at hand. Edjop's own views about the issue had been enriched by the discussion, and by the ideas of other comrades. What came out, in the end, was an idea, not just of Edjop's, but of the entire collective.

"During the discussions, Edjop would always be smiling. He never showed any sign of being troubled or irritated by the views of other people, or the length of the discussion. We talked about and planned so many things in those days, yet we never felt burdened."

Conferences on various concerns and lines of work were called. In May 1980 a meeting of key urban cadres, codenamed "Mayflower," was held in Davao del Sur. The White Area Conference was held a few months later. There were conventions to discuss conditions in the different sectors; to assess and formulate policies on NPA operations; to sum up experiences in alliance work with the Moro forces.

In this period of reorganization, plenums were convened and leading committees formed at the regional and provincial levels throughout Mindanao. In September 1982, two weeks before he was killed, Edjop presided over the first Mindanao-wide Cadre Conference in Davao del Norte, which capped more than two years of organizational streamlining and consolidation. Leading cadres from different regions and different lines of work assessed the state of the Mindanao organization and drew up plans and projections for the coming years.

"Never before had so many underground conferences been held in Mindanao," says Mark, a cadre from Southern Mindanao. "Of course, Edjop was not responsible for all of these. But he was definitely instrumental in regenerating the organization in this period."

Heated debates were as common in the Mindanao underground as they had been in Manila. There were disagreements on the tactics to use in guerrilla warfare; the handling of middle-class allies; and the dominant mode of production in Mindanao. Some discussions lasted days and months; some, years. Others have never really been resolved.

In these verbal tussles Edjop, as he had been when he was still in Manila, was the cadre in the middle, always trying to synthesize contending points. Having had more experience by then in underground polemical brawls, rarely was he caught flat-footed while trying to mediate. When Edjop entered a debate, according to Horace, one of the cadres involved in the discussions, it was "always well-calculated and well-timed." Edjop picked his words carefully and never raised his voice. Comrades always welcomed his views.

This perhaps is the reason why Abel and a few comrades, in one informal chit-chat about the Party leaders of Mindanao, concluded that "if the rebolusyon was a road, Edjop went through a very smooth path."

"We saw how well he related with other kasamas," explains Abel. "We could have been wrong, of course. But as far as we knew about him then, he was one kasama who never got into a misunderstanding or a bitter dispute with another comrade.

Everything seemed right with him, compared with the others in the leadership, most of whom had very strong, overwhelming personalities. But Edjop was a very gentle person. *Wala siyang nakabangga.*"

The conclusion is not entirely accurate. Edjop also walked the rugged trail. But he knew how hostile and impassioned debates could wreck the camaraderie in the movement, and this may have been the reason for his consistent conciliatory posture in intra-party disputes. Edjop never forgot the lessons of the 1979 Manila-Rizal struggle.

Also from his stint in the Manila-Rizal region, Edjop brought with him to Mindanao the concept of an underground workers' organization with a national democratic orientation. He and Domingo had pushed for the implementation of this project in Manila, but were overruled by comrades who believed that, in the Communist Party, the workers already had a revolutionary organization. In 1981, the *Katipunan ng Rebolusyonaryong Manggagawa* (Association of Revolutionary Workers or KRM) was formed in Mindanao.

"It was Edjop who spearheaded the formation of this organization, although he consulted union leaders and organizers about it," says Manding, a trade union cadre. "The KRM was one of Ka Gimo's major contributions to the workers' movement in Mindanao."

34
A Plenum

In July 1980 Edjop, Leon, and Fidel left for Luzon to attend the eighth plenum of the CPP Central Committee. The meeting of about 200 leading party cadres was held in a guerrilla zone, along the Quezon-Bicol border. A camp was set up in a forested area where cadres built a pavilion-like structure, made of rough tree branches, trunks, and anahaw leaves. This served as the session hall.

As a security precaution, the huts for the delegates were built far apart. Ten cadres stayed in each hut, where they were grouped in three squads: Abe, Bakking, Kaloy (Filipinized version of Able, Baker, Charlie). The squads remained in battle formation even during sleeping hours. Each delegate slept in a stretcher made of rice sacks and tree branches, which were suspended on the beams of each hut.

It was about a 30-minute hike to the nearest house of a barrio resident, and about two hours to the next barrio. The meeting, which lasted three months, received support from surrounding barrios. Five cows were slaughtered, and supplies from the lowlands constantly arrived. Barrio folk contributed gabi, nangka, eggplant, and other vegetables to the plenum. The cadres bought rice from the town. Sometimes, there were special deliveries—canned goods and medical supplies—from allies in Manila.

Some peasants were surprised at the enormous amount of cigarettes the cadres bought. The preferred brands of some cadres—Marlboro and Philip Morris—also drew sharp criticism from the masa. "Why do you have such luxurious tastes?" the peasants sneered. Other cadres, such as Edjop, settled for rough-tasting but cheaper brands like Peak, Champion, or Union. In Mindanao, guerrillas smoked a brand of native tobacco called Tres-B. Its taste was so atrocious even Edjop could not take it. "If it comes to a point where I would have to settle for Tres-B, I'd rather quit smoking altogether," he said.

High spirits prevailed in camp. The conference was called to assess the revolutionary struggle in the past ten years, and the cadre-delegates had a lot to be optimistic about. After eight years of martial law, the movement had not only survived the regime's most vicious onslaughts, but it had advanced to a notable level of strength and influence. Guerrilla fronts had been set up in almost every province in the country. The NPA had become a regular guerrilla fighting force, capable of regularly launching bold offensives against AFP units. There was a mass-based underground network in almost every region.

As Mauro, who worked with Edjop in the NDF Prepcom, puts it, "The trench-building stage was over. In 1980, we were already planning the endgame. The foundation of the revolutionary movement had already been laid down. It was time for the big advance."

The cadres were still holding the conference on September 21, 1980, the eighth anniversary of the declaration of martial law. They decided to observe the historic event. The plenum was adjourned for one day so that representatives of each region could prepare a cultural number. Edjop, Leon, and Fidel formed themselves into a "combo" and, using improvised instruments, performed revolutionary songs in Cebuano.

Lorenzo, a cadre from Quezon province, noticed the distinct camaraderie of the Mindanao group: "They were obviously very close friends, a barkada. During discussions they consulted with one another, but this did not prevent each one of them from taking a different position in a debate. It seemed natural for them to disagree, without it affecting their personal relationships. This was unusual."

Edjop and company also performed a playlet loosely based on Mao Zedong's essay, "The Foolish Old Man who Removed the Mountain." A favorite of KM activists during the First Quarter Storm, the playlet tells the story of an old man who wants to tear down a mountain so he can build a house and a farm on the spot where the mountain stands. Another old man chides him for having such an absurd objective: "You fool. Before you can tear this mountain down, you will die and be buried beneath it." The foolish old man replies, "I know that, my friend. But after I die, my son will continue the task; and, after him, his son, and the sons of his sons, will carry on the work. For every lump of soil we dig up, the mountain becomes less formidable. Eventually, it will be torn down." Other players, representing the worker, peasant, youth, and other sectors, come to the aid of the old man, and they all bring down the imaginary mountain.

To cap the program, Edjop was asked to deliver a speech before an audience consisting of delegates to the plenum and peasants from nearby barrios who had joined in the festivities. It had been eight years since he last spoke before a mass demonstration at Plaza Miranda or at Mendiola Bridge, but his skills as a public speaker had not been diminished. He maintained the stance learned as a college orator at the Ateneo, one foot forward as he spoke; but this time he was speaking as a *rebolusyonaryo*, clenching a fist to emphasize a point, and speaking in fluent Tagalog, no longer getting tongue-tied in the language.

Before peasants and cadres, Edjop made his last public speech:

"Walong taon na ang batas militar. Walong taong naghasik ng Puting lagim ang estado laban sa mamamayan, sa Partido at Hukbo. Walong taon ding ipinakita ng mamamayan na sila'y handang tumindig at lumaban . . ." [It has been eight years since the declaration of martial law. In those eight years, the state sowed White terror against the people, the party and the people's army. But the people have also shown that they are ready to stand up and fight . . .]

His talk, which lasted almost half an hour, reviewed the history and achievements of the revolutionary movement under martial law. He cited victories and defeats. He said the movement was about to enter the "advanced sub-stage of the strategic defensive," when it would "launch bigger and stronger blows against the dictatorship, and bring the conflict closer to a stalemate." He called on his comrades to prepare for such a leap, emphasizing the need to consolidate the revolutionary forces.

The masa, he said, were "the key to the movement's survival and growth":

"Ang masa ang nagtanggol sa atin sa mga pinakamahihirap na taon

pagkapataw ng batas militar." [The people helped us survive the most difficult years of martial law.]

The eighth anniversary of the declaration of martial law, Edjop affirmed, had as much significance for the revolutionary movement as it had for the dictatorship:

"Sa araw na ito, ipinagdiriwang ni Makoy ang batas militar sa Malacañang. Siguro meron pa silang kuntodo alak at bangkete. Naroon siyempre ang kinatawan ng Estados Unidos. Naroon ang telegrama ng presidente ng Estados Unidos sa pagdadaos ng anibersaryo ng batas militar. Nagpupupugay sa kanya ang mga panginoong maylupa at komprador burgesya na malaki ang pakinabang sa batas militar.

"Tayo rin ay nagdiriwang. Ipinagdiriwang natin ang mga nakamit na tagumpay ng rebolusyonaryong kilusan' nitong huling walong taon. Pinaghahandaan natin ang mas mabilis nating pag-abot sa mas mataas na yugto, nang may kumpiyansa't determinasyon."

[On this day, Marcos and his cohorts are celebrating in Malacañang. They are probably having a banquet, with a lot of wine and food. Of course, the representative of the United States will be there. Marcos will probably receive a telegram of greetings from the U.S. president. The landlords and compradors, who benefited the most from martial law, will hail and praise him.

[We are also holding a celebration. We are celebrating the victories and gains of the revolutionary movement in the past eight years. And we are also preparing, with confidence and determination, for the next higher stage of the struggle.]

Edjop ended his speech on a light note. *"Hanggang dito na lang siguro, mga kasama. Medyo nauubusan na ako.* I think I've run out of things to say, comrades," he said, with a smile, to the applause and cheers of his comrades.

"Edjop had been involved, one way or another, in the events and developments that he recounted," says Lorenzo.

Other delegates shared this view. At the end of the conference, they overwhelmingly elected Edjop to the Central Committee's Political Bureau (Politburo), the second highest organ in the CPP hierarchy.

The plenum ended in late October; the cadres went their separate ways. A number of them, like Fidel, headed for other provinces to visit friends and relatives. Others went back to their respective cities and towns by bus. Some walked to other guerrilla fronts, while a few headed for Manila, from where they traveled, by ship or plane, back to their provinces.

Edjop and Leon were both wanted men. To avoid military agents posted at airports and harbors (and also to save on money), they returned to Mindanao—by motorcycle.

It was an amazing feat in human courage and endurance. More than 700 kilometers separated the Bicol region from Davao City. It was also the middle of the wet season, in one of the most typhoon-vulnerable regions in the archipelago. The journey took three days. Edjop and Leon traveled with another comrade called Delfin. All three wore identical raincoats, which allies in Naga City had given them. They rode for more than 15 hours a day, stopping for lunch and snacks at turo-turo restaurants. They carried backpacks filled with dirty clothes and packages containing underground documents. They were unarmed.

The trip was even more remarkable in Edjop's case. When the group set off from Naga City, he did not know how to ride a motorcycle. He had to learn along the way.

It didn't take long for Edjop to learn to ride a motorcycle. But the long hours of riding also took its toll on him. They were still in Sorsogon, in the Bicol region, when he lost control of the motorcycle during a sharp turn. The bike skidded on the rocks and crashed to the side of the road. Edjop suffered cuts and bruises on the face and arms.

"He had a nasty fall," recalls Leon. "But he was all right. Later, I even kidded him about being too ambitious for a beginner. 'You shouldn't perform stunts like that. See how you ended up kissing the road.' He just laughed."

From a town on the southern tip of Sorsogon, the motorcyclists took a ferry to Samar Island. There was a military checkpoint at the ferry port. While crossing the San Bernardino Strait, the Coast Guard also made a random inspection of the boat.

The three cadres became suspicious. In the past, the military never put up checkpoints in the middle of the sea. It was only about a month later that Edjop and his comrades found out that the military had been tipped off about the plenum in Bicol. Knowing that it was a national gathering of CPP leaders, the AFP had set up checkpoints with the hope of catching cadres on their way back to the Visayas and Mindanao.

Upon landing in Samar, Edjop, Leon, and Delfin rode southward to Leyte. They spent a night in the house of a comrade in Tacloban City.

On the ferry ride from Leyte to Surigao City, they reached the critical point of their journey. NISA agents boarded the ferryboat just before it docked at Surigao City. The inspection was stricter than at any of the previous checkpoints. Books were checked, page by page. Leon's harmonica case was carefully scrutinized.

The agents became suspicious of the dirty laundry which Delfin had in his bag. They demanded that a package, which contained underground documents, be opened. Delfin did a poor job of trying to talk his way out of the crisis. Leon decided to take charge of the situation. "If you insist on opening the package, then we must do it in the mayor's office, in front of a government official," Leon asserted. "We were given strict instructions that these packages should not be opened until they reach their destination."

The gamble paid off. The agents were probably not inclined to go through the tedious process proposed by Leon. They let the three go, without bothering with the packages.

It was more than what Leon himself had hoped for. His original plan would have led to another dangerous adventure for the three of them. "If that agent had called my bluff and agreed to take us to the mayor's office, we would have gotten a little time to plan our moves," Leon says. "Once we reached shore, we could grab their guns and fight our way free. We could then head for the mountains and probably make contact with other comrades."

Edjop, he adds, remained cool, as he always did in tight situations.

The three spent the night in Surigao. The next day they set off for Davao City.

35
Fine Points of Revolution

At around four o'clock in the afternoon of April 22, 1982, Edjop and his comrades sailed off, in three pumpboats, from the shoreline of Davao City. They were on their way to Davao Oriental for a dialogue with leaders of the Moro National Liberation Front. The trip would take four to five hours, and the comrades expected to reach their destination at around nine o'clock in the evening.

They could have taken a shorter land route. But the military had set up checkpoints on the main roads. Though it took a longer time, a boat ride through the Davao Gulf exposed them to fewer risks.

At around eight-thirty, the boat Edjop was sailing in developed engine trouble. The pilot signalled the two other boats to stop. The damage was not serious, but it took more than an hour to make repairs.

For one whole hour, three wooden bancas carrying the top leadership of the revolutionary movement in Mindanao drifted idly in the dark open sea. A Coast Guard patrol would have put an end to their mission right there and then. But that night, luck was apparently on Edjop's side—though, perhaps, balance was not.

After waiting for about an hour, a cadre named Lenny, who was seated beside Edjop, began to feel restless. He suddenly stood up, violently rocking the boat. Lenny lost his balance and fell into the dark waters. Edjop, expecting the boat to capsize any moment, jumped in after Lenny.

When he surfaced, Edjop was surprised to see the boat still afloat. His comrades were doubled up with laughter.

"You see how much we can learn from the Moros?" Edjop remarked, as he was helped back into the boat. "They are masters of sea travel, while we are clumsy amateurs who cannot even keep our balance."

272

The boat fixed, the cadres sailed off once again. At around ten they had the shoreline of Davao Oriental in sight. They did not use flashlights or lanterns, to avoid being spotted by military patrols. They calculated their approach to shore based on the outline of the mountains and hills, silhouetted against the evening sky.

As a result of the pilots' inexperience, they missed the rendezvous point several times. Their hosts from the MNLF were already getting worried when they finally made it to shore.

But the dialogue did not happen. The MNLF leaders with whom the National Democratic Front panel was supposed to meet, and who also had to come from other parts, failed to reach the camp.

Edjop must have been disappointed. The meeting was supposed to be the first formal "panel-to-panel talk" between the NDF and the MNLF.

Before that, there had been dialogues between guerrilla commanders of the NPA and the Bangsa Moro Army (BMA, the military arm of the MNLF) in specific localities. But these were informal meetings, to forge agreements on areas of control and the conduct of military operations, and to share combat experiences. In some areas, NPA and BMA guerrillas were known to have played basketball together.

The natdem movement had yet to formulate a clear position on the Moro question. Some Muslims joined the Communist Party, but even they were disappointed with how little the movement understood the problems of the Moros. Some of them reacted against Amado Guerrero's description of Islam, in *Philippine Society and Revolution,* as a "feudal religion." Islam, these cadres of the Muslim faith asserted, could also be "liberating."

By the time Edjop joined the Mindanao Commission, Party leaders were showing greater interest in the issue. Edjop actively participated in these debates. Though no specific position on the Moro question can be attributed to him, he facilitated discussions on the issue by supplying statistical data and readings on historical experiences of other countries. In fact, according to his comrades, he helped raise the discussion to a more theoretical level.

To gain more practical insights, Edjop contacted Dicky Castro, his former colleague in the NUSP. Dicky grew up in Marawi City and had been living with his parents in Iligan. During his NUSP days Edjop often visited with the Castros, and Dicky's father, a retired Philippine Constabulary colonel, grew fond of Edjop.

Colonel Castro, Dicky, and Edjop spent a whole night talking about the Moros. As Dicky recalls it, Edjop asked how the Castros lived with the Moros and what was their attitude toward them. He asked Dicky about his childhood experiences: "Did you ever get into fistfights with Moro children?" He asked why Colonel Castro refused to return to active service when the Marcos government asked him to help out in quelling the Moro rebellion. The colonel explained: "The problem is not the MNLF, but the way the Moros have been treated in their own land."

"Edjop," says Dicky, "was actually picking our brains on the issue, while at the same time gathering information."

Edjop prepared the preliminary social investigation on the Moro question, more popularly known in the underground as the Moro PSI. It was, like the Mindanao PSI, a significant document that presented the facts and different positions on the Moro issue.

The Moro PSI described the plight of Muslims and other minorities in Mindanao and Sulu, and the struggle of the MNLF-BMA for Moro independence. It cited the programs of revolutionary governments in the Soviet Union and China regarding national minorities in their respective countries. It also listed guidelines for comrades on how to conduct formal "panel-to-panel" talks with leaders of the different Moro groups.

The document affirmed an earlier position of the party, which recognized the Moro people as a nation and supported their struggle for "national self-determination." The party also recognized the Moros' right to secede in "conditions of national oppression."

But in the Moro PSI Edjop stressed "unity in struggle" between Filipinos and Moros. This, according to Mindanao cadres, was Edjop's basic position on the Moro question, still the subject of debate in revolutionary circles to this day. In the document, Edjop used the term "Moro-Filipinos," and described as "flawed" the belief that the Moros and the Filipinos cannot live as one nation, even under a democratic state.

Other formal NDF-MNLF dialogues were held after April 1982. Edjop, however, never had the opportunity to participate in any of them. A few months after the suspended talks, another meeting was set in Cotabato. But just as Edjop was about to leave Davao, he received a telegram from comrades who told him not to proceed to Cotabato City. The MNLF liaison man had been arrested.

For a series of dialogues set in late 1982, Edjop asked Ernesto, a party cadre from Iligan, to make arrangements for six different houses in Iligan. He gave specific instructions that there should be no pork in the meals to be prepared.

Another dialogue was scheduled in Lanao in September, when Edjop and Leon were supposed to meet with the famed Commander Solitario of the MNLF Lanao Revolutionary Command.

Solitario is committed to the establishment of an independent Moro republic. With years of experience in guerrilla warfare, he is a legend among the Moros, perhaps the equal of Dante of the NPA. But Solitario also had a high regard for the cadres and guerrillas of the NDF, whom he considered—he still does—as "fellow revolutionaries."

A few days before the scheduled dialogue was to take place, Edjop told Leon he would not be able to go. What would have been a historic meeting between Solitario and Edgar Jopson never took place. While waiting for the NDF representatives in an MNLF camp in Lanao, Solitario heard the news of Edjop's death.

In the early and mid-seventies, the MNLF had put up the fiercest resistance to the Marcos regime in Mindanao. In 1975 the MNLF had more than 30,000 armed men and was in control of a great part of Mindanao and the entire Sulu archipelago. Up to 1978, two-thirds of the government forces were committed against the Moros.

In many ways, the NPA benefited from this situation. As an underground document on the history of the Moro struggle (based on the Moro PSI Edjop wrote) puts it: "The MNLF-BMA helped dissipate the strength of the reactionary armed forces. The CPP-NPA was provided a very favorable condition, as it spread guerrilla warfare on a nationwide scale."

By the early eighties, the NPA had become the military's primary target of operations even in Mindanao, as the guerrilla army began to inflict more damage on AFP units there. More than 20 AFP battalions were deployed against the NPA in Mindanao.

As it expanded to the strategic areas on the island, the NPA had acquired a wealth of combat experience. In preparation for bigger operations, the first Mindanao-wide military training was launched in May 1981.

Not since 1971, when Victor Corpus taught young recruits the basics of jungle fighting in Isabela, had guerrilla fighters undergone a major military training course. Guerrilla commanders and cadres from different fronts converged on a spacious clearing in the Zamboanga peninsula, then the strongest and most consolidated NPA zone in Mindanao.

The trainees came from different walks of life. Horace was a mine worker and a parish volunteer before joining the NPA. Buddy, who had gone up to the mountains after the declaration of martial law, came from a rich landowning family in Southern Mindanao; it was said that in the fishponds owned by his family, a fish that hit the ground after being caught was no longer considered fresh. Other trainees were of the Higaonons or Subanens, tribes in Mindanao collectively known as Lumads. Still others used to be factory workers and out-of-school youths from the cities and town centers. Most were of peasant origin, descendants of homesteaders and pioneers who had come to the island from the Visayas and Luzon.

The course was divided into two parts: the theoretical·and the practical.

Leon took charge of the practical training. He designed an obstacle course patterned after the one used by Scout Rangers. It involved different rigorous exercises and dangerous maneuvers—monkey crawl, ravine jump, sliding rope. Most of the commanders in the camp had never tried any of the drills. Many of them were overwhelmed, and not a few thought that Leon was "crazy" to expect them to go through the course.

In the sliding rope drill, for example, a fully-armed guerrilla, with a backpack, had to slide down a rattan rope with only an iron ring to hang on to. The rope extended from the hillside to the ground, and it was a 50-foot drop from the peak. "*Siguradong tepok pag bumitaw ka,*" Buddy describes it. "It was sure death if you let go."

The guerrillas complained: "We'll go through the exercise only if the trainers try it as well."

Leon and the other trainers agreed. With backpack and rifle, Leon went up the hill, got a good grip on the iron ring, and slid down, like a rock falling, to the ground. He landed feet first with a big thump. Leon hurt his knee; the rope was too steep.

It was adjusted, and Leon tried again. This time, he landed smoothly. Assured by his example, the other guerrillas agreed to do the exercise.

In the ravine jump drill, a guerrilla in full gear had to jump down from a wooden platform, roll to the ground, and get up on his feet. The trainee had to maintain his balance despite the heavy load and the depth of the descent. He should not grip his rifle too tightly, for his shoulders and arms might become too stiff, resulting in a heavy landing. Nor should he grip it too loosely, for the rifle might slam against his face when he landed.

Edjop gave the drill a try. He ran to the top of the 10-foot platform, his backpack heavy and bouncy, his AK-47 swinging unevenly as he held it diagonally across his body. When he reached the top, he leaped off the wooden deck, and as he descended he hugged the rifle closer to his chest. His inexperienced hands, however, could not control the rifle. When he hit the ground, the AK-47 snapped sharply upward, hitting him on the lower lip. Blood flowed down his chin as comrades rushed to give him a hand. Edjop wore a bandage on his chin for the rest of the training.

Abel, a friend of Edjop's, watched him make the sloppy descent. More than a year later, when news broke out that Edjop had been killed, she would lament that had Edjop done better in the training, he might have survived the raid.

At another point in the training, Edjop pulled out the magazine from his AK-47 rifle. Unaware that there was still a bullet left in the chamber, he squeezed the trigger, and the rifle went off. Fortunately, he had been oriented never to aim at people.

The training was capped by "war games," combat drills on jungle warfare tactics. The guerrillas were divided into two platoons: one, to act as the hunter; and the other, as the hunted. Edjop volunteered as one of the referees.

"The exercise took a lot of stamina, which the Red fighters naturally had," Buddy relates. "Edjop had experience in walking in the jungle, but not in swift military maneuvers, which meant running in rough and rugged terrain. But he kept up with the guerrillas, crossing fallen logs and going over ravines and creeks, steep hills and second growth areas of stumps and trees with sharp dry branches. Sometimes, he asked for a short break, and was allowed to rest a few minutes. But he was never left far behind."

Part of Edjop's job was to keep score of "casualties" in mock encounters.

"*Out ka na, kasama,*" he would announce. "*Ikaw rin, kas, nabaril ka na.* You're out, comrade. You too, comrade, you have been shot."

"Despite the cuts and bruises he got," says Buddy, "Edjop really enjoyed the experience."

Edjop, alias Ka Gimo, served as the facilitator in sharing sessions among guerrillas. He also gave lectures on the history of other armed movements, from which he drew comparisons with the development of the rebel army in the Philippines.

As always, Edjop asked a lot of questions. The guerrillas were amused at his childlike naivete. At times they thought him too eager to see the triumph on the horizon, and many of them were taken aback by the conclusions and projections he drew from their stories and reports.

Edjop, says Horace, was obviously unfamiliar with guerrilla warfare. In one of the sessions, he computed the number of rifles that the NPA should have captured in a year, by multiplying by 12 the number of weapons that NPA units recovered in a month.

"Talagang lalakas at lalawak na tayo, mga kasama!" Edjop exclaimed. "We get stronger every day!"

"But, Ka Gimo, it is not as simple as that," Horace explained. "For every tactical offensive we launch, we should expect the military to launch retaliatory operations which may lead to loss of lives and arms in our ranks. The hukbo moves forward, yes. But sometimes, it also moves backwards, and even sideways."

Armed struggle, Edjop was told, was as rugged as the Mindanao terrain.

36
= *A Different Kind of Guerrilla* =

Edjop was the first member of the Mindanao Party leadership who was not, at the same time, an accomplished NPA commander. Not only did he not have a noteworthy military record, Edjop did not have any combat experience at all.

Other members of the Mindanao Commission, like Fidel, Leon, Magtanggol Roque, alias Vic, and Merardo Arce, alias Perry, were military cadres and veteran commanders of the NPA. As Abel explains, "In the past, comrades rose to positions of leadership because of the many sacrifices they had undergone as NPA commanders. They earned the respect of other kasamas for their courage and military exploits."

Fidel was with the handful of NPA squads which opened the first guerrilla fronts in Mindanao. Leon joined the guerrilla army right after it was formed in 1969 and took part in the campaign to establish a Yenan-style base in Northern Luzon.

That campaign had been a near disaster. Superior government forces hunted down the ragtag army from one end of the Sierra Madre mountains to the other. Constantly harassed by government soldiers, the rebels were forced to retreat to unknown and uninhabited parts of the wilderness. They went hungry; malaria and other diseases plagued their ranks. Every day, they fought and ran.

Leon was among the few who survived this grim period in the history of the movement. In many battles, he saw buddies, alive just a second before, suddenly slump dead right beside him. "We could not even give them decent burials since we were always on the run. I used to feel very angry whenever someone died, was arrested, or went over to the other side. But I eventually accepted deaths, arrests, and betrayals as part of the cause."

Leon was transferred to Mindanao, where he became known for his courage and military skills, the epitome of the guerrilla-cadre. In NPA operations, or even just meetings in guerrilla camps, cadres always felt safer with Leon around. Once, during a sudden report of enemy presence near their camp, Leon grabbed the petite Ruby, a Davao-based cadre, and, with one arm, carried her upland, toward the jungle, where the whole party had retreated.

"When he is around, the comrades suddenly become courageous. *Tumatapang bigla ang mga kasama pag nandiyan siya,*" says Ruby. "*Ang pakiramdam nila'y ligtas na ligtas na sila.* They begin to feel very safe." Thelma, a Party cadre based in the countryside, adds, "*Pag nandiyan siya, parang hindi ka na mamamatay.* It's as if it's impossible for you to be killed."

Edjop, nevertheless, earned the respect and admiration of cadres in Mindanao despite his less glamorous background. "He did not have the strong, sometimes overwhelming, personality of the other party leaders," says Abel. "But his personality and leadership were an inspiration to many of us."

Edjop was also different in bearing and appearance. Formal and refined in manners, he had none of the roughness of a gerilya. He looked more like a college boy than an underground fighter. The first things that comrades, especially those based in guerrilla zones, noticed upon meeting him were his fair complexion and the smooth texture of his skin. *"Halatang hindi tagabundok. Halatang mula sa mataas na uri,"* Horace of Northeastern Mindanao notes. "He was obviously of the affluent classes. He didn't seem like someone who could break a drinking glass."

Being short and roly-poly, he looked less belligerent—less macho—to comrades on the island who were accustomed to the sinewy features of leaders like Leon and Fidel. In Mindanao as in Manila, Edjop's height became the butt of jokes. During long hikes in the jungle, comrades noticed how the M-203 rifle he was carrying was as tall as he was. During one trip, he was asked to stay in the cramped far-end portion of the van, because he was the smallest in the group and occupied the least space. But, says Horace, "Edjop was always a good sport. *Hindi pikon.*"

When he found himself in guerrilla zones, Edjop chatted for hours with peasants, organizers, and NPA fighters. At first, cadres were not comfortable with talking to someone from a higher organ. But they eventually warmed up to Edjop, who engaged them in marathon conversations that often lasted late into the night.

Edjop once had a long talk with an elderly peasant guerrilla during a meeting in the Diuata Mountain, along the Agusan-Surigao border. Weeks later, the elderly peasant was surprised to receive a letter from Edjop, who expressed his appreciation for the experiences the old man had shared with him. "Who was I that he should bother to write to me?" the elderly cadre wondered. "I didn't even expect him to remember me."

In spite of his burgis background, Edjop took to the hard life. At times, he endured even more hardships than veteran guerrillas. Leon, for one, admits that "there were many things Edjop did while in a guerrilla camp that I myself could not do." Once they were served snake meat. Leon would not even taste it, but Edjop went ahead and ate it.

As in Manila and Samal, he never complained about the food, and he insisted that comrades, especially those based in the cities, show their appreciation for whatever the guerrillas or the masa had to offer.

In the first plenum of the Southern Mindanao regional committee held in a mountainous area in Davao del Sur, dog meat was served after other food supplies ran out. Lenny, in jest, commented, "The best way to eat this is to gaze at the trees, the mountains and the hills after every bite. That way the beauty of the terrain will more than make up for the taste of the dog." Edjop didn't find this funny. "We should be grateful to the people here that we still have something to eat," he scolded, quite serious.

Another time, during a Mindanao-wide military training in Zamboanga, rice wine was served. There were no cups in use. The wine was in a big jar with a white bamboo straw protruding from it. To have a drink one had to fall in line and take a sip using that one straw. The squeamish Leon saw how the straw, after being used by so many people—there were about 200 cadres in the training—had begun to turn red from the *nganga* (beetle nut) that the old peasant cadres chewed. Leon decided to stay thirsty. But Edjop, whether out of curiosity or *pakikisama*—he did not drink any kind of alcoholic beverage—fell in line, took the scarlet-stained straw in his mouth and took a sip of the native liquor.

Nor did Edjop fall short of his comrades' expectations in moments of danger. They still remember his courage and presence of mind in the long march of July 1982. That month, while attending a major conference on Mount Apo, news of enemy presence reached the camp. The military had apparently been tipped off about a mass underground meeting in the area, and soon the roar of helicopter gunships echoed in the vicinity, as four battalions of government troops were airlifted to the mountain.

There were more than 200 cadres in the group, half of whom were noncombatants. Mindanao Commission members, led by Edjop, Leon and Mer Arce, made plans for an organized retreat. Guerrillas launched diversionary tactics to attract the soldier's attention away from the main bulk of retreating cadres.

As they marched down mountain trails, they sometimes saw government platoons conducting search patrols on a road below them. The thunder of Huey helicopters constantly reminded them of the presence of enemy troops sent out after them.

"It was like playing a deadly game of hide-and-seek," Veronica, a cadre based in the front, recalls.

Merardo Arce got separated from his wife in the confusion. He wanted to go look for her in the groups assembled in the camp, but as a member of the Mindanao Commission, he had to stay put and help make decisions about the conduct of the retreat. Edjop was aware of Mer's predicament. After one of their planning sessions, he himself instructed the kasama, "Go and look for her, Mer. You might not see each other again. We can handle the work here for now."

It was an act of friendship that Mer Arce never forgot. "Even in an intense crisis situation, Edjop is sensitive to how a kasama feels," he would later tell Veronica and his wife.

For three days, the beleaguered cadres marched from one end of Mount Apo to the other. The military would have easily caught up with them if the peasants had not provided them with shelter, food, and reports about military movements.

"The masa would send word that a certain number of soldiers had just passed through Aling Piring's house," Veronica recalls. "Edjop and those in the central command, naturally, didn't know who Aling Piring was, and where her house was. Local cadres were then consulted and necessary evasive actions planned."

After one long march, they paused for a rest at the house of a peasant family. Suddenly, they heard the thunder of an approaching Huey helicopter.

"Everybody hide! Away from the skyline, comrades!" the commanders yelled.

Most of the cadres, including Edjop, ran inside while some hid under the house. Guerrillas took cover in the nearby bushes and trees. But not all of them could find a hiding place in time. Among them was Veronica, who relates: "If just one of us was exposed, a battle would have surely taken place right then and there. We didn't know what to do, until a peasant woman grabbed some mats and laid them out on the ground. She took a sack of corn and emptied it on the mats. She then yelled to us, 'Pretend you are sifting through the corn! Quickly!"

Veronica and the other comrades caught in the open did as they were told, and not a moment too soon. Just then, the Huey helicopter roared in sight. "*Patay na.* This is it," Veronica said to herself when she saw the gargantuan iron machine. Her comrades felt the same way as they nervously pretended to work on the corn. Guerrillas in the bushes and trees prepared to open fire.

The helicopter hovered menacingly above them, its 50-mm machine guns trained on the ground. But after a few minutes of aerial inspection, the helicopter flew off without firing a shot. As soon as it was out of sight, the rebels dispersed and marched quickly into the jungle.

"That incident boosted our morale," says Veronica. "Later, comrades were sending each other notes which said, *Ang galing talaga ng masa, ano?* Aren't the masses great?' Edjop and other members of the Commission conducted snap discussions on the developments. Mer even taught us some new songs."

NPA operations helped the main bulk get through the military cordon. While the guerrillas engaged government troopers, Edjop and the other members of the Commission supervised retreat operations. After three days, all noncombatants had been taken out of the battle zone.

Despite the dangers he faced as a leading cadre in Mindanao, Edjop became less rigid in the lifestyle he imposed on himself and on his comrades.

To a kasama who believed that a "true cadre must make absolute sacrifices," Edjop said. "A comrade's welfare is just as important as the work he or she does. We must always care for a kasama's health, his emotional and psychological well-being. We cannot wage revolution if we are weak and unhealthy. If we do not take care of ourselves, how can we expect to fight side by side with the peasants and workers, who are strong and sturdy in their day-to-day struggles?"

When they met again in the 1980 plenum, Mauro, Edjop's former deputy in the NDF Preparatory Commission, noticed a change in attitude in Edjop. "He was no longer as grim and determined as he was in the past. 'You know what, I now go to the movies. *Nagsisine na ako ngayon,*' he told me. 'And I'm no longer a cheapskate. *Hindi na ako masyadong matipid ngayon.*' I guess he realized that one doesn't have to deprive oneself of watching movies and things like that in order to be a real cadre."

Before they parted, Edjop invited Mauro to come to Mindanao, enticing his comrade-friend with images of mangosteen, rambutan, and nice, clean beaches.

Mauro believes that "the time he spent in Mindanao were the best years of Edjop's life."

37
Last Days

Though hundreds of miles away from home, Edjop maintained links with his family and some of his friends. In 1981, when he learned of the death of Inday's husband, James Espadero, Edjop wrote his sister: "We thought of you and the heartaches you have experienced in the past. And now, this sudden blow. Crises make or destroy men. Like fire, which burns things to ashes, but at the same time makes steel out of ordinary iron."

Inday accepted her brother's invitation to visit him in Davao, and is glad she had the chance to talk to her kid brother before he died.

Freddie Salanga had also moved to Davao, where he worked as editor of the *San Pedro Express*. One day, Salanga was in the supermarket when somebody tapped him on the shoulder. He turned and there was Edjop smiling at him. "I didn't think it was wise for me to greet you," Edjop said. "But I wouldn't have forgiven myself If I had passed up this opportunity to talk to you again."

Edjop and Joy had been affected by what their son Nonoy went through when his father was captured in 1979. When the couple moved to Mindanao, they decided to leave the boy and his newborn baby sister, Joyette, with Edjop's parents. But Nonoy would visit with his parents in summer or during the Christmas holidays, and they would go to the beach and the Shrine, where they spent whole afternoons together.

During the school months, Edjop and Joy would send their children letters or taped voice messages. One cassette sent to Nonoy on his fifth birthday on February 16, 1980, is worth quoting in detail:

EDJOP: "How are you, 'Noy? And your sister Joyette? Are you also taking good care of her? I hope you are, so she would grow up faster.

"How about you? Can you already jump high and far? Can

you already walk long distances, so you can come along with Tats [short for *Tatay*, father] in going around the ricefields, in climbing mountains, right? Of course, Joyette will also come along with us, when she is bigger.

"As Nanay and I told you before, on your next school vacation, you will come visit with us again. And when you're already here, we'll surely have a lot of stories to tell one another. We will also sleep together at night.

"We are still living in a probinsiya, but it's different from the place you visited before. But here, we also have a lot of friends, the poor, the masa. Ordinary people. They are very good to us. They share their food, their blankets, their pillows, with us. They let us stay in their houses. They help us in many ways. When you come here, we will introduce you to them.

"Did you get the bullet necklace you asked for, which we sent you? You know what, a friend of ours from the NPA made that necklace. Nanay and I told him, 'Our son Nonoy wants a bullet necklace.' And he said, 'Is that so? Then we'll make one for him.'

"We were then in the mountains. We asked another NPA friend to give us a bullet from his Armalite. Then, in one of the huts, our friend split the bullet in two. What you actually have is just the pointed edge of the bullet. The case, which is the part which makes the bullet fire, has been removed.

"We also got rid of the gunpowder from the case, since we didn't really need that. Then we heated one end of the bullet over a fire, until the lead melted. The rest of the bullet didn't melt since it was made of brass. Then we got a piece of paper clip, which we inserted into the lead, to create a hole. Then we got a piece of string, and inserted this into the hole. The string is not so good, but I guess it will do."

JOY: " 'Noy, if you don't like the string, you can also replace it with a better one."

EDJOP: "That's right. We even polished the bullet, so it is clean and shiny. We even put—"

JOY: "Nail polish."

EDJOP: "Right, the stuff girls put on their fingernails. Then

we wrapped the necklace, and we asked a kasama, who was on
the way to Manila, to give it to you. We hope you have already
received it. If you have, then we hope you wear it—but only
when you're inside the house. Well, I guess it is also all right to
wear it outside the house—"

JOY: "But keep it inside your shirt."

EDJOP: "Right."

JOY: "Now Tats and I will sing you a song, entitled *Karaniwang
Tao* [Ordinary People]. It's also your favorite, right? Okay, here
we go.

EDJOP AND JOY (*singing*):
> *Karaniwang tao ang nagiging kawal*
> *Mga magsasaka na karet ang tangan*
> *Mga manggagawa na walang sandata*
> *Kundi ang bisig lamang . . .*
>
> *Kayong walang yamang sukat ipagtanggol*
> *Walang pag-aari ni silong o bubong*
> *Magbuklod, kumilos, maghandang masawi*
> *Sa pagsasanggalang ng sariling bayan . . .*
>
> [It's ordinary people who become soldiers
> Peasants with sickles in hand
> Workers with no weapons
> Other than their arms . . .
>
> [You who have no wealth to defend
> No property, no roof over your heads
> Unite, act, be ready to suffer
> To defend your country . . .]

EDJOP: "All right, son. That's it for now. We hope you will
also send us a tape of your voices. You can even include the
voices of Mommy, Daddy and your other titos and titas."

JOY: "Maybe you can also ask Joyette to tape her voice. She
probably can speak a few words by now. Tats and I would surely
like to hear her speak. Goodbye for now, son. *Maraming yakap at
mga halik.* Many hugs and kisses."

In late 1982 Edjop invited his mother to visit with him in Mindanao. "I immediately packed my bags," Mrs. Jopson recalls. "Ed's comrades picked me up at the airport, then brought me to a house. Ed welcomed me there. I noticed that he had just had a haircut and looked real neat."

The mother teased her son: "Wow, you look very handsome—*plantsado*," and Edjop replied: "Because that's the way you want your son to be, right?"

That night, when they were about to sleep, Mrs. Jopson noticed she was the only one with a pillow. "I bought it at the marketplace this morning," Edjop explained. "I got it especially for you. We don't really use pillows around here."

Later that night, Mrs. Jopson saw her son in the bathroom, soaking his feet in warm water. He said he had twisted his ankle while walking in the jungle, and his comrades even had to carry him in a stretcher. "Before sleeping," Mrs. Jopson recalls, "he let me massage his feet."

Mrs. Jopson says Edjop worked every morning, typing all sorts of documents. When she gave him some M & M chocolates she had brought with her from Manila, he teased her: "Mommy, I wish you wouldn't spoil me with this imported stuff, because we don't eat them here. But I'll have some, anyway."

"We were together for three days," says Mrs. Jopson, "and we were very happy. I would have stayed with him forever."

When she was about to leave, Edjop said he couldn't see her off at the airport because he was a wanted man in Davao. But he assured her: "Don't worry, Mommy. I am being assigned back to Manila. I'll be home for Christmas. We'll have a grand family reunion this year. I promise."

The promise buoyed up Mrs. Jopson's spirits: " 'I was already excited about the coming Christmas."

Edjop was set to return to Manila in June 1981. But a few days before he was to leave Davao, an underground house in Guadalupe subdivision was raided. Magtanggol Roque, alias Vic, had just entered the gate of the bungalow when military men pounced on him. They dragged him into the house and beat him up. It was later reported that Roque had been shot dead while trying to escape, but his comrades believe he was tortured to death.

The military also arrested Benjamin de Vera, whom they accused of being the chairman of the Party organization in Mindanao.

With Roque dead and Edjop reassigned to Manila, the Mindanao Party leadership lost two very valuable cadres at a very critical period. In the June 1981 Politburo meeting, Edjop asked that he be allowed to return to Mindanao. Leon, who was left with the burden of running the Mindanao organization, also made the same request.

Arman, a Central Committee member, describes how Edjop pleaded his case: "He was very concerned about comrades in the Mindanao Commission. But I think he also wanted to complete his own development as a revolutionary in Mindanao."

Edjop's request was granted. He was given another year in Mindanao, where he was tasked to head the Commission. Now known as Ka Phillip, he returned to the island in November 1981.

The Cadre Conference in September 1982 was the last underground convention Edjop attended. After the meeting, he went back to Davao City where good news greeted him. Joy had given birth to their third child, a baby girl, whom they named Teresa Lorena, or Risa for short.

Edjop's stint in Mindanao was to end in December, during which he would return to Manila. In September, he and Leon were to leave for Cagayan de Oro City, where the Mindanao Commission was moving its base of operations. But at the last minute, Edjop decided to stay behind in Davao, asking Leon to proceed without him.

The reason for Edjop's decision was that he wanted to help resolve the problem of a collective which he was directly in charge of. The problem involved Laura, head of the research and translation staff of the Mindanao Commission.

Before that, she had been contentedly doing peasant mass work in a guerrilla base area in Davao del Norte. But then Edjop and other Commission members had asked her to head one of their city-based units.

At first, Laura had turned down the assignment: "I told Edjop there were other kasamas who could do the job. I said that I was more effective in organizing work. But the Commission insisted."

Edjop had told Laura: "We are asking you to take this assignment, not just because of a specific need, but also because of our concern for your safety. There have been too many kasamas who insisted on working with the peasants and who were assigned to dangerous areas in the CS. Many of them ended up dead. We don't want the same thing to happen to you or any other comrade."

"Although he didn't say it directly," Laura says now, "I think he was trying to make me realize that my love for that area was a romantic illusion—that I was glamorizing the idea of being in a zone of danger."

But Edjop had also stressed the importance of the new assignment: "Please consider what this could mean for the advancement of the revolution in Mindanao, and in the entire country as well."

"It was," says Laura, "this argument—and the way Edjop explained it—that made me more open to their proposal. Although I still had reservations, I was eventually convinced to take on the task."

Laura had subsequently gone to Davao City, where she stayed in an underground safehouse in Skyline subdivision, together with two other cadres, Mer and Thelma. Day in and day out, they worked in an air-conditioned room, soundproofed (to keep neighbors from being suspicious about the continuous typing) with blankets nailed to the walls. From morning to night, their faces were buried in piles of documents, writing, translating into Visayan, and churning out underground literature on typewriters and semi-functional mimeographing machines. They went out only to buy groceries and office supplies. Sometimes they watched a movie or went to the beach, but such times were rare.

It didn't take long for Laura to start hating the assignment.

"I was simply overwhelmed by the work. It felt like someone was breathing down my neck saying, '*Resulta! Resulta!*' I felt suffocated, and found the daily routine excruciating. I was sick and tired of seeing the same faces, of working with documents every day. I felt isolated, as though I was in prison."

Laura requested a return to her former task in the countryside. "*Hindi ko na talaga kaya.* I can't take it anymore," she told Edjop. He listened, but asked her to be patient and wait a little longer.

One day Laura simply had enough: "I started going out of the house often, supposedly to deliver materials or buy supplies. But I actually used that as an excuse to get out of the house. I didn't show initiative in my work. I just couldn't function anymore. I was really burned out."

Her relationship with the other members of her staff began to suffer. Thelma and Mer resented Laura's repeated requests to be transferred, and her miserable performance as head of the group.

"I tried to explain my situation to them. But they could not understand what I was going through. There were many barriers between us—class, cultural, even language. Thelma was of working-class origins; Mer came from a lower-middle-class family in the countryside. I guess mine was the gut-level dilemma of an urban petty bourgeois. Other comrades called it *kaburgisan,* or the tendency to vacillate and be undecided. Only Edjop tried to understand my problem, from my point of view."

Edjop and the other members of the Commission eventually decided to let Laura go.

"I was relieved to go. But somehow I also felt guilty."

Before leaving, Laura agreed to complete an underground primer. Edjop took over her other responsibilities; he began to spend more time in the UG house in Skyline.

By then, members of the collective were already worried about the security status of their UG house.

"We stuck out like a sore thumb in the neighborhood we were in," explains Laura. "We kept the stereo on the whole day to drown out the noise of the machines. We told neighbors that the house was owned by a businessman, and we were his caretakers—a weak and worn-out cover. Since we would only stay in the house for a few months, we didn't even try to establish a more solid cover."

The house was vulnerable to surveillance. About 20 meters away was a waiting shed where an operative could hang around and case the area. Commuter buses, the only means of public transportation available in the subdivision, passed close to the house. The cadres often got off a few blocks away and walked the rest of the way. But they still had to pass the waiting shed on the way home. If one of them were spotted by an agent, the UG house could immediately be pinpointed.

Once a man came to the house and tried to sell them Coke. Another time, it was someone peddling bottled fruit juices. "They were very persistent," says Thelma: "They said we didn't even have to pay for the drinks at once. We decided to move after that."

Edjop helped in the preparations. "At that time, he was like our dad," Laura recalls. "He suggested places where we could look for a new place. He made sure that we had enough money. He asked about the plans of Thelma and Mer, and even encouraged them to take a vacation before moving into the new house. No matter how busy he was, he showed his concern for us."

Laura got permission to visit a comrade-friend who was about to give birth. She promised to have the primer ready by the time she returned. By then, Edjop would have been on his way to Cagayan de Oro.

"This may be the last time we'll see each other," Laura told Edjop. "I know that you are disappointed with the way I behaved. *Nahihiya ako sa iyo.* I feel bad about what happened."

"It's nothing to worry about," Edjop said. "Just take good care of yourself."

That was the last time Laura saw Edjop alive.

About a month earlier, two of her former comrades in the countryside had surrendered to the military. When Laura was head of the translation staff, the two collaborators were already moving about the city as informers, tasked to spot and squeal on people they recognized to be UG cadres.

Unknown to Laura, she had been spotted in one of her previous errands. The surveillance that the informers maintained on her led them to the translation staff house. As Laura walked out of Skyline subdivision, operatives lingered unnoticed, monitoring her movements and those of the people inside the bungalow on San Vicente Street.

As in 1979, there had been signs. But again, Edjop and the other kasamas misread them.

38
The Major

Major Nelson Estares would later gloat that Edjop and the other cadres never knew what hit them that night. "We stalked them like leopards," he says. *"Wala silang kamalay-malay."*

In the seventies and early eighties, the major boasted a perfect record—"Nobody ever escaped from me," he crows—and he meant to keep that record unblemished. With 21 soldiers under his command, he waited in an empty lot in Skyline Subdivision in Matina, Davao City, early in the evening of September 20, 1982.

Major Estares, a portly fellow with a pot belly, wore a maong jacket that night. He was constantly handling his walkie-talkie. His men were in civilian clothes. They were about four kilometers away from Number 10 San Vicente Street, a small, ordinary-looking bungalow, with a low concrete fence of pointed steel bars.

A covert team "harbored" (military term for conducting surveillance on) the house, giving reports by radio about the people moving inside, about the weapons they possibly had, about any sign that they had been alerted to the forthcoming assault.

No alarming reports came; movements in the house remained normal. For the major, the komunistas were easy prey.

He went over the plan of attack with his men. By eight, the trap had been set. The major had only to wait for the right time to spring it. He was about to have one of the biggest breaks in his career.

The movement has always believed that the military never found out that Edjop was in Mindanao. Estares, now a colonel, maintains that he knew it all along. He speaks of a letter recovered in the raid where Magtanggol Roque was killed. The secret communication referred to the deployment to Mindanao of a leading Party cadre who had just escaped from detention.

More leads came Estares' way. According to the major, they

were able to "put one and one together," and conclude that the CPP's new man in Mindanao was Edgar Jopson.

"I had an inkling that he was Edjop," Estares says. "My operatives looked for him and, when he was located, we put him under surveillance. This was about three or four months before the raid."

Knowledge of Edjop's presence in Mindanao excited Estares. Edjop was known to the military as a top-ranking leader of the CPP, a "big fish" worth the P180,000 price on his head. For any ambitious officer, Edjop's capture meant, not just a big purse, but a promotion in the stiff AFP hierarchy.

But the major had other reasons, related to neither money nor military glory, in wanting to get the CPP leader. There was a time when Edgar Jopson represented what Estares had always wanted to be, and to have, in life. Now he was his faceless, nameless enemy in a bitter civil war. It was, for the major, a most baffling irony.

As he waited with his men in that vacant lot, on the eve of the 10th anniversary of the declaration of martial law, Nelson Estares was about to play a key role in the conclusion of what, to him, was the strange and unfortunate odyssey of one of the most celebrated figures of the First Quarter Storm.

From the moment they met at the 1969 NUSP Congress in Iloilo, Estares admired Edgar Jopson. "To be student council president of Ateneo, you had to be really brilliant," says Estares. "You must be part of the cream of the crop. And Edjop was exactly that. He had a clear, sharp mind. He was articulate in expressing himself. He was, of course, lucky to have come from a rich family. To have the abilities he had, you need the proper intellectual and academic atmosphere, where you are not hampered by the problem of where to get the money to pay for your tuition fee or for the rent at the dormitory."

The second of five children, Estares dreamed of becoming a lawyer. But his father, a government employee in Cotabato, earned barely enough to put all his children to school. When Nelson graduated from high school, he took, and passed, the highly competitive entrance examinations at the University of the Philippines in Diliman. Delighted with Nelson's achievement, his grandfather agreed to pay for his schooling at the prestigious university.

Nelson packed his bags and headed for Manila. Barely two weeks later, his father came to his dormitory and broke the sad news that his grandfather had just died: no one would be able to pay for his education at UP.

Disappointed, Nelson returned home. His former high school classmates mocked him for not having made it. Estares still hoped to return to UP, to take up law or a masteral course. He never did. The only time he ever went to study at the state university was when he took a two-month course in preparation for his training in counter-insurgency and intelligence at Fort Bragg, in the United States. During that short stint, according to a friend, Estares sometimes took long walks around the Diliman campus, appreciating its serene and intellectual ambience, and contemplating how he once almost became part of it.

Nelson got a scholarship at the Notre Dame University in Cotabato. His former classmates, over whom he had always excelled, went to UP and other prestigious universities: they had the money. It was a reality Nelson became very bitter about—that affluence, not academic excellence, determined the quality of education a person could have.

To Estares, Edjop had everything. He was not like other students from rich families, who had only a fancy accent to brag about. Edjop had both the brains and the bread.

In his student days, Estares was, ironically, drawn to the radicals. At the Notre Dame University, when the radical activists preached national democracy, Nelson Estares listened.

"I was also curious. I wanted to read the Red Book of Mao and other materials. But these were not available in the provinces. KM was then presented as a nationalist student organization. They put up a chapter in our school. I talked with some of them. They were very eloquent, although they dominated the discussions."

But Nelson couldn't be a member of the radical movement. He was cadet corps commander in Notre Dame. This made him suspect in the eyes of the radicals—a *pasista*, a fascist. "I knew about their secret meetings, but they isolated me. As a student, I also wanted to learn about nationalism. I wanted to be involved. But they would not let me join them."

In Edjop and the moderates, Estares found an alternative. He was indignant about the way the radicals lambasted Edjop.

"Our position then was, if you wanted reforms, you had to join the government. Then, as you went up the ladder, you could make the changes yourself. That was our philosophy. But the radicals believed you had first to destroy the government and then build a new one. In effect, they wanted to kill all Filipinos, and evolve a new Filipino. We challenged other students to join the government and be as clean as they could be. Then you could start changing the system. That's why I am still with the PC now."

The military was another important influence in Estares' life. His father and other uncles had been in the army, and Nelson often listened to their stories about the military. From them he learned arnis, boxing, and fencing with bolos. He grew up in a town where there were frequent clashes between Christians and Muslims. As a boy, he watched soldiers in a military jeep drive down from the PC station on the hill toward their town. He was impressed with the way the troopers took care of *huramentados,* so-called Muslim troublemakers.

Immediately after graduating from college, Estares joined the military. He was already a regular officer in the Philippine Constabulary when he learned that Edjop had joined the underground.

"I was confused when I learned that. But I guess, after Marcos imposed martial law, he had no other option. Only the CPP would take him in."

39
"They're Here!"

In the afternoon of September 20, Edjop, alias Ka Phillip, was having a meeting with Bruce in the latter's UG house. "He borrowed five pesos from me. He said he was going to have a haircut," Cindy, Bruce's wife, recalls.

Edjop left on a motorcycle with Teddy, his bodyguard. They went to a subdivision adjacent to Skyline, called Montemaria, to the house of Dr. Alfredo Buenavista (not his real name), a dentist who was Edjop's friend. While Major Estares and his men were waiting in Skyline, Edjop was barely two kilometers away, having a chat with another former colleague in the NUSP.

Buenavista, like Estares, attended the NUSP Congress in 1969. He, too, was a great admirer of Edjop's, though he never personally knew him in their student days.

They met again in Davao City in 1979, through a kasama who was Buenavista's cousin. Edjop was introduced to him as Gimo. After ten years, Buenavista had already forgotten what the former student leader looked like. But later, as Gimo came to visit him more often, Buenavista sensed something familiar about his new acquaintance.

During one of his visits, Gimo asked Buenavista if he was familiar with the NUSP.

"Yes. In fact, I was a delegate to the NUSP Congress in 1969," Buenavista answered. "Edgar Jopson was our president."

"Did you personally know Edgar Jopson?" Gimo asked further.

The doctor was intrigued. The process of recollection of his NUSP days suddenly made him realize what he had found curious about his new friend. With an amused but uncertain look on his face, he asked, "*Teka muna.* You're Edgar Jopson, aren't you?"

Gimo simply smiled and said, "No, I'm not, Doc. You're mistaken."

But the doctor was not convinced. He went over his collection of old pictures and saw that, indeed, Gimo looked very much like the young Jopson. Soon after that, Edjop himself revealed his true identity.

They became good friends. Ed visited him to talk, drink and eat kilawin. "I was also his official dentist," Doctor Buenavista chuckles. Once he pulled out an impacted tooth from Edjop's mouth. The doctor wanted to do the operation in his clinic, but Edjop, for security reasons, asked him to do it in his house.

Doctor Buenavista knew of Ed's underground links, but says he was not aware just how deep Ed's involvement was: "*Hindi ko alam na mabigat na tao pala siya.* I didn't know he was that big a personality."

Doctor Buenavista was not a man of definite political views. Like most people then, he was against the dictatorship. But this was never translated into any concrete political action (except, perhaps, when he watched from the sidewalk on Mendiola the student assault on Malacañang on January 30, 1970). He was a family man who led a quiet life in the Davao suburbs.

He was aware of the risks involved in being identified with somebody from the underground. The military, the doctor knew, would probably not take the time to make a distinction between a cadre and a friend of a cadre. He was pursuing a potentially dangerous friendship. Still, he accepted Edjop and treated him like a brother. Ed sometimes spent the night in his house; he became a part of the dentist's family.

"He was so easy to get along with. My wife and children were very fond of him. My kids called him Tito Gimo."

Doctor Buenavista says they never really talked about politics or ideology. "*Walang ganoon sa pagsasama namin.* Ed was a very humble person. He did not force his ideas on me. We treated each other as equals, respecting each other's views and position in life."

In one of their last conversations, the doctor kidded Edjop: "What do you think about my joining the underground, Ed? Do you think I can already pass for one of you?"

Edjop's reply, spoken with an amiable Visayan intonation and with the sincerity of an older brother, revealed much of how he viewed their friendship: "*Huwag na, bay.* You don't have to, my friend. It is better for you to stay where you are now. *Kita mo naman ang hirap ng buhay namin.* You can see how hard our life in the underground is. If you join us, you may have to leave your family. That would be very difficult for your children."

After a brief pause, Edjop added: "Besides, if you join us I won't have any house to visit anymore."

They both laughed.

"*Binibiro lang naman kita, bay,*" the doctor said. "I was only kidding. But I want you to know how much I really admire you and others like you. *Bilib talaga ako sa iyo at mga kasama mo.* You have courage. Unlike me who may be brave one day, but not the next. But you are brave one day, and even more courageous in the succeeding days."

That evening of September 20, Doctor Buenavista was glad to see Edjop. His underground friend had not paid him a visit for months, and now they embraced like brothers.

Doctor Buenavista remembers how young Edjop looked. "You look like a schoolboy," the doctor had teased. "Like a seminarista."

"*Ikaw naman, bay,*" said Edjop. "Is that what you're going to say after we haven't seen each other for a long time?"

Edjop had dinner at the doctor's house. Later, over beer, they watched a boxing match on TV. Doctor Buenavista says Edjop was a "very moderate drinker." He had one bottle that night.

At around eight o'clock, one of the doctor's maids reported that, on the way home, she saw military men along the highway.

"The military may be conducting an operation in the area, so there may be checkpoints all over," the dentist worriedly told Edjop. "You better spend the night here. Tell your companion to bring in the motorcycle."

"I don't think that's necessary, *bay,*" Edjop said. "They are just probably preparing for the martial law anniversary tomorrow."

The doctor and his wife continued to urge Ed and Teddy to

spend the night at the house. But Edjop said he had things to attend to that night. "Believe me, *bay*," said Edjop, "there is nothing to worry about. These troop movements are just routine. I'll tell you what I'll do. I'll come back tomorrow with some fish and we'll make kilawin. We can talk the whole afternoon."

Doctor Buenavista, though still concerned, could do nothing but agree:" All right. I'll take care of the drinks. But be sure to come back."

"I will, my friend. I promise. Don't worry about anything."

"We were both in a jolly mood that evening," the doctor recalls. "But my wife and I were really worried about him. *Hindi kami mapakali.* It was the first time we ever felt that way.

Edjop and Teddy left at a little before nine. They crossed to the neighboring subdivision in Skyline, to their UG house on San Vicente Street. They were practically neighbors with Doctor Buenavista, but only later that evening would the doctor find out.

The covert team saw the two cadres on a motorcycle enter the UG house. One of them radioed their commanding officer. Major Estares immediately ordered his men to get ready.

"I was afraid that they might leave again," Estares relates. "So we made our move at once."

The raiding party split up into two groups. Estares led one squad to the front of the house, while the other team went around the block and took their position in a vacant lot right outside the concrete fence at the back of the compound.

While Estares and his men were closing in on the house, Beatriz de Vera was in her room listening to jazz music. She had grown "allergic" to raids. The rushing, the alarming noises in the middle of the night, the banging and breaking down of doors and the armed men who suddenly and threateningly appeared from out of nowhere—she had a certain lingering trauma from all this. The wife of accused CPP leader Benjamin de Vera, she was one of those arrested in the raid on a UG house in Guadalupe. She had just been released from detention in March 1982. Barely six months after that, her husband had escaped from prison. By then, all the excitement in the past months had taken its toll on her nerves.

There were five other people in the house. Father Dong Tizon was writing letters in another room, on the other side of the duplex. Thelma, who was down with a fever and had gone to bed early, was asleep in the room she shared with her husband.

Edjop, who only had his shorts on, was in the living room, in a meeting with Mer and Teddy. Mer was telling his comrades about their new house. He said he had already paid the rent and had made other arrangements for their transfer. It was decided that they would move to the new neighborhood in a week's time.

Estares' team was close enough to see some activity inside the house. As he sat on a bench right in front of their target, Estares says he recognized the top of Edjop's head, leaning against the jalousie-type windows in the living room. He took an M-16 from a soldier and aimed at Edjop's head, marveling at the thought of how it could be all over for that Communist right then and there.

But the major wanted his prey alive. He ordered one of his men to climb over the railing in front of the house. His plan was simple. The trooper was to stealthily approach the front door, barge in and aim his rifle directly at Edjop. The operation would then be over, and Edjop and his comrades would have been taken prisoners.

But it was not a night for brilliant coups and military precision.

The trooper Estares had sent over the railing got his pants caught in one of the steel points. He lost his balance and fell, his M-16 slamming noisily against the fence.

Edjop quickly looked out the jalousie-type window. He saw armed men with white bands on their foreheads.

"*Andiyan na sila!* They're here!" he cried out. (To this day, why Edjop didn't yell "Raid!" or "*Kaaway!*", as any other cadre might have instantly blurted out, remains a mystery to his comrades.)

Edjop ran toward the back of the house. Teddy and Mer ran to their respective rooms. Teddy went to get his .45-caliber pistol, which happened to be the most high-powered weapon they had in the house.

Mer woke Thelma up by tapping her on the shoulders. Thelma groggily got up. She had heard the commotion outside the room, but had thought that it was because of a burglar being chased by neighbors; there had been a series of robberies in the neighborhood in the past weeks. When she saw her husband stuffing letters and money into his pockets, she realized what was happening. She got dressed and started helping Mer gather all sensitive documents.

Betty de Vera was also awakened. She had just opened the door of her room, when she saw Edjop running down the hallway. "What's going on?" she asked nervously.

Edjop repeated the warning: "*Andiyan na sila!* Raid!"

"I didn't know what to do," Betty recalls. "I felt like I was melting. My whole body became numb—my arms, feet, ears, everything."

Teddy and Betty followed Edjop to the kitchen. Edjop unbolted the door, and the three of them ran out to the backyard.

It was dark outside. Edjop held Betty's cold, shaking hands as they ran, saying, "Be brave. Just follow me once we jump over."

From the backyard, the wall was only about seven feet high. But on the other side it was about a 10-foot drop to the vacant lot, overgrown with tall cogon grass.

"Let's go!" Teddy said, as he quickly leaped up and over the wall. Edjop followed after him. But while Teddy, who had spent years as an NPA guerilla, jumped swiftly and without stopping to the other side, Edjop hesitated—he stayed a second too long on top of the wall.

Suddenly, there was a burst of automatic fire.

40
Dying Moment

Major Estares heard Edjop yell out a warning when the trooper from the assault team fell off the railing. Estares immediately led his men over the steel fence. He was watching the people running in the living room when he heard the shots. Estares took cover beside the door, while some of his men redeployed back to the sidewalk.

"We thought the gunfire came from inside the house," he recalls. "We were taken by surprise. It was even funny the way my men took cover on the street. They hid their heads behind the pavement—but they had their buttocks raised."

The major radioed the officer in the second team to ask what had happened.

"Two men went over the fence, sir," came the reply. "We hit one of them. A little guy, in shorts, with a balding head."

Estares worried that the man who got shot was an ordinary resident, scared off by the sight of armed men.

"What's his name?" the major asked on the radio.

"Caguiat, sir. He said his name is Caguiat." Caguiat is the name of Edjop's nephew in Davao City. Estares now thinks that Edjop was probably trying to say, "Let my nephew, Mr. Caguiat, know what happened to me."

But Laura, who was picked up a day after the raid, says that Edjop may have refused to give his real name to protect the identity of his other kasamas in the UG house: "The military didn't really know what kind of a house it had stumbled on. If Edjop had admitted who he was, the raiding party would have immediately verified that it was a major UG safehouse." Laura believes that, in concealing his true identity, Edjop had made a final act of sacrifice and commitment.

Later, the major drove around the block to the vacant lot. There, Estares claims, he saw Edjop's broken, battered body.

"I tried to talk to him," he says, "but he could no longer speak.

305

His eyes were closed and his entire face was contorted. Why did he have to resist? I thought then. He could still be alive now if he had just given up. But he really didn't want to be captured. He had already been in prison, and I guess he didn't want a repeat of that experience."

Edjop sustained nine bullet wounds in the chest, legs and right arm. According to Estares, he died before reaching the hospital.

"Had he lived we would have talked about politics, about the old days. Looking back, I guess I can understand him. He just had too much of Marcos. The system is not perfect and it was complicated by the dictator. But Marcos is not the system. Edjop should have known that."

There are other versions of how Edjop was killed.

The major dailies reported that he shot it out with government soldiers. According to Estares, Edjop was already wounded when he jumped off the wall. But he was still able to grab an Armalite from one of the soldiers, and he was shot in the ensuing scuffle.

"We were not able to conduct a recon of the vacant lot," Estares explains. "It was dark and had a lot of tall cogon grass in it. My men didn't know that there were also parts which were soft and muddy. So when they tried to advance to the wall, some of them stumbled and fell."

The soldiers may have been alerted when Teddy jumped over, and were ready to shoot the next man they saw on the wall.

"Edjop himself was trapped in the grass and mud. His bodyguard was luckier, for he ran in the other direction where the ground was solid, and he could hide behind the cogon grass while making a run for it to the other street. That's why he was able to escape."

Cadres and Edjop's own father believe that Edjop was still alive when he was captured.

According to Betty de Vera, minutes after the first burst of gunfire, she heard soldiers yell, "*Tinamaan sa paa iyong isa!* One was hit in the leg!"

Teddy, the only one who succeeded in escaping during the

raid, told his comrades that Edjop was wounded, but alive, after he fell off the wall.

The Jopsons commemorate Edjop's death on September 21 instead of the 20th, believing he was killed sometime early in the morning of the 21st.

Those arrested in the raid believe that Estares really wanted Edjop alive, but that soldiers, without the major's orders, liquidated him. According to Betty and Laura, Estares admitted to them that he was not in complete control of the operation, claiming that there were other officers in the raid who gave their own commands, without consulting with him.

Mer would have another theory. While under detention, he learned that some of the soldiers who took part in the raid were survivors of an AFP-NPA encounter in which government troopers had suffered heavy casualties. During the Skyline operation, some of these troopers may have been itching to get even with the first rebel they got their hands on.

A cadre who also happens to be a relative of Estares suspects the major himself ordered Edjop's execution: "I know Estares. He has a very sophisticated military mind. He knew that Edjop was more dangerous to them alive than dead. He probably believed that, as another martyr of the revolution, Edjop was harmless."

Estares claims that Edjop was armed when he tried to escape. His men found a gun—a .38-caliber Smith and Wesson snub-nosed pistol made of stainless steel—on the spot where Edjop was shot. Leon admits that it was the weapon he had given to Edjop, but he and other cadres are not sure if Edjop had it on him during the raid. They believe it may have been the gun Teddy got from his room, which he dropped as he jumped over the wall.

The soldier who picked up the .38 had planned to sell it, but someone tipped off the major, who immediately confiscated the weapon. Estares still keeps the gun as a souvenir of the successful raid in Skyline—and as a souvenir of Edjop.

Estares casually affirms, "All those who join the insurgency must accept the fact that, since they hold the gun, they'll die by the gun. Like Edjop."

About a half hour after Edjop and Teddy left, Dr. Buenavista heard two bursts of gunfire. The first round sounded like it came from an M-16 rifle; the second, from a .45-caliber pistol. He learned from a neighbor that there was a raid in Skyline. He also learned that a man, in his mid-30s, short and bald, was shot.

When he heard the description, the doctor felt his heart sink.

"I wanted to go to Skyline," he says. "But I was also afraid. I was able to confirm later that it was indeed Edjop who had been shot."

The doctor could not sleep that night. In bed, he tearfully recalled his last moments with Edjop.

"I still think about that night—how, a few minutes before he died, Edjop was my visitor and friend, laughing and joking with me in my own house."

Later that evening, he heard someone running in his back-yard. It sounded as if the intruder wanted to enter, but decided to move on. The next morning, military elements came to Buenavista's house. They asked if he had seen or heard anybody running past his house the night before. The doctor said he had, but added that he didn't see the person.

"I later found out that Teddy had escaped, and it must have been he who had tried to enter my house. He was apparently hurt, for he left behind a trail of blood as he ran. The military found bloodstains in my backyard. That's why they paid me a visit."

Teddy was indeed wounded, but he was able to slip past the military cordon. He made his way to the countryside of Davao City. In a remote wooded area, he ran into a farmer who, luckily, was also a member of the local underground organization. The peasant gave Teddy food and helped him get in touch with local cadres.

Betty hit the ground when she heard the shots. She didn't know what had happened to either Teddy or Edjop. She lay in the backyard, shaking with fear. She thought that Thelma and

Mer had also escaped, and that she was the only one left in the house.

There was a door leading to Father Tizon's room in the other half of the duplex. Betty ran toward it and tried to open it, calling the priest's name. The door opened and, to Betty's surprise, Thelma pulled her into the room.

Outside they could hear a soldier calling through a megaphone, "Those in the house, give yourselves up! You are already surrounded!"

For Father Tizon, Betty, Thelma and Mer the situation was hopeless. The main thing left for them to do was to limit the damage that the raid could cause to other comrades and to the organization as a whole. They gathered all sensitive documents—underground memos, minutes of meetings, letters—and tore them to pieces. Most of the scraps of paper they flushed down the toilet; the rest they burned with a cigarette lighter, or chewed and swallowed.

It took another half hour before the military actually made their move. In fact, Father Tizon almost succeeded in bluffing their way out of the situation. He went out and, with an arrogant air, demanded to know what the armed men were doing in his frontyard.

Feigning innocence, Thelma also came out. She asked Estares his name.

Estares lied: "I am Major Esparagosa."

"We're sorry to trouble you, miss," a soldier said apologetically. "But we saw two men on a motorcycle enter this house. Did you see them?"

"No. Nobody came through here."

"Does anybody named Adel live around here?"

"Adel" had been Laura's codename on the guerilla front where she was formerly assigned. Thelma said, "No. I don't think there's anybody here by that name. Why don't you ask the people in the other houses?

"The raiders weren't sure if they got the right house," Thelma relates. "We could have fooled them if one of the soldiers had not spotted the motorcycle which Edjop and Teddy had used, parked in the garage."

Estares instantly gave the order to enter the house. Fully-armed soldiers came through the front door like a storm.

A trooper spotted Betty hiding in one corner. "Yes, we got the right house, sir!" the soldier yelled, triumphantly. "De Vera's wife is here!"

41

Laura

The damage—or "fire," as cadres would say—that the Skyline raid caused did not end with Edjop's death and the arrest of his four comrades. One more cadre was "burned" the following day. The sixth victim, Laura, could have been spared if the other people in the UG house had been able to knock off a Nido milk can which hung from a steel bar on the backyard wall. The can could be seen from a block away. If a cadre on the way to the house did not see it, then he or she was warned not to proceed to the house.

Laura came home the next day, at around four in the afternoon. As the bus she was riding drove past the back of their house, she saw the can on the wall. Laura got off a few blocks after San Vicente Street. She noticed that two men also got off the bus after her.

As she opened the front gate of their underground house, she saw their pet dog scrounging for food in the garbage can. She noticed how scrawny it looked, "as if it had not been fed for days."

She was about to open the front door when soldiers pounced on her, yelling, *"Huli!"*

"They were naked from the waist up, " she recalls. " I saw one of them holding a deck of cards. I figured they had been waiting in the house since the previous night.

"Who are you? What's going on ?" Laura asked, confused.

A soldier slapped her in the face. She knew the slap was meant to keep her from thinking clearly, and she remembered Edjop's advice, given when he related his own experience in the 1979 raid: "Think of a simple story and stand by it."

Unfortunately for Laura, her landlady came to confirm that she lived in the house.

"Putang'na mo! Ikaw ang hinahanap namin! You're the one we're after!" a soldier said, giving her another slap.

Laura tried to act and sound defiant. "Are you with the police?" she asked. "Where is your warrant?"

"We don't need a warrant, you bitch!" a soldier replied. "We have enough evidence against you! We even killed one of your companions!"

"I was frightened when I heard that," Laura recalls. "Maybe they were lying, I thought. Maybe the others had escaped and I was the only they had captured. But maybe all of them—Thelma, Mer, the entire Mindanao Commission—had been taken."

"Maybe you don't believe us," a soldier said. "We'll even show you the blood."

"Where?" Laura answered with all the arrogance she could muster.

"Come in and see for yourself," one of the soldiers said, pushing her into the house.

"Once inside," says Laura, "they started beating me up. Some of them tried to take off my clothes. But I resisted. They held my head still, to keep me from looking around the house."

One of her tormentors pointed to the piles of documents in one corner of the house. Laura could only curse to herself, remembering all the sensitive materials they had in the house.

"I desperately wanted to know what had really happened," says Laura, "so I would know how to handle the interrogation. I clung to the hope that I was the only one who had been captured, that the soldiers were merely using some psywar tactic on me—that no kasama had been killed."

Laura was brought to Camp Katitipan where she went through a nightmare. Soldiers blindfolded her with masking tape and a piece of string. They banged her head with two thick encyclopedia volumes, making her nose bleed. They undressed her and watched her shiver in front of the air-conditioner. They mashed her breasts and put sili and a piece of eggplant in her vagina.

The military also used a torture technique they called "dry submarine."

"What kind of supermarket bag would you prefer, Felcris or

Gaisano?" a soldier mockingly asked Laura, referring to two popular Davao supermarkets.

A soldier then put a plastic grocery bag over her head, taping it shut around her neck. She could only hear voices afterwards:

"*O, 'day, kawawa ka naman.* Oh, you poor thing. *Mga salbahe talaga itong mga ito e. Ako, ineng, mabait. Magsalita ka na.* You can trust me, dear. I'm not like these other guys. You can talk to me."

"How can she talk with her mouth covered?"

"*Sige na, ineng, magsalita ka na.* It's all right, dear. Do you want to say anything?"

"Yes," she answered through the plastic bag. "I want my lawyer. I have rights as a human being. I want to sleep."

They started to beat her up again.

One evening the soldiers brought in two men, both gagged and badly beaten. "They were the two men who had gotten off the bus after me. The soldiers mistook them for my companions. I learned that they were pedicab drivers and that soldiers had been beating them with a metal chain. I could hear them crying out in pain at night."

From the soldiers' conversations, she also confirmed that there had been a raid, and that some of her comrades had been arrested. But she still didn't know who it was who had been killed.

"On the third or was it the fourth day—I had completely lost my sense of time—they interrogated and tortured me for eight straight hours. I already had a fever then, and had not been eating well. I felt so weak, physically and psychologically. My captors had hit on my weakest point. I come from a very conservative family. Even Edjop and the others had teased me for being such a prude. And then the soldiers made me go through such a humiliation.

"I constantly reminded myself of my oath to serve the people and to protect my comrades. But I no longer had any will power to resist. I was ready to surrender, to cooperate with my persecutors."

But one night a soldier showed her the front page of a Davao newspaper. The headline read: "TOP CPP MAN KILLED IN DAVAO CITY RAID." Beside it was a large photograph of Edjop.

"*Putangina,* I said to myself. The memory of our last days together suddenly flashed in my mind. I was the last problem he had had to deal with, and I remembered how he had been so understanding. I felt guilty. I had failed to live up to his expectations of me as a cadre. And now he was dead.

"I thought of how, as he was about to die, he still refused to reveal his own identity, to protect other kasamas. *Biruin mong mamamatay ka na lang, ipagkakaila mo pa ang tunay mong pangalan.* Remembering all these gave me strength. As I stared at his picture, I thought: I will not fail you this time.

"I became enraged. I began to hate those who were persecuting me, who had killed a good man like Ed. I began to fight back. I didn't care anymore about dying. Edjop had given up everything for our cause, I thought. I could do no less.

"I tried to get hold of a bottle which I could smash, so I could use one of the broken pieces to slash my wrists with. I wanted to kill myself, so that I wouldn't be able to give away any damaging information and be a dishonor to what Ed had died for."

Meek and frightened in the first days of her captivity, Laura became unruly and defiant towards her torturers. She started to yell at them and curse them: "*Mga putangina n'yo! Mga baboy! Kaya maraming sumasali sa rebolusyon, dahil mga hayop kayo!* You sons-of-bitches! You pigs! This is why so many join the revolution, because you're all animals!"

Laura says the whole camp must have heard her, because she was shouting at the top of her voice. She knocked down chairs and whatever she could reach. She kicked and spat at her torturers. She even deliberately urinated on the floor of Estares' office, sending the soldiers scampering to clean up the mess, all the while cursing her: "You bitch! Now we'll have to wax the floor!"

"The soldiers eventually got tired of beating me up," says Laura. "They moved me to another part of the camp. By then

I had calmed down. I began assessing my performance under interrogation, to see if I had done my best to protect other comrades."

After a few days, Laura was reunited with the others who had been captured in the raid. Each one had suffered one form of torture or another.

"For about a month, we bore with the pain of living with Edjop's death," says Thelma. "Our morale was very low."

The most painful torture they had endured was to see military men with some of Edjop's belongings—his watch, his clutch bag, even his clothes.

"Nakakainis talaga," recalls Thelma. "We were all so mad. They did not even show any respect for him."

Raids and the apprehension of top leaders of the movement are big business for the different military intelligence units.

"When the documents captured from our house were brought to Camp Katitipan," relates Thelma, "intelligence officers scampered to get as many papers from the pile. *Agawan talaga.* They didn't want to share bits of information which they could use to nab other top-ranking leaders of the movement."

Edjop was worth P180,000 to Estares and other officers of his unit. Fat sums were also in store for the capture of other suspected CPP leaders: Rodolfo Salas, suspected CPP Central Committee chairman, was worth P250,000; Rafael Baylosis, suspected CPP secretary-general, P200,000; Antonio Zumel, P125,000; Chito Santa Romana and Ericson Baculinao, exiles in China, P100,000 each.

On their first week in Camp Katitipan, Mer and Thelma could hear Major Estares singing to the tune of Elton John's hit song: *"Kung gusto mo ng promotion, manghuli ka ng Skyline pigeon.* If you want a promotion, go catch a Skyline pigeon." A few months after the raid, Estares got his promotion. He is now the provincial commander of Davao del Norte, with the rank of lieutenant colonel.

Laura and the other detainees wrote letters to Edjop's son and family.

To Nonoy, they said: *"Mga kasamahan kami ng tatay mo. Gusto naming ipaabot sa iyo na mabuting tao ang tatay mo. Mahal namin siya. Minahal niya rin kami. Dapat nating ipagmalaki na namatay ang tatay mo para sa bayan."*

[We are your father's comrades. We want you to know that your father was a good man. We loved him. He loved us. We should be proud that your father died for the people.]

To the Jopson family, they wrote: *"Gusto naming malaman ninyo na kahit sa huling sandali, ang mga kasama at ang kapakanan ng bayan ang pinaninindigan ni Ed . . . Bagamat hindi na niya dinanas ang aming dinanas sa aming pagkadeteyn, malaking tulong ang kanyang alaala para mapanghawakan namin ang tortyur, gawing pampalakas ng loob ang kanyang sakripisyo at kabayanihan para matagalan ang pahirap ng mga militar . . . . Maraming salamat sa pagbibigay ninyo sa bayan ng isang anak at kapatid na tulad niya."*

[We want you to know that, up to the last moment, Ed stood by his comrades and for the welfare of the people. . . . Though he did not go through what we went through under detention, his memory helped us endure torture. His heroism and sacrifices helped us withstand the brutality of the military . . . . Thank you for giving the people a son and brother like him.]

42
Farewell
Under a Red Banner

News of the raid and of Edjop's death spread to other underground units in Mindanao.

Leon learned about it over the phone. "After having lost so many friends and comrades, I had stopped crying over the death of a kasama. But I couldn't help shedding tears over Edjop's death, for we were very close and he was an extraordinary comrade. I regretted, and was even angry, that he did not come with me when we were supposed to leave for Cagayan de Oro."

On September 21, a very nervous cadre came to Bruce's house with the news. Cindy broke down in tears. Bruce recalls suddenly feeling weak: "My wife and I hoped it wasn't true, that Edjop had just been captured or perhaps wounded. Then we tried to reach Laura, to tell her not to return to the house. But it was too late."

Joy also heard the news. She went to her niece's house in Davao, to ask her help in confirming the report. Cornelio Caguiat, an executive in a local logging company, and his wife, Eden, accompanied Joy to a friend's house, while they went to the different morgues in the city.

"We still feared for Tita Joy's safety," Eden relates. "We thought that the military could also be after her."

After inquiring at two funeral parlors, the couple went to the Cosmopolitan Funeral Homes, where the caretaker informed them that the military had just brought in the body of a "short man wearing shorts." The body was Edjop's.

"His body had already been wiped clean of the blood," Kune, as Mr. Caguiat is called, recalls. "It was badly bruised and riddled with bullet wounds."

He and Eden went back to their friend's house where Joy was waiting. "Tita Joy, it's him," Eden said.

"Nanamlay siya," says Kune of Joy's reaction. "She suddenly felt weak. But she was still composed. She sat down and wept, but

she was not hysterical. She seemed to have been prepared for it."

In the afternoon of September 21, the Jopson family was celebrating the birthday of one of Edjop's younger sisters.

" 'I wasn't feeling well then," says Josefa Jopson. "But we were having fun. We even had a program where everybody sang. I didn't know why, but somehow I couldn't sing, despite being the singer in the family."

At around six in the evening, one of the Jopson girls received a call from a journalist from the *Bulletin Today,* who told them about unconfirmed reports from Mindanao that Edjop had been killed in a raid. The journalist promised to call back with more details.

"I prayed that it wasn't true," says Hernan Jopson. "In the past, we had heard numerous reports about Ed being captured or killed. But they had all turned out to be false."

At around one o'clock the following morning, Joy called up from Davao to confirm the news.

"Everybody in the family was shocked," relates Inday. "The first thing we did was to take care of Mommy. She really took the news hard."

Mr. Jopson left on an early morning flight to Davao, where Kune met him.

Meanwhile, the Jopsons' long-time maid, Sianing, was asked to get Edjop's clothes ready. As she went through his things, she remembered how she had also helped Edjop, then NUSP president, prepare his clothes for out-of-town trips. She began to cry.

That same morning Kune and Mr. Jopson went to the morgue to see Edjop's body.

The medical examiner showed Mr. Jopson a copy of the autopsy report. Edjop had sustained nine bullet wounds—five in the chest and stomach, two in the right arm, one in each leg. According to Mr. Jopson, the doctor told him that many of Edjop's wounds were inflicted at close range. It reinforced suspicions that Edjop had been taken alive—and later executed.

"It takes one bullet to kill a man. Why did they have to shoot him so many times?" The people who killed my son were sadists," a bitter Mr. Jopson says.

Military authorities would not immediately release Edjop's body; they referred Mr. Jopson from one office to another. But with the help of influential people in Davao—some of them Edjop's former colleagues in the NUSP; others simply admirers of the former student leader—Mr. Jopson finally claimed his son's remains.

At the funeral parlor, Mr. Jopson picked out and bought a beautifully crafted coffin made of narra. "I know my son would have appreciated resting in a coffin made out of our national tree."

In the morning of September 23, Edjop's body was flown to Manila and brought to the Jopson residence.

"When we opened the coffin, we noticed how handsome he looked," relates Mrs. Jopson. "We all touched his face and hair. We all wept."

The gates of the Jopson home were locked. A guard politely told sympathizers that the family wanted to be left alone for a day, so they could mourn Edjop's death in private.

The Marcos government hailed Edjop's death as a major victory in the counter-insurgency war. According to a news item in the *Bulletin Today*, (September 24, 1982), the AFP Chief of Staff himself, General Fabian Ver, reported to Marcos and Defense Minister Juan Ponce Enrile that the killing of Edjop had "dealt a big blow to the dissident movement in the south." Earlier that year, NDF leaders Horacio Morales and Father Edicio de la Torre were captured in a military raid in Manila.

At the Ateneo, the school which once hailed Edjop as a model student and leader, administrators initially refused to let his body lie in the college chapel. They said they were concerned about military surveillance and the security of their students.

Only criticisms from Ateneo alumni, who, in the words of Reli German, were "bewildered at our alma mater's taking such a fraidy cat stance," made school authorities reluctantly allow the wake to be held on campus—but only for one day.

And it was hardly a warm reception, as Freddie Salanga would later relate in an article on Edjop's funeral (*Mr. & Mrs.*, October 19, 1982):

"The mass over, I opted to go in and join the line queueing up for a last view of the friend in the long brown coffin. When my turn came I could hardly make him out under glass, for the Jesuits had sprinkled too much holy water. As I made a turn past the altar I stopped to look back and suddenly heard this Jesuit practically pleading with the family to please decide when to close the coffin and take it out. He had a stupid smile on his face and anyone could plainly see that he was nervous. It took all I could to keep myself from pushing him away. There was still a long line of mourners and all he could think of was hustling everyone away."

In the same article, Freddie wrote: "They may not have agreed with his brand of seeking justice, but the man had, undoubtedly, stood for the same thing many of them had been (sometimes triumphantly) preaching about, albeit under better protective cover, for Loyola Heights is hardly any sane man's idea of a guerrilla jungle."

Wrote columnist Ninez Cacho-Olivares (*Bulletin Today*, October 26, 1982): "One wonders: Who taught this Atenean the strength to stick to his convictions? Who nurtured this same man's idealism?

"As one Jesuit said afterwards, 'How terribly sad it is. While we may not share his ideology, he must be admired for sticking to his convictions.' "

The wake at the UP chapel, where Edjop's body lay for three additional days, achieved more meaning. People of different ages, sectors and political beliefs, whose lives Edjop had touched in one way or another, came to pay him tribute.

Edjop's enemies also made their presence felt. The inscription on a wreath, believed to have been sent by military elements, read: *"Kay Edjop, Pulang Mamamatay-tao."* (To Edjop, Red Murderer.)

Joy attended the wake in disguise, but she was apparently recognized by military agents. A brief scuffle took place outside the chapel, with Mr. Jopson himself taking the initiative to block the car of the agents out to get his daughter-in-law. Joy got away.

Despite these incidents, the salutations for the fallen leader echoed in the UP chapel and beyond.

"We are not gathered here to mourn Edjop," said nationalist leader Jose W. Diokno Jr. "Instead, we should mourn for ourselves and a society which has made it necessary for a young man like Edjop to give up his own life."

Joma Sison, then in prison, wrote, "A system that hunts down and kills a man like Edgar M. Jopson is thoroughly wrong and unjust. By his accomplishments and martyrdom, he inspires more people to fight for the national democratic revolution."

Joaquin "Chino" Roces, who worked with Edjop in the relief operation after the Bantay burning incident in 1970, as well as in other civic campaigns, was there. He approached and saluted Edjop's body in the coffin for about two minutes, and would have prolonged this gesture if people had not assisted him back to his seat when he began to shake with emotion.

In his column in *WE Forum* (October 4, 1982), Joaquin "Titong" Roces wrote:

> They could not buy your mind
> So they put a price on your head
> They thought that this would bring you shame
> And make your friends disdain your name
> But they made it obvious instead
> They did not want you to survive
> To avoid having to face you alive.

"There's one thing I quite admire in Edjop," says Father Raul Bonoan, who has served as a board member of the Edgar Jopson Memorial Foundation, "and that is his firmness of conviction. There were many of his peers who were more radical than Edjop—much more radical than Edjop. But many of them did not pursue the convictions which they had then. Some of them have gone to government and private business. Some have gone abroad and stayed there. But Edjop stayed in his country and continued to work in activities and organizations that are in direct touch with the people."

"It's strange," comments Romy Chan on the way things have turned out. "It's not something that makes you feel better. It just makes me realize that, in those days, we didn't know any better."

Some of Edjop's former comrades who were still active in the underground dared to go to the UP chapel to pay their last respects to their fallen comrade. Jackie, who had worked with him in the NDF Prepcom, was teary-eyed as she viewed the body for the last time. "When I learned that he had tried to escape," says Jackie, "I thought, yes, that was Edjop. He did not give up so easily."

In guerrilla camps and UG houses, cadres learned of the death through radio or the newspapers. Some were disheartened by the loss. In one camp, kasamas were about to have lunch when they heard the news. "*Hindi na kami nakakain.* We couldn't eat," recalls Doy of Mindanao. Months later in Mindanao, cadres were heard to comment in times of crisis, "If only Ka Gimo were still alive. . . . "

But Edjop's death had the opposite effect on others.

"I didn't feel demoralized by his death," says Jackie. "*Mas lalo pa akong tumibay.* I felt even stronger."

"He was such a gentle person," relates Louie Jalandoni, who was in Europe as NDF international representative when Edjop was killed. "I could not imagine Edjop dying such a violent death."

Some of Edjop's admirers were surprised to learn that he had joined the underground movement. Marcel, the cadre who welcomed Edjop to the party, tells of a friend of his who considered Edjop his *idolo:* "The main reason he would not join the movement was because we had been critical of Edjop in the FQS. It was only when Edjop died that my friend learned Edjop was one of us. Now he helps us out in his own way."

Workers and labor leaders, some of them in tears, also came to the wake. "I have no doubt in my mind that Edjop took the right path," says Ka Felicing, the union president who became

Edjop's ninong in matrimony. "And he showed us this road, taught us how to liberate ourselves and our fellow workers."

Ellen, a member of the CPP Central Committee, worked closely with Edjop in the mid-seventies. "After we went our separate ways, Edjop and I only met a few times a year, during important meetings. When he died, I didn't immediately feel the loss. Somehow, I still felt that he was just in some far place in another part of the country, still fighting for our cause. That's how I usually feel about comrades who become close to me. It was only at our next national conference, where Edjop was not present, that I really felt he was gone."

Olive, a cadre now based in Southern Luzon, also became close to Edjop. A few months earlier, she had sent him a letter in which she confided her wavering commitment to the revolution. Edjop never got a chance to answer her. But as she viewed his body at the wake, Olive thought, "Why did you have to answer me in this manner?" She stayed on in the underground.

Political detainees sent cards and drawings. One had the inscription: "They have not silenced a just man just because they have killed him."

Another card said:

> Ang magbuhos ng dugo para sa bayan,
> Ay kagitingang hindi malilimutan;
> Ang buhay na inialay sa lupang mahal
> Mayaman sa aral at kadakilaan.

> [To shed blood for one's country
> Is gallantry not easily forgotten
> A life offered for the motherland
> Is rich in wisdom and heroism.]

Edjop's friends from NUSP days were also there.

"I was, of course, saddened," says Jun Pau. "But somehow, it wasn't totally unexpected, knowing the kind of risks his work entailed."

As he looked at the body of his friend, Edros observed how

"Edjop didn't seem to have changed at all, physically—he looked the same as when we were still together."

"It was obvious that they [the military] didn't just kill him," says Romy Chan. "They did all sorts of things to him."

"By then, other fellow Ateneans had offered their lives in the struggle," says Alex Aquino. "Sonny Hizon was killed in Panta-bangan, Ferdie Arceo in Iloilo, Billy Begg in Isabela. Manny Yap was made to disappear in 1975, and has not been found since. Still, Edjop's death was no less saddening."

In an article for an American Jesuit magazine, Joseph O'Hare, Edjop's professor in college, had this to say:

"It seemed much more likely that Edgar Jopson would leave school and, like many of his contemporaries, go on eventually to an executive office in one of the international corporations in Manila. Instead, he found himself in the end in a small house far from Manila, huddled with others who dreamed of changing a society where most people are poor and where the poor are powerless.

"What changed the mild, rational idealist of 1970 into the revolutionary of 1982? It is difficult to resist the argument that his journey was inevitable, that when repression frustrates all attempts at reform, a more radical logic will prevail. One tragic truth, however, is beyond question: The Philippines cannot afford to so waste its valuable resource: gifted and dedicated idealists like Edgar Jopson. No nation could."

"Some people say Edjop is a hero," says Father William Kreutz, Edjop's high school teacher. "Some people would say, 'No, he acted against the national interest.' It's very hard to make these judgments. They have to be made many many years after it all occurred. My own feeling is, yes, anyone who follows through and dies for what he or she believes in, especially if it is for the benefit of the nation—I think that person deserves to be called a hero."

"I was mainly shocked to learn that [Edjop] had turned to communism as a way of life, a way of life diametrically opposed to the things we imbibed at the Ateneo," wrote columnist and

Ateneo alumnus Ernesto Rodriguez Jr. "Of course he was not the first, nor the last, Atenean to embrace atheistic communism."

On her brother's beliefs, Sucel Jopson Samonte wrote in a conservative Baptist newsletter: "Was Ed an atheist? I don't know. We had prayed much for him. We had tried to share our faith with him. But if indeed he was an atheist, while I am a Christian who has all the access to God's power, doesn't God expect from me greater LOVE, greater SELFLESSNESS, greater COMMITMENT to His cause, than what an atheist had offered to his cause?"

"What do I think moved him?" says Adel Musidora. "I think it was, simply put, an honest-to-goodness desire to serve the people."

Sometime before his own untimely death, Freddie Salanga recalled: "How did his death affect me? Shock . . . shame. I think shame more than shock, because this man you had grown up with had taken that step . . . and here you were alive, not doing very much and afraid to speak out. I did speak up at Edjop's wake. I guess his death put a little spine where there wasn't any spine at all. I think that's what happened to many of his classmates."

Salanga was most memorable in his "Eulogy for My Friend, Edjop" (Mr. & Ms. magazine, October 12, 1982):

"The problem with you, of course, Edjop, is that you never blinked. Even when the times began to change and the activist's life no longer was romantic because we were growing old and aching for the comforts our Jesuit education made us feel heirs to. We were the romantics then and you the pragmatist. There's no other way of putting it. We were in love with the romance of activism, while you had a romance with activism itself. That should make all of us a little smaller, I think, in view of the ideals that we shared.

"Then, too, the funny thing is that you were always the small one. I mean physically small. Short as a stump of a tree. That's a fitting image, I think, because you remained rooted while we all allowed ourselves to roll down to the log pond, there to be towed to the lumberyard to be cut, sawn, hewed and polished to uniform lengths and breadths. It was you who stayed on in the forest—short as a stump, yes, but strong. Were you stronger then, in the face of temptation, in front of the blandishments of the good life whose attainment we knew would be denied us if we stuck to our ideals?

"We were taller, yes, but you always cast the longer shadow.

"Because you were more faithful to your ideals.

"Because you had the guts to turn your back on what you had because you always felt that you had something better to do.

"Because you refused to let your ideas fade.

"Because you stayed on in the forest, rooted to the ideals you felt were worth more than all that the good life had to offer.

"We stand under that shadow now.

"We will be standing under that shadow for some time to come.

"And while standing under your shadow, Edjop, we will try to understand how and why it had to come to this.

"In the final analysis, we may not agree with what you died for. Your circle of friends will remain divided on that question as will, sadly enough, your country. But one thing we will always be sure of: you died a brave man, a just man and a good man. You died believing in what you lived for and that is an honor we may never even have the privilege of sharing."

"I grieved when Ed died, " says Josefa Jopson. "But at his wake and funeral, so many people praised him and related so many of the good things my son had done. Some people we did not even know told us that they really loved Ed because of how he had helped them. It's amazing how he had to die for us to know how much he had really done for people. Instead of being sad, I was elated. I felt like I was being lifted up by the people who paid him tribute. It was as if they were rejoicing for the strength that Edgar gave them when he was still alive. They had been inspired to go on. That was the time when I offered everything and thanked the Lord for giving me such a son."

"Edgar lived a full life," says Hernan Jopson. "We feel no

bitterness about his death. In fact, we even envy him. *Naiinggit kami dahil hindi namin magaya ang ginawa niya. Tumanda na lang kami, wala pang nagagawa.* We have gotten old without doing much. But we try in our own way to help our people. But, of course, it can never be as big or as much as he gave."

"Ed's death awakened us," adds Josefa Jopson. "I even agreed to help form MARTYR. [Mrs. Jopson is the chairperson of MARTYR, Mothers Relatives and Friends Against Tyranny, a human rights group that helps relatives of victims of political repression.] I didn't even know anything about running an organization. But if my son offered his life for a great cause, then I thought I could contribute in this way. I have always told my fellow mothers, those who have also lost a son or daughter in the struggle, 'We have only a few years left. We must help the masa, those whom our loved ones died for.'"

On October 1, 1982, Edjop's family, friends and comrades— monitored closely by military agents—led the funeral march to the Loyola Memorial Park. A nun and a student draped a red banner over the coffin made of narra.

Edjop was finally laid to rest. It was a bright sunny day.

Epilogue

The assassination of Ninoy Aquino, less than a year after Edjop's death, sparked a massive awakening in the cities. But in the months just before and immediately following the takeover of Corazon Aquino, the revolutionary movement committed mistakes and miscalculations that led to confusion and disagreements among the kasamas.

There were critical mistakes, such as the overreaction of cadres in Mindanao to the "zombies," leading to the arbitrary execution of kasamas suspected of being deep penetration agents.

There were debates on strategy and tactics. Some cadres resigned, disillusioned. Others, while still critical of policies, stayed on.

But the reasons and passions that made Edjop take the radical path have remained.

Workers have borne the brunt of the new government's economic policies, which have stressed cheap labor as an incentive to foreign investors. Strikes have erupted all over the country, and have been brutally suppressed by police and military authorities.

Twelve years after the La Tondeña strike, the historic battlecry of the workers—*"Tama na! Sobra na! Welga na!"*—echoed once again, but from a different perspective. In October 1987, President Corazon Aquino, speaking before businessmen and capitalists, proclaimed her government's new thrust with the slogan: *"Tama na ang Kudeta! Sobra na ang Komunista! Ipaglaban ang Demokrasya!"* [Enough of Coups d'etat! The Communists have gone too far! Let's fight for Democracy!]

Included in Cory Aquino's "komunistas" were organized workers who would not accept the government policy of putting the interest of local and foreign capital above theirs. They were considered an obstruction to "development" and, as one of the first results of Cory's call, state troopers moved in to break up picket lines.

But if there is a lesson to be derived from Edjop's odyssey, it is that the word *despair* is not in the vocabulary of those who seek change.

In 1986, as the final confrontation between Marcos and the people approached, Freddie Salanga, speaking before a group of UP academics in the Edgar Jopson Memorial Lectures, underscored this point:

"But what about Edjop? And what about the great lesson he has left us? It is this: he has shown us that we are capable of growth, that we are eminently capable of escaping the confines of our class consciousness and that there is good reason to have hope."

In October 1988, Freddie died of pneumonia after undergoing a kidney transplant operation.

By then, some of Edjop's other comrades were also gone. Nobody had blamed Teddy for Edjop's death, but he felt a deep sense of guilt that he had survived the raid, while the kasama he was supposed to protect perished. He swore that the incident would never be repeated.

Two years later, in 1984, military elements raided the Mindanao Commission's underground house in Cagayan de Oro City. Teddy, Leon, and other ranking leaders were trapped, as soldiers pinned them inside with heavy automatic fire. "We had only one long rifle and we did not not have enough ammunition," Leon recalls. "We could fire only single shots, against their continuous heavy blasts."

As the situation worsened, Teddy commanded his comrades to make a run for it, through the back, while he provided them with cover fire. "I thought Teddy would follow us out," says Leon. "But I guess he stayed behind to make sure that the military would not be able to advance."

Leon and the others escaped unharmed. Teddy died in the shoot-out.

In 1985 Mer Arce, along with some comrades, fell when the car they were riding in was ambushed by military elements in Cebu City.

In the face of so much death, life continues. Many people who derived inspiration from Edjop still pursue his ideals.

Ka Felicing is now an official of the Kilusang Mayo Uno (May First Movement or KMU), the beleaguered labor federation advocating "genuine trade unionism."

Josefa Jopson is still chairperson of MARTYR, whose membership continues to increase with the rise in the death toll of progressive leaders and activists.

Hernan Jopson served as board member of the *Partido ng Bayan* (People's Party or PnB) and continues to assist the families of detainees and victims of political repression.

Luis, the 15-year-old lad whom Edjop advised on his relations with his parents, is now a member of the leading committee of the NDF in Bataan.

On September 12, 1987, Samal became the scene of an epic battle, when 24 NPA guerrillas were trapped in Barrio San Juan by more than 200 government soldiers. Most of the guerrillas managed to escape, with the help of Aling Osang and the other "fighting people" of Samal.

On March 29, 1988, Joy was arrested together with her second husband, Romulo "Rolly" Kintanar, accused by the military of being commander-in-chief of the New People's Army.

Later that year, on September 21, the sixth anniversary of Edjop's death, she came out with her first public statement on her late husband, which their daughter, Joyette, read during commemorative rites at the Ateneo. "I have no regrets about our life together, except perhaps, that we were separated so soon," said Joy. "But Edjop lives in the hearts of all who are still struggling for a more just society, where ordinary people, the workers and the peasants, will truly be free."

On November 12, a day before Joy's birthday, she and Rolly Kintanar escaped. In a letter to family and friends, Joy wrote:

"I know that what we have done has caused you deep anxiety. But rather than rot in the Aquino government's prison and being relatively passive in that condition, we have taken the necessary risks to be able to rejoin our comrades and people in the common struggle to make our country a better place to live in.

"To Nonoy, Joyette and Risa, I say hold your heads high. There is absolutely nothing to be ashamed of. On the other hand, I know that you are very proud of your Tatay and of the sacrifices that he—and all of us—have had to bear as a result of his martyrdom in the service of our country and people. The cause for which he lived and so unselfishly gave up his life is the very cause which I, your Tito Rolly and other comrades are now striving to carry forward. We are animated by the same convictions that he held so dear; we carry the same banner of struggle that, in life, he so proudly held aloft.

"I do not, of course, expect you, Nonoy, to be some kind of 'superboy,' and you, Joyette and Risa, to be 'supergirls.' You are as human as the next boy or girl, and as such, you do miss the love and guidance that is directly bequeathed by parents. But I beg you to understand. From childhood, almost from babyhood, you have been taught the right values. And as you grow older and come to comprehend the dire problems that beset our country, their causes as well as their solutions, I know you will come to fully understand why your Tats was in this great movement for national freedom and democracy, and why I am in it too."

AFTERWORD

Edicio de la Torre

Around midnight on September 21, 1982, the colonel in charge of the Bago Bantay military detention camp asked to see Horacio "Boy" Morales and myself. I don't recall what we talked about, except that the phone rang. After taking the call, he sounded pleased: "We got Ed Jopson." "Where did you arrest him?" we asked. He corrected us: "He was not arrested; he was shot."

I can still remember most of the feelings, but not the words I managed to say—some muttered regrets that such a good person was killed. Unable to release the turmoil within, I felt even more imprisoned.

All nine prisoners at the camp worked on a condolence card. Our artist suggested the image of candles, with wax running down like tears and faces half-lit in mourning. In a letter to Edjop's family, I added a few lines about the passion, death, and resurrection of a middle-class Christian, saying Edjop was one of those who had undergone such a passage.

Less than a year later, Edjop's larger-than-life picture was carried through the streets of Metro Manila. On August 21, 1983, Benigno "Ninoy" Aquino was assassinated at the international airport that now bears his name. The initial reaction of most traditional opposition leaders was panic. Worried that Marcos would come gunning for them next, they sought out their contacts in the clandestine resistance and were offered sanctuary, should they need it, in selected guerrilla zones. Before they could take up the offer, massive protests in Metro Manila gave them reason to stay in the city. A loose alliance, Justice for Aquino, Justice for All (JAJA), organized a funeral march that lasted a whole day and involved over a million people. The main canvas mural had Edjop in its gallery of martyrs, together with Ninoy Aquino, Macli-ing Dulag, the leader of the Igorot people's opposition to the Chico river dam project in the Cordillera, and Dr. Juan Escandor, a cancer specialist who

333

had joined the New People's Army (NPA). (In response to criticism against gender bias, later murals included Maria Lorena Barros, a feminist poet who was killed while leading the NPA in southern Tagalog).

The mural reflected the initial dominance of national democrats as the organized core of the protest movement. But the anti-Marcos protests included a variety of political tendencies, from conservatives to a mix of liberal and social democrats. In addition to politically "conscious" organizations, there were a lot of "spontaneous" participants, including highly visible middle-class groups and even some upper-class personalities. Even inside prison, we could feel the energy and quickening flow of the popular movement—a mixture of anger and laughter, slogans and jokes, creating new acronyms and protest forms, manifestos and songs, proving that "fear is contagious, but also courage is contagious." The economic crisis further fed the political crisis; after 1981, the economy had negative growth, with a sharp downturn in 1983 as foreign credits dried up, and capital fled at a faster rate. (After Marcos' departure, economists from all schools of thought calculated that the economy could recover its 1981 level only by 1991.) The critical mass of organized political tendencies sustained the momentum of the protest movement. The unprecedented numbers of unorganized participants magnified the impact it had on the popular consciousness, especially on the mainstream media.

The different political tendencies struggled to interpret and give direction to the popular movement. Some traditional political clans who had been excluded from the spoils of Marcos' martial law project saw the protest movement as an electoral base for their return to power and for their project of restoring pre-martial law democracy; they did not see much need for other social changes. Newer opposition forces, who defined themselves as neither conservative nor revolutionary, saw the protest movement as central to their evolving strategy of "pressure politics" that would force Marcos to resign in favor of a government that was more progressive but not revolutionary. Unlike the conservatives, they saw the need for social reforms, especially agrarian reform, and for changes in the existing relations between the United States and the Philippines.

National democrats agreed on many points with the second strategy, but saw the value of the protest movement within the framework of a "people's war" strategy and a revolutionary transformation of Philippine society. That strategy gave first priority to armed and clandestine forces. The protest movement was part of the open legal movement that sought to involve a wide range of progressive and "middle forces," but directed toward an armed perspective, couched in formulations such as "we must be open to all forms of struggle."

The contradictions among these different political tendencies and projects explain the energy spent on what seemed like petty debates among the opposition. Even JAJA leaders couldn't agree on what central slogan should express the political objective of the alliance. The initial proposal was "Marcos Resign!" National democrats thought that was too passive and reformist; they proposed "Oust Marcos!" But despite their debates, JAJA leaders were united on drawing a sharp line between themselves and traditional politicians, notably Salvador Laurel, the best-known of the old elite, and currently vice-president. They welcomed some of the more progressive of the old nationalist leaders, especially Jose Diokno and Lorenzo Tañada, regarded as the most honest and committed to developing a "new politics."

When Marcos called for elections to a national assembly in 1984, JAJA split on the issue of participation or boycott. The majority—including most of the national democrats—opted to boycott the elections and formed a new alliance, the Coalition of Organizations for the Realization of Democracy (CORD). The split in the opposition extended to the two Aquinos who had emerged as political figures in the period of protest: Ninoy's brother "Butz" and his wife "Cory." Butz joined those who advocated a boycott, partly because of his closer link to the street protestors, and to Diokno and Tañada. Cory, after some hesitation, opted for participation, reflecting the greater influence traditional politicians such as Laurel had on her political outlook.

In 1978, the question of whether or not to participate in the national assembly elections bitterly divided the national democrats. Initially, most of those in Manila wanted to participate, including Edjop; but he later decided to follow the Communist Party's directive to boycott. Although demoralized by his change of stand, his comrades defied the order to boycott and pursued an acrimonious debate. In 1984, however, the political situation did not encourage many national democrats or other political tendencies to advocate electoral participation. It helped that the more progressive traditional politicians within the opposition—such as José Diokno—advocated a boycott and joined CORD. But the clear-cut electoral strategy of their conservative opponents forced the "new opposition" to think through their own strategy.

Some, including Diokno, tried to develop a strategy of "pressure politics" that avoided a premature choice between elections and revolution. From prison, we proposed the concept of "popular democracy" as a coalition project. National democrats in the open movement had a more complicated task, since their strategic center of gravity was not the open legal struggle, much less the struggle in the cities. Also, unlike those who advocated the other two contesting strategies, they worked with the calculation that the balance of forces placed the revolutionary movement only on the "strategic defensive."

As the protests escalated, however, new experiences of the national democrats and the broader popular movement began to blur the sharp distinction between pressure politics and people's war. In Mindanao, the urban "sparrow units" set up by the NPA, by means of selected assassination of military and police officers, succeeded in putting the military and police on the defensive, especially in Davao City. And the theoretical discussions that came out of the successful struggle in Nicaragua and the growing insurgency in El Salvador led to proposals for an insurrectionary strategy.

In late 1984, the national democrats began to elaborate and test the strategy of *welgang bayan,* or people's strike. The strategy was spectacularly successful in Bataan, where popular protest was able to permanently stall construction on a nuclear plant. The protest brought thousands of people into the streets, unarmed; people were even pushing back military tanks. It was practically a rehearsal for the uprising of 1986. One difference was that the NPA were also blowing up electricity towers. Long marches or *lakbayan,* involving up to 100,000 in Negros island alone, forged closer links between the rural and urban movements.

By 1985, the different political tendencies in the popular movement thought that they had built sufficient unity to formalize a coalition, *Bayan* (*Bagong Alyansang Makabayan* or New Patriotic Alliance). *Bayan* was intended to embody an alternative to the electoral project of the traditional politicians and also to act as a sort of "unified command" for the open legal movement. The coalition did not hold; those who refused to join, or left afterward, accused the national democrats of trying to dominate it organizationally. More than organizational factors were involved, however, and before fence-mending measures could succeed, even sharper political differences surfaced when Marcos unexpectedly announced "snap elections" for the presidency. As a result, the rift deepened.

After some debate, the Communist Party of the Philippines (CPP), which exercised overwhelming influence on the national democrats, decided on a boycott, arguing that the elections would be rigged by Marcos and would not substantially change the system anyway. But many national democrats (including communists) who worked with CORD and *Bayan* were inclined to support the candidacy of Cory Aquino. From prison, most political prisoners argued for participation. It was not simply because Aquino promised to release political prisoners if she won; we shared the belief that Marcos would cheat his way to victory. But we argued that if we wished to influence the post-election protests, we should be with the people if they chose to take part in the elections campaign.

A large number of individual national democrats did participate in the electoral campaign, but organizations identified with national democracy publicly advocated a boycott stand; as a result, they were not invited to the post-election protest campaign called for by Cory Aquino. They might have recovered their influence in the protest movement, had it lasted longer and escalated to the planned general strike. But another unforeseen factor intervened. Directly after the election between Marcos and Cory Aquino in February 1986, plans for a coup by Juan Ponce Enrile and his supporters in the Reformed Armed Forces Movement (RAM) were uncovered. Enrile and RAM took a stand of open rebellion and declared support for Cory, thus sparking the "people power revolution" of February 22–25. The uprising on the highway called EDSA (Epifanio de los Santos Avenue) ushered in an unexpected and complicated new political situation.

After the departure of Marcos, Cory Aquino ordered the release of all political prisoners. Most of these were known to be national democrats. But that did not prevent us from joining in the celebration and taking part in the debate about the new "democratic space." Not that we had illusions about the limits of the post-Marcos order; we simply chose to concentrate on pursuing its possibilities. We expressed our qualified optimism by comparing the new situation to a "premature baby": it came sooner than we expected; it was smaller than what we wanted. But we were part of its multiple parentage, and claimed the right to take part in the struggle to define the direction of its growth.

But it was obvious that the main national democratic organizations, both illegal and legal, were on the defensive, burdened by the mistakes of *Bayan* and the boycott. Conservative forces used these mistakes to further marginalize them from the democratic debate. Many liberal and progressive forces seized the chance to get back at them for past hurts. (A recent visit to Berlin reminded me of the mood of those days. I met Germans who sadly observed that many who proclaim their adherence to democracy also viciously prevent those who called themselves socialists or communists from joining the democratic debate.)

There were other sobering reminders that the situation was even more complex than it seemed. A friend from Mindanao said that she had written to people in Davao del Norte about a talk I had given on democratic space; they had written back: "What greater democratic space? We are being bombed for the first time!'' The departure of Marcos had also released the fifteen battalions he had kept for his defense in Metro Manila; they were immediately thrown by the new Armed Forces command into active combat against NPA guerrilla fronts in Cagayan, Bicol, Negros, and Mindanao.

The CPP leadership issued a rare public self-criticism, admitting that the boycott position had been an error and had violated democratic procedures within the party. But the national democratic movement was in a dark and self-critical mood for quite a while. How could a movement and party that had played such a central role in the struggle against the dictatorship so miscalculate the mood of the people and the balance of forces, and be left out of the climax of the struggle? More important, what should they do to "reposition" themselves and get back to their accustomed place in the popular movement?

The heated debates about the boycott error, as well as over new tactics, drew attention away from a much more serious problem in the movement. In 1985, the Mindanao CPP organization discovered that it had been infiltrated by military agents up to intermediate leadership levels. The deep penetration agents (DPA) had sabotaged NPA military operations and alienated the mass base and allies by deliberately offensive behavior. A campaign was waged against the DPA, also called "zombies," but this inflicted more damage than what the infiltrators had done. By the time the campaign was ordered to stop, only one-third of the 9,000 CPP members in Mindanao remained. At least 300 had been killed; the rest fled to other areas, resigned, or simply stopped operating. It would take the Mindanao CPP another three years just to double their depleted numbers. The damage to the rest of the national democratic movement is harder to quantify. At that time, the revelations about the killings did not arouse the furor they deserved. Three years later in 1988, about sixty people were killed in another anti-DPA campaign in southern Tagalog and Metro Manila. This time, the impact on the public and especially on the movement itself was much greater, because the killings added to the accumulated doubts and dissatisfaction about the movement's efforts to cope with the new situation.

Up to the present, mid-1990, the fortunes of the national democratic movement since 1986 receive conflicting judgments. On the negative side, military officers, government officials, liberals, and some progressive intellectuals deliver variations on a common theme—the movement has suffered continuing organizational decline and political marginalization; its leadership is divided and unable to adjust to the changed situation. This is quite a contrast to the judgment in the early 1980s, when conventional wisdom tagged it as "the only insurgency growing in Asia with a chance of entering the corridors of power."

These critics cite the capture of key communist and national democratic leaders, resignations and dissent among cadres, the lack of enthusiasm (outside of their own organizations) for purely national democratic initiatives, declining sympathies in the mainstream media, and public criticism of such NPA tactics as indiscriminate sparrow killings in Metro Manila. Their judgments are also partly colored by their political options. This is most obvious in the case of the military, who have declared their intention to crush the insurgency by 1992, or at least contain it. Government officials, faced with mounting public disaffection, cite the results of the 1987 plebiscite, elections, and public opinion polls, saying that even if they are not doing well, the people still reject other alternatives as worse, whether they are rightist coup plotters or leftist guerrillas. The same line is taken by some bishops who recently met with leaders of the National Democratic Front (NDF). Liberals hold on to fading hopes for a centrist alternative, still suspicious of the national democrats' ability to accommodate them. The same is true of progressives who nurse past resentments; their theoretical critique of the national democratic line indirectly justifies their choice of purely legal and gradualist politics.

Leaders of the CPP and the NDF do acknowledge that the movement has suffered losses, and reiterate the need for "consolidation and rectification." But they see no reason to change their line. They reject the conclusion that they are "politically marginalized," and express confidence that the worsening social and political crises precisely vindicate the logic of national democracy, and will eventually bring people around to join or rejoin the movement. Hence, they pursue a "back to basics" campaign, to reassert and propagate the national democratic critique and alternative. Toward the end of 1988, there was even talk of possible victory within a decade.

My own judgment is also based on a mix of indicators and my own choice of politics, which is identified with the "popular democratic" tendency in Philippine political discourse. I hold myself accountable to the broad popular movement, which includes the national democratic movement as its largest section. My stay in Europe has also given the impact of recent changes in Eastern Europe greater immediacy. (The same is true of the "new thinking" going on in the popular movements and liberation movements in South Africa and Central America.)

From this perspective, I think that the sweeping picture of a much weakened movement needs major retouching, especially in the rural areas. The NPA has maintained its peasant guerrilla force of about 10,000 regulars and has even developed bigger formations for fighting. There is one operational battalion each in Northern Luzon and Samar; most of the fifty-plus guerrilla fronts have regular companies, and the NPA continues to operate in sixty-three out of seventy-three provinces. Anticommunist vigilantes and the paramilitary force called Citizens Armed Forces Geographical Units (CAFGU), together with unrestrained military assaults, have put heavy pressure on the NPA and the organized rural base, but the NPA can rightly claim to have survived the worst attacks so far. However, the rate of increase of full-time guerrillas and high-powered rifles has slowed down. This has led some NPA leaders to argue that buying or capturing weapons from the Armed Forces has reached its limits; they push for arms procurement from abroad, especially of heavier weaponry.

But if the NPA can show some growth, the same can not be said of its clandestine rural mass base. The escalation of military assaults (including bombing and artillery) and paramilitary attacks has dis-

placed a cumulative total of 250,000 to 500,000 "internal refu-
gees" in the past three years, many of them from guerrilla zones.
This has influenced a broader debate within the NPA and CPP. One
side argues for even faster NPA regularization and procurement
of heavy weaponry to enable the NPA to protect the base areas
and to carry the fight to exterior lines. The other side emphasizes
the deepening and widening of guerrilla war, with smaller regular
units (platoons), enough local guerrillas, and political work by the
NPA and by unarmed cadres to strengthen the mass organizations.
The last published figure for the clandestine rural bases (last quarter of 1987) was 750,000, quite small compared to the total population classified by the military as "threatened, infiltrated or
influenced" by the NPA. Barangays, the smallest political units, include about 2,000 people; estimates of those so threatened range
from 9,000 to 12,000 out of a total of 40,000—for a total population of about 10 million. Both sides of the debate also recognize
another problem: bigger NPA formations mean that the rural base
must produce greater surplus to support them.

The organizational picture needs further refinement when we take
legal rural organizations into account: peasant associations, rural
workers unions, cooperatives, and base Christian communities
(BCCs). These organizations have grown to a few million members,
despite the pressure, and most of them are in the Congress for a
People's Agrarian Reform (CPAR), a coalition which is critical of
the Aquino government's agrarian reform program. CPAR represents
different political tendencies, but they are united in a direction that
is not antagonistic to the national democratic line, at least not to
its rural program. The biggest member organization, *Kilusang Mag-
bubukid ng Pilipinas* (KMP), is in fact tagged by the military as a
front of the clandestine movement. Its head, Jaime Tadeo, has recently been arrested on trumped-up criminal charges; other KMP
provincial leaders have been killed. The sister organization of rural
women, *Amhan,* has had some of its members horribly disem-
boweled; so with a number of BCC leaders.

The organizational and political strength of the national democratic movement in the rural areas cannot be calculated without taking

account of such coalitions as CPAR, even though CPAR is not dominated by national democrats. The initiative to form it came from social democrats, and they continue to run CPAR's secretariat. To add
further nuances, we have to evaluate the attempt to form cooperatives among rice farmers in Tarlac, an experiment run by former
NPA commander, Bernabe Buscayno ("Dante"), and the program
run by the Philippine Rural Reconstruction Movement (PRRM), one
of the country's largest nongovernmental organizations (NGOs),
to bring credit, health care, and self-help projects to rural areas.
These are attacked by some of the left as "reformist"; they are
also suspected by the armed forces as "fronts" for the underground.

The national democratic strategy has always given a privileged
place to rural arena of struggle, to the point of heavily influencing
even urban (Metro Manila) debates. In the early months of 1986,
I asked a ranking CPP leader why their statements kept stressing
that things had not essentially changed, instead of addressing the
changes that have happened. "Eighty per cent of CPP members
are in the countryside. We get more questions from them about
continuing the armed struggle or not, given the new government
and talk of ceasefire." He added that he was concerned about
the difficulty of resuming fighting once the ceasefire ends, as happened to the Moro National Liberation Front (MNLF) when they
agreed to a ceasefire in return for government concessions to their
demand for autonomy.

And yet it is the urban arena that plays a bigger role in the
judgment of the "political marginalization" of the national
democratic movement by its critics. National politics do tend to
mean Metro Manila politics in ordinary Philippine discourse, and
the negative judgments about the movement's political influence are
strongly affected by its performance in Metro Manila. Since urban
struggle even within a people's war strategy is primarily open and
legal, this is where the national democrats are more vulnerable to
competition from other political tendencies, especially those that
concentrate on purely open legal lines. Personalities also tend to
play a bigger role in open legal struggle, without rigid correlations
to organizational numbers. The media plays a key role in expand-

ing perceptions about political influence, inside and outside the Philippines. No wonder TV stations have become prime targets of attempted coups and popular uprisings everywhere—together with military arsenals.

National democrats suffer from the simplistic counterposing of the concept "democratic" to that of "revolutionary," with democratic interpreted to mean legal and open, or even narrowly electoral, struggle. Such counterposition is associated with liberal democratic thinking; unfortunately, revolutionaries often reinforce the contradiction. Until very recently, national democrats were always warned about a hierarchy of dangers that had reformism, parliamentarism, and "right" tendencies on top. Their leaders rarely worried about ultraleft tendencies and "revolutionism." The clandestine character and shadowy image of the NDF are disadvantages in an open market contest for democratic credentials. Even the profiles of legal national democratic organizations suffer, for they are seen as "fronts," without their own organizational integrity or independence in political initiatives.

Given all its limitations in urban open legal politics, it is still an overstatement to call the national democratic movement "politically marginalized." It would be fairer to say that it does not occupy the hegemonic place it used to enjoy in the broad popular movement, which is the source of a new democratic legitimacy ("people power") that expands and deepens the traditional democratic legitimacy based on elections. But it remains the biggest organized section of the urban popular movement, and its critique and proposals have to be incorporated into any coalition that seeks to be the "people's alternative."

The political marginalization of the national democratic movement is sometimes attributed to its failure to participate in pursuing the democratic and progressive potential of the post-Marcos order when there was still hope for it. Instead, it is blamed for emphasizing the structural limits rather than the conjunctural possibilities, and of counterposing revolutionary power to people power.

I was one of those who argued for critical support of progressive or even just liberal programs and tendencies of the coalition government headed by Aquino, at least in the first months of 1986, and I think that the national democratic movement, especially its legal section, could have done much better. But its failure or default must be judged in the context of the times. National democrats were generally not welcome in the broad coalitions that claimed the franchise of "people power." Efforts to exclude national democrats in turn strengthened tendencies within the movement to sulk and stress the objective limits and reformism of initiatives that did not include them. They concentrated on "repositioning" themselves at the head of an oppositionist line and tried to force the pace of "exposing the reactionary essence of the Aquino regime."

It was easy enough to criticize all initiatives of the Aquino-led coalition against the revolutionary standards of national democracy, but many national democrats failed to appreciate that they were in no position to define the terrain of struggle in their terms, at least not that early. "People power" was perhaps the concept that defined the terrain, and it had its possibilities, if only because it was difficult for conservatives and military forces to coopt it. Liberals and other progressives did try to monopolize it, proving that sectarianism was not peculiar to national democrats. But even if they had upheld the coalition character of people power, national democrats most probably would have found it difficult to emphasize its potential rather than its limitations.

Part of the reason for this failure was the people's war framework that the NDF elaborated under the Marcos regime; this strategy did not lend itself easily to the kind of tactics called for by the particular conjuncture and transition of 1986. Another reason was the structure of the movement; while this structure had served it well under repression, with a strong clandestine network that permeated the open legal organizations, it proved unwieldy in the fast-changing and complex competition of a purely open legal arena. In a strategic framework that considered armed struggle as "the main form" or "the highest form" of struggle, open legal struggle tends to be quite secondary. Organizations and persons who restrict themselves to purely open legal politics are at best tactical (not strategic) allies, if not suspect. In a structure that "follows the law of gravity" and gives greatest weight to the underground, legal formations and cadres are not partners but servants, with limited margins of maneuver, always reminded about the dangers of reformism.

And yet the movement need not have confronted the conjuncture of 1986 with this strategy and structure. According to a cadre from Mindanao, in 1982, just before his death, Edjop wrote a paper that defined the national democratic strategy as involving "three strategic combinations"—of rural and urban struggle, of armed and political struggle, and of the struggle on the home front and on the international front. These ideas were not Edjop's personal discoveries; they were supposed to reflect discussions in the leadership collectives he belonged to, within the CPP. I expressed regrets that we did not get to hear about them before 1986; perhaps because we were in prison? They offer a much more flexible and appropriate framework for national democrats to understand many of the concerns raised by popular democrats and other political tendencies after the February 1986 uprising, often called simply EDSA.

Even more interesting was another piece of news, again involving Edjop, that I received on my release. Edjop was supposed to have attended a series of meetings from 1980 to 1982 which discussed research findings on the following questions: How urbanized is the Philippines and what is the percentage of urban and rural population? How large is the urban working class and petty bourgeoisie? How strong is the legal and electoral tradition among the middle forces and the rest of the people? How capitalist is the Philippines compared to its characterization as "semi-feudal"? How significant is religion (both religious consciousness and religious institutions) in the life of the people? The study was an effort to advance beyond the pioneering work of Amado Guerrero, "Specific Characteristics of Our People's War," written in 1974. The tentative conclusions were that all the factors mentioned—urbanization, capitalism, workers and middle class, legal and electoral tradition, religious influence—were much greater than had been presumed within the national democratic framework. When I first heard this,

I couldn't help exclaiming: "Those are the ingredients that came together at EDSA!"

It is tempting to speculate on what might have been, had the research and discussions succeeded in adapting the national democratic framework in time for the transition. Or had the framework of "three strategic combinations" been translated structurally, so that urban and open legal formations and methods were given their due strategic weight and distinct logic.

The question, however, about strategic framework and structure is less about what could have happened than what can happen. As the Aquino-led project unravels and exhausts its possibilities, a new flow of fresh ideas and energies will seek to create a viable alternative, in competition with other more conservative and militarist projects. The national democratic movement will face a challenge quite similar to the one it confronted sometime after Edjop's death, although in quite dissimilar circumstances. Will its current framework and structure prove adequate and flexible enough for the coming conjuncture?

One element of the coming conjuncture is the presidential and national assembly elections scheduled for 1992. This advance notice gives national democrats more time to debate policy than they had in 1978 and 1985. But it is not really time that they need most; what they need is a framework that allows them to consider the place of elections and avoid divisions around the issue of participation, whether in 1992 or in earlier "snap elections" preferred by some Aquino rivals and supporters. It is definitely not a matter of choosing between electoral participation or armed struggle. After all, in addition to the ongoing counterinsurgency "total war," there is the threat of a military coup, including a new variant called "coup-cum-revolution" advocated by the Young Officers Union (YOU). Even the imposition of some sort of martial rule can not be totally ruled out, although the likely shape of governance as 1992 approaches is *democradura*—the Latin American description of post-dictatorship regimes that are a *mestizo* coalition of conservative democratic and outrightly dictatorial elements.

The struggle for a democratic state might require a combination of forms that has not yet been theorized or verified by standard sources of the national democratic movement. The challenge of democracy, however, extends beyond even the democratic state, to the broader terrain of "people's empowerment." This is the key item in the debate associated with popular democracy. The popular democratic proposal to "institutionalize people power in non-governmental centers of direct democracy" is a necessary foil to the statist tendencies of left models that influence national democratic thinking. Another challenge is to recognize pluralism and coalition work as essential not just for future governance but for advancing the popular movement. The criticisms against gender-blindness and gender-bias, and the search for alternative nonpatriarchal structures and relationships further push the debate about democracy beyond present boundaries.

A similar push beyond boundaries is happening to the development debate. National democracy's development paradigm (as a transition to socialism) is not only affected by the critique of previous socialist experiments and new "planning versus market" debates; it needs to address the question of "sustainable development." This means more than taking on board the issues of environmental degradation. The recently formed Green Forum is exploring alternative "scales of sustainability," including the concept of bio-districts based on ecological and economic, rather than political-administrative, boundaries. A sustainable development paradigm would have a better appreciation of indigenous communities. Instead of being "minorities" who are marginal to national development issues, indigenous communities become central to the search for development alternatives that are more appropriate to the Philippines.

Another challenge that faces the national democratic movement is the question of peace. This is, ironically, a very conflictual item. There are proposals for "zones of peace" (initially put forward by a group of popular democrats in Bicol and picked up by church leaders), covering a whole town and city or only one *barangay*, where neither government troops nor the NPA would enter with their weapons. Even more crucial for the movement are lessons from the peace negotiations currently being undertaken in other revolutionary struggles, especially those in El Salvador and South Africa.

Questions about democracy, development, and peace underline what is possibly the weakest point in the present national democratic framework—the third strategic combination that Edjop cited, "combining the struggle on the home front and on the international front." Even this afterword reflects this weakness, since it concentrates on the internal dynamics of Philippines without spelling out their interaction with international structures and conjunctures. But people's empowerment, sustainable development, and peace cannot be achieved in the Philippines without a sophisticated combination of international and internal initiatives. In this connection, 1992 has a further symbolism as the 500th anniversary of European (Northern, Western) colonization and Christianization of the third world. Given the consequences of such dependence, third world nation-states like the Philippines have no choice but to look for another way forward. Is the path opened by the first socialist nation-states a dead end? How do we accept the current trade, investment, and lending arrangements and still pursue a "delinking" strategy that tries to use such international linkages without yielding our internal needs and markets to their logic? Have the ideas of "diversifying dependence" toward OECD economies and South-South cooperation more than rhetorical value?

So many questions, and they are bound to generate even more debate than already exist inside the national democratic movement and within the broader popular movement. Mistakes will surely be made, and new wounds added to old wounds that have not yet fully healed. And more deaths, many not at their chosen hour.

A last word about Edjop and a role he continues to play among many circles of the movement. When cadres get depressed, feel exhausted, become disillusioned with comrades and leaders, they try to recover their spirits in different ways. They may find strength with select comrades who are also friends, or go to the grassroots, in lowland and mountain villages, urban slum communities and factories, to renew their resolve through fresh contact with the people's poverty and everyday resistance. Sometimes they think of martyred friends, and vow to continue what these friends did not finish. I remember my first months in the clandestine resistance in 1973; I was reading some old magazines, doing research for *Pilipinas,* the publication of the Christians for National Liberation (CNL). I saw photographs of Filipino revolutionaries at the turn of the century. One showed a pile of dead bodies, with some U.S. soldiers posing beside them like trophies; another had hundreds lined up before a battle, looking like a graduation class picture. At that moment, I felt an almost mystical link. They died, I thought to myself, not knowing that we would be continuing their fight. I guess others will, too, after us.

When friends come to Europe and we get to talk about problems in the struggle, I ask, "But are there any bright spots? Any sources of hope?" Among the answers these last two years is Edjop's story, his life and death reminding us of what changes we can undergo as we struggle to help change our world.